Dole Scrounger   *Drongo*

Poet   New Ager

MEDIEVAL
BRIGAND   PERFORMER

Artist   **CRUSTY**

Brew Crew   PARTY ANIMAL

PACIFIST   Cheesy
                                        Quaver

HIPPY   **ORBITAL**

"Actually it's Adam wearing a pullover his granny knitted him."

'A Time to Travel?' Fiona Earle, Alan Dearling, Helen Whittle, Roddy Glasse and Gubby.
First published in 1994 by Enabler Publications.
ISBN 0 9523316 08

© Enabler Publications
Distribution through Russell House Publishing, 38 Silver Street, Lyme Regis, Dorset DT7 3HS

The publisher and contributors would like to point out that many of the photos are of very varying quality, since they were mostly taken by Travellers and were not originally intended for publication. We hope you enjoy their inclusion, anyway!

Credits:
Fiona Earle: writing the majority of chapters 1, 2, 3, 4, 6, 7; contributing to chapter 5; photos pps 30, 62, 81, 103.
Helen Whittle: writing the majority of chapter 5; contributing to all other chapters; cover photos; all other photos except those listed individually.
Alan Dearling: contributing to all chapters, editorial work and design; photos pps. 3 & 151, and drawings pps 56 &150.
Roddy Glasse: photos pps 55, 65, 78, 98, 112, 136, 148, 156, 170.
Gubby: line drawings of the convoy, the park-up and the gathering!
Linette: chapter quotations art-work.
Andy: photos pps 5, 11, 13.
Gary: photo page 109.
Lizzie: photo page 159.
Bert: (and the police service): photo page 34.
Sharon: photo page 146.
Nicola Beechsquirrel: drawing on page 58.

Acknowledgements
The authors and the publisher would like to thank the many people and organisations who have offered help, encouragement, advice and criticism along the evolutionary path of 'A Time to Travel?' Apologies if your name isn't here; we've tried to remember most of you, but the brain cells do get depleted over time!

From Fiona: John Harrison of Monolith Publications and Bruce Garrard of Unique Publications, for their comprehensive collection of small press books; LCTR, SCF, FFT, Liberty, TSC for information. Dave and family for my park-up; Janine, Blair, Sue and Herring for conquering the word-processing; Alison, Duncan, Diane, Katrina - my family, for forwarding mail; Shirley, Joyce and Linda for taking my phone messages; Jo for support; Arthur Ivatts, Rowena Fuszard and Bev Gutheridge for professional contributions; Ian, Phil, Jill, Andy and Sally for hours of valuable recollections; Linette, Gwen, Alan Moorehouse, Pete, Liz, Richie, Celia, Cheryl, Bob, Jenni, Gary, Roddy, Gubby, Lizzie, Sharon, Bernard, Michael Eavis, Sid, Jane and everyone else who offered constructive criticism and stories; Polly and Ria for rewriting their work; all those who donated or allowed us to use, photos, songs, poems and artwork; CG and Ferdia, with love and thanks for putting up with my research and writing.

From Herring: Pete and all from Park Lane Youth Centre, Woodside, Telford for darkroom facilities; everyone at DRUG HELP, Wellington, Telford for office facilities, help and support; Derek MacConnell of Bobbetts & Maclean, Bristol, for helping to keep a safe site together; Steve, for being chief cook and bottle washer and general dogsbody; Cori for being 'mum'; Es, for info, advice, lateral thinking and insanity; Planet-Telecommunications HQ; Liz and Jeff - other telecommunications; Janet, Patsy and Kathleen - encouragement and mail forwarding; Pete Mercer, Anne Bagehot and everyone at LCTR, SCF and NGLE for all the help and support, and for news cuttings etc. Many thanks to everyone who contributed their stories, info and and constructive criticism or agreed to let me use their mugshots. Cheers!

From Alan: Jackie Nike and Steve Redhead for interesting reflections on where the Rave scene and music fits in; Vicki Stangroome for her views on health matters; in different vehicles and boats: Alwyn, Mikki, I and P, Brian, Kathy, Simon and Don - long may they survive; Bert, Juilet and Laurian, who keep their shit together; Luke Clements and Jeremy Sandford for support and advice; Andy Hemmingway and his crew at 'Fevered Imaginings'; Amanda at Bridestone; Steve Staines at FFT; Tom Odley and the British Romani Union and ACERT; Jennifer Boyd-Cropley, Bill Forrester, Thomas Acton and Donald Kenrick for listening to and helping all types of Travellers; Geoffrey, Martin, Jacqui, Scott H and all the 'parts' of Russell House Publishing', who have helped to make the book a reality, and finally to Christine, my unlikely travelling companion through 'adventures'.

A Time to Travel?

An introduction to Britain's newer Travellers

**Fiona Earle, Alan Dearling, Helen Whittle,
Roddy Glasse and Gubby**

**An Enabler
Publication**

Publisher's Intro

There are many books I'm involved with which are just plain 'work'.

'*A Time to Travel?*' is much more. It's a personal statement about choice and freedom. Publishing the words and pictures contained here is an act of sharing. Many people have travelled, many others have wished they could. The current breed of Travellers are distanced from the traditional Romani Travellers by upbringing and culture. To my mind, though, it doesn't disbar them from a right to be heard, and more than that, a right to find space and freedom to live a lifestyle of their own choosing.

I have spent a lot of my forty-three year old life attending festivals, roughing it in fields and on hillsides, driving and parking-up all over the UK and in some bits of Europe. I lived full time for a couple of years in a narrowboat on the Severn and round the canals. This brought me in the nineties into much greater contact with Travellers who the media dubbed 'crusties', 'brigands' and 'New Agers'. As I travelled in my boat, pub and shop staff would stereotype me and say "No Travellers wanted here." At about that time, Fiona and I were in contact about education and Travellers' children. I'd worked with and written about youth work for over twenty years. What came out of the conversations was the framework for this book. We approached over twenty mainstream and small press publishers. Two were initially interested, but nothing came of their interest, and they wanted to attach all sorts of strings to the project. We decided to go ahead and do it ourselves. Self-publishing feels about right for this book anyway. It also feels like money well invested in something which should matter to a lot more people.

I hope you find something in the book which offers you a new insight or two. Successive governments have urged the homeless and the unemployed to 'get on their bike'. Strangely, when people like the Travellers make an effort towards a self-help solution, they are branded as subversives, villains and outcasts to be hunted down, outlawed and punished. It's a sad and sorry reflection on the United Kingdom when it cannot offer a little more toleration and caring of young (and not so young) people, many of whom are making a considerable effort to treat the earth more gently; attune with the environment, and find alternative ways of living and working. Sure, some Travellers are dirty; some get busted for dealing; some are suffering from mental health problems and drink and drug-related problems. Unfortunately, the same is true for many other members of society. But, many Travellers are out there searching for better ways of living and education for their children and themselves, and thankfully reject much of the materialistic mayhem that traps the majority.

Anyway, that out the way, here it is, Fiona's 'A Time To Travel.' READ IT - DO IT!
                                                                          Alan.

CONTENTS

◆◆◆◆◆◆◆◆◆◆◆◆◆◆◆◆◆◆◆◆◆◆◆◆◆◆◆◆◆◆◆

"This book is dedicated to Travellers everywhere"

◆◆◆◆◆◆◆◆◆◆◆◆◆◆◆◆◆◆◆◆◆◆◆◆◆◆◆◆◆◆◆

Author's Note

Writing about an enigma is very difficult, especially one as diverse as the modern Traveller scene.

The phenomenon of a group of people who adopt a nomadic lifestyle, instead of being born into its tradition, is hard to explain to anyone who has not experienced the urge to travel, and/or live unconventionally. This book has been put together for several reasons. Primarily, it is for our children, who need and deserve a written history, as well as oral re-tellings. Also, however, it is for those who want to read about us - especially our families, and the increasing floods of students, to whom we seem to be a new subject for theses and discursive essays.

There are always questions, and 'A Time to Travel?'' may answer some of them.

Although there are a plethora of small-press publications dealing with particular issues linked to the broad travelling scene, the prominent commercial publications have been composed by non-travellers. In this book, the authors, photographers, artists, contributors and editor are all part of the travelling scene.

I cannot pretend to put forward all points of view, but I have tried to include a range of opinions relating to important aspects of our lives and culture.

The interested reader will need to turn to the bibliography to search out other voices and material; or talk to Travellers. Everyone has a different tale to tell. Events experienced by hundreds, or thousands, will have that many interpretations, and I can only offer those which I have read or heard.

Read this with an open mind and make of it what you will.
Fiona.

Chapter One:
The Origins

When the earth has been ravaged and the animals are dying, a tribe of people from all races and creeds shall put their faith in deeds not words. they shall be known as Warriors of the Rainbow Protectors of the environment

Hopi Indian prophecy

Perhaps, in the beginning..........................

Trying to trace the origins of the current Traveller scene is very difficult. There is no clear moment when people took to the road 'en masse', and the scene itself has constantly evolved. Our approach is to look at a number of different social events happening throughout the 'seventies, and show how they converged in some ways in the 'eighties. This is not a definitive history, but a few suggestions of how it may have originated.

Almost all Travellers pinpoint the start in 1974, with the first Stonehenge People's Free Festival; but how did that all come about? It is thought by some to have evolved out of the Isle of Wight festivals in the late '60's and early '70's.

In 1970, over 200,000 swarmed onto the island for Jimi Hendrix's last U.K. gig; and an alternative free fringe event was established outside the security fence in an area known as Desolation Row, and Desolation Hill. Eventually, successive near-terrorist attacks on the fence caused it to be removed, and the event declared a 'free festival'.

Similarly the organisers of the early Phun City festival lost control to the audience, and it was made a 'free' event. In 1972, the first Windsor Free Festival was organised, and it was strongly linked with the squatters' slogan : 'Pay No Rent'. It attracted about 7,000 people in '72; but about 15,000 turned up the following year, when it became a rally and petition against cannabis laws. The even larger 1974 event, an 'Ecological Fair', backed by the United Nations, was broken up by police after only a few days.

> *"The police staged a vicious early morning attack on the sleeping festival goers. Hundreds of people were hurt as police randomly and brutally laid into anyone unlucky enough to be in their way. People were dragged from their tents to be treated to a breakfast of boots and abuse."*

The event brought together many strands of alternative society, which later evolved into the Traveller scene. The festival newspaper 'Sunday Head' offered the Albion Free State national anthem:

> *"Giants built Stonehenge, giants built this land, Let's sprout up like mushrooms and seize the upper hand."*

William Blake was frequently quoted as the source of this mythical Albion Free State. Police arrested Sid Rawles and Ubi Dwyer in 1975 for breaking an injunction on the Windsor Festival; so the event was held instead at Watchfield; in 1976 it was at Seasalter; and in 1977, at Chobham Common. But by then, Stonehenge had become the 'official' People's Free Festival.

As a postscript, it is worth noting that 7 picnickers did turn up for the 'Windsor Feast' in 1975, joined by 5 others - as well as 9 journalists, 4 welfare organisations and over 350 police!

▢*Bring what you would like to find!*▢

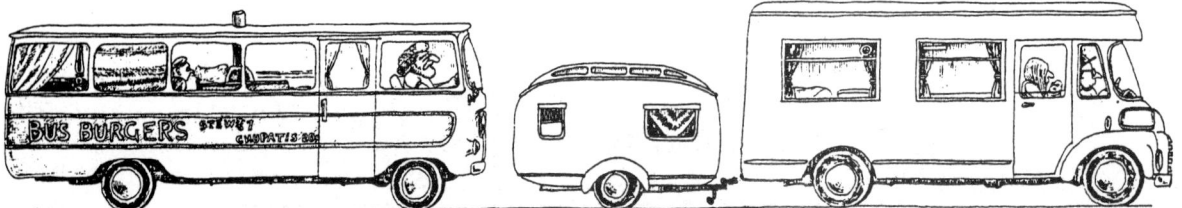

The Free Festival movement was clearly allied to the squatting movement, in which Dr.John, Wally Hope, Bill Ubique Dwyer, Nic Alberry and Sid Rawles were prominent figures. Political action and statements, often imported from the U.S., blended the acid mysticism of Timothy Leary with the street anarchy of Jerry Rubin's Yippy movement. His 'Fuck the System' book proclaimed :

"Take what you need
take what you want
there is plenty to go round
everything is free."

Typical early festival scene

By the mid '70's the 'love and peace' philosophy was being replaced by more political activity. There were clashes between organisers of festivals and the members of the audience who wanted to:

"Create a free festival movement that can't be stopped"
Watchfield Freek Press '75.

Site meetings about permanent sites, and whether land should be 'bought' or 'liberated' echoed the words of Gerrard Winstanley, leader of the Diggers, the True Levellers, who in the 1600`s tried to reclaim common land for the oppressed:

"The Earth (which was made to be a common treasury of relief for all,
both beasts and man) was hedged into enclosures.... is bought and
sold and kept in the hands of a few."
1649 True Levellers Standard

Still true and relevant today.

Strictly commercial festivals, such as Reading, Knebworth, Bath, Weeley et al, were part of the music scene, but had little to do with present Travellers. Many experimented with European and world-wide travel, using small buses or vans, motorbikes, or simply hitching, and working their way around. India and Morocco were popular, for a mixture of spiritual, mystical and

drug-related reasons. Holland became the youth-culture capital of Europe, with it's tent village in Vondelpark, liberal drugs law and the Paradiso Hotel. Christiania in Copenhagen, the largest squat in Europe, became a home for over a thousand summer residents.

Amsterdam '73, Queen's Day Street-trading

Communes and communities were also seed-beds for the later Travellers. Tony Kelly, of the Selene Commune in Wales founded the U.K. Commune Movement- members grew from 8 in 1968, to 354 in 1970, with a 3,000 circulation of the 'Communes' journal. Communes and arts/spiritual communities have come and gone ever since, but with many philosophies paralleled by Travellers.

There was a rise in interest in religious movements, ancient sites and ley-lines. Hare Krishna, Chinese Taoism, Japanese Shinto, Paganism, Buddhism, the Maharishi Yogi; all provided many with challenging ideas, and occasionally, with enlightenment. There was a concern for ecological and green, or conservation issues; the relationship between man and the universe. The Native American culture provided sources of wisdom:

> *"We saw the Great Spirit's work in almost everything: sun, moon, trees, wind and mountains.....Indians living close to nature and nature's ruler are not living in darkness."*
>
> *Tatanga Mani, Walking Buffalo. Stoney Indian*

Earth harmony was adopted by many as an alternative consciousness to materialism- and this is reflected in current Traveller culture. Increasingly, green gatherings were held to promote awareness of the earth.

When the last tree has been uprooted
The last flower has been stamped on
When the last waters have been polluted
And the last fish has gone.
When the life of the last animal has come to an end
And the last bird has left the sky
When your last breath has been poisoned
What will your money then buy?

With unemployment rising through the 70's and an increasing level of alienation, both contributed to festivals becoming an alternative lifestyle. It wasn't too long before summer on the road became a nomadic lifestyle all year round. Whilst Glastonbury and Stonehenge are most commonly associated with Travellers, the majority spent much time at small local gatherings developed from rural community festivals - including May Hill, Meigan Fair, Strawberry Fayre, and the Psilocybin Fair.

Tipis at festival

From about 1978, radical street culture of punk had an influence on events - young new bands with a harder edged political statement adopted festivals as a natural stage. Young people who adopted the poses of anarchy, self-destruction and nihilistic high energy, moved from squats onto the road. They brought a 'new' dimension which had little to do with love and lunar energy, but it did reflect the growing disenchantment with, and opposition to Thatcherite policies.

The rest of this chapter focuses more closely on a few specific places and events which have been instrumental in shaping public perception of Travellers, and indeed, our own daily lives. It cannot be fully comprehensive, but is a general reflection on what was happening nationally at the time.

Glastonbury Festival

Held at Worthy Farm in Pilton, 5 miles from Glastonbury town, the festival valley has views west to the Tor. In the years 1970-1984, it grew rapidly from a small free gathering to a considerable commercial enterprise in aid of C.N.D.

Michael Eavis, a Somerset dairy farmer, hoped originally that:

> *"There might be a way of combining the*
> *traditional country fairs with the ideals*
> *of the pop festival culture.... by adding*
> *theatre, drama, alternative politics and*
> *kids' entertainments...it could become*
> *part of a regular midsummer festival of joy*
> *and celebration of life."*

Inspired by the Bath Showground event of '70, the Glastonbury event was held annually for four years, initially with locals organising a range of attractions of all kinds. Spiritual considerations worked alongside practical solutions, and the site of the original pyramid stage, for example, not only drew an audience into the valley; but also stood on a Stonehenge / Glastonbury Abbey ley line.

Nothing else happened until 1978, when Travellers gathered for an impromptu party at the farm. The enthusiasm for the fortnight prompted the organisation of subsequent festivals. The sale of £5 weekend tickets in 1979 allowed the organisers to make a donation to the 'Year of the Child'; but in 1981, C.N.D. became the benefactor. With an attendance of 18,000, the future of the event was assured, and C.N.D. became increasingly involved in its promotion, organisation and running. By 1984 about 50,000 attended. Generally held around the solstice, the festival attracted Travellers and New Age sympathisers, as well as music fans. The immense amount of work to prepare, then clear the site, forced people to live nomadically, if only for that period. It was also ideal labour for Travellers, who could then use their entertainment or craft skills during the main event itself.

It was one of a number of potential places to go, and no group particularly dominated the festival. Some weekenders, seduced by sunshine, meadows and music; abandoned conventional lifestyles for that of the road. Others enjoyed this chance to live freely, if only temporarily. So through the 'seventies and early 'eighties, Pilton provided earning potential for some Travellers, and even encouraged others to join them.

The Albion Fairs

These were held in Norfolk and Suffolk, and seemed to grow in popularity in a similar way to the Glastonbury event. Organised by a local committee, the fairs sought to revive traditional rural festivals; and the first was Barsham Fair in 1972, bringing people together in a medieval type event. Gradually, the number of annual fairs grew, and contributors included local

inhabitants of all kinds, not only those with New Age philosophies - though names such as Albion, Sun, Moon, Faerie and Tree Fairs reflected a pagan nature.

> *"When you walk into a fair , you enter another world, welcome in an atmosphere of fantasy and Bohemia.......when people from all walks of life, colour and creed have been able to mix in harmony for a few hours from the grief stricken world of jealousy, greed and hate."*   P.Tynan. 'The Sun in the East'.

By 1982, a representative of the Albion Fair committee said at their open meeting:

> *"Problems are going to arise regarding the Peace Convoy..."*

And one of the convoy responded to the media, saying:

> *".....they are making us into a separate ghetto. We find all the things we had hoped for years ago but are still outcasts because we carry a political ethic into Society."*

By 1984, the Albion Fair organisers limited their advertising, and actively discouraged **all** people from outside the local area from attending, including Travellers.

So who were the 'Peace Convoy', and why were they seen as such a threat to the predominant, mildly-commercial festivals of the time - Glastonbury and the Albion Fairs?

Stonehenge and the 'Peace Convoy'

The first Stonehenge summer solstice festival was held for several weeks in 1974. Wally Hope, fired by a vision of claiming the site back for the people to celebrate freely, instigated a campaign of posters and leaflets - and succeeded! The Wally Tribe became the first 'prophets of the road' and squatted Stonehenge for much of the year. The tipis flew their Union Wally flag, and epitaphs abounded, such as:

> *"Home Sweet Dome"*

Thousands of people turned up the following year, for a fortnight of festivities. There were wood fires amongst the tents and tipis; children ran naked on the grass; adults gathered wood and water; everywhere there was singing and dancing. a celebration of life. Wally Hope was no longer around, but the dream that he had held, his hope for the future, continued to grow for another eleven years; until the State could tolerate it no longer.

← This is the 'WORLD' →

This is what the World going to turn out like IF you dont look after. So be Carefull

KALi

Something about Phil (Wally) Hope
(Reprinted with grateful acknowledgement to: CRASS and the Existential Press. From: 'A Series of Shock Slogans and Mindless Token Tantrums'. (1982))

"Phil Hope was a smiling, bronzed, hippy warrior. His eyes were the colour of the blue skies that he loved, his neatly cut hair was the gold of the sun that he worshipped. He was proud and upright, anarchistic and wild, pensive and poetic. His ideas were a strange mixture of the thinkings of the people whom he admired and amongst whom he lived. The dancing Arabs. The peasant Cypriots. The noble Masai. The sad and silent North American Indians, for whom he felt a real closeness of spirit.

'Our temple is sand, we fight our battles with music, drums like thunder, cymbals like lightning, banks of electronic equipment like nuclear missiles of sound. We have guitars instead of tommy guns.' **Phil Hope '74.**

The various inhabitants of the festival '74 had agreed that, should the authorities intervene, they would answer only to the name of 'Wally'. The ludicrous summonses against Phil Wally, Sid Wally, Chris Wally etc. did much to set the scene for the absurd trial that followed in London's High courts. Wally Hope jubilantly left the courtroom to face waiting reporters announcing: "We have won, we have won...."

◆ ◆ ◆

Wally Hope came away from Windsor '74 bruised and depressed. Once again he had danced amongst the boys in blue in a vain attempt to calm them with his humour, and he lost - he was beaten up for his efforts..... Wally spent much of the early months of '75 handing out leaflets in and around London.... In May, he left our house for Cornwall... we had done all that we could to prepare for the Festival (Henge) and Wally wanted to rest up in his tepee until it began. The day of his departure was brilliantly hot; we sat in the garden drinking tea as Wally, glorying in the golden sun, serenaded us, and it, with a wild performance on his tribal drums. He was healthy, happy and confident that this time round we'd win again...........

The next time that we saw him, about a month later, he had lost a stone in weight, his skin was white and unpleasantly puffy, he was frail, nervous and almost incapable of speech. He sat with his head hung on his chest.... his tear-filled eyes had such a dull and dead look.....his hands shook constantly....Wally Hope was a prisoner in one of Her Majesty's Psychiatric Hospitals, a man with no future but theirs. This time round, he was not winning.........

Wally was prescribed massive doses of a drug called largactil which he was physically and often violently forced to take.

A couple of days after the last person had left the festival site, Wally was, without warning, set free.......... we got Wally to a doctor friend who diagnosed his condition as being 'chronic dystenesia', a disease brought about through overdoses of modecate and similar drugs. Wally had been made into a cabbage and worse, an incurable one......

On 3rd September 1975, unable to face another day, perhaps hoping that death might offer more to him than what was left in life, Wally Hope overdosed on sleeping pills and choked to death on the vomit they induced."

Stonehenge.

"The one thing about Stonehenge about which everyone is agreed is that it is primarily a temple....." R.J.C. Atkinson, archeologist, 1956.

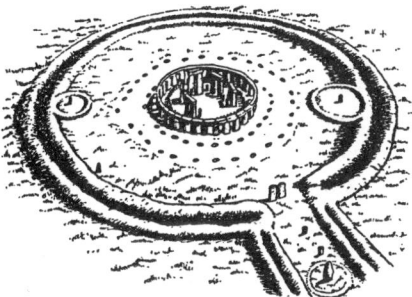

Although now in a state of ruin, it is the most impressive prehistoric monument in Britain. The outer Sarsen circle was built of 30 huge stones from the Marlborough Downs. Precisely positioned mathematically, the means of construction has never been ascertained. The bluestones of the inner circle came from Milford Haven and the Welsh mountains. These trilithans- one stone resting upon two - were technically constructed. The alter stone marked the centre of the circles, from which the rising of the summer solstice sun could be viewed directly above the outlying Heelstone. Other markers, individual stones and holes, indicate eclipses and equinoxes. The complex discussions surrounding the monument are fully explored in many publications; but it remains true to say that the stones have a power many of us have experienced, and really are a sacred site of major importance.

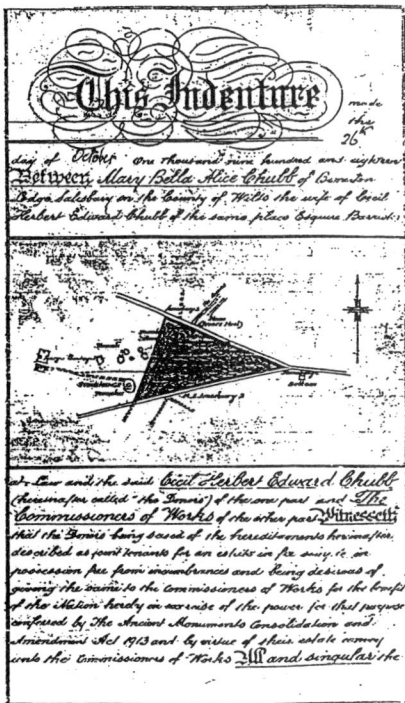

It was on 26th October 1918 that Stonehenge was 'gifted' by Mary and Cecil Chubb to the nation, in the guise of the Commissioners of Works, later to evolve into English Heritage. Parts of the deed of gift are reprinted here and the ways in which the intentions of the donors have been flagrantly ignored are self-evident.

Recent history of Stonehenge.

By 1976, the summer of the long drought, many people were realising that vehicles provided the necessary means of travelling nation-wide to the very full programme of free festivals. Combined with socio-economic factors of the time, and the belief that life on the road was better, cheaper and healthier, some individuals became full-time Travellers.

> *"What happened was each week we'd have a fiver*
> *or a tenner to ourselves. After we'd paid the rent,*
> *paid the gas, the lecky and such, fuelled the car up,*
> *got in the food.... and I was on the average wage of*
> *the land at the time, eighty pound a week... we were*
> *still poor. We talked about it; we decided to sell*
> *the contents, get a Commer and go on the road and*
> *we did, and I've never looked back since."*
> *Phil, 1992, about 1979.*

The travelling culture became a community as people forged bonds and started living together.

> *"There was a lot of people who'd share a vehicle,*
> *and use it to move all the tat for benders and stuff*
> *together... loads of us communally moving." Andy.*

The mood was still hopeful, very positive. Although soft drugs were quite commonly used, there was a definite abhorrence of hard drug use, and,

> *"You didn't see people around site with alcohol all the time,*
> *there weren't loads of drunks." Andy.*

Strong characters who had consciously decided to change their lives for the better, refused to tolerate sloppy habits; and enforced site clearance each time they moved. Without the media hype and legal powers of today, the whole emphasis was on a peaceful existence in harmony with nature and local people, even the police.

> *"There was lurcher racing at Inglestone in '81*
> *with local guys on the common....and the*
> *farmer who leased the land at Stonehenge, he'd*
> *cash giros for us, if we needed it." Andy.*

Although the Stonehenge festival had continued to grow, there were still very few vehicles present in the early years:

> *"My truck was there in `76, and two others... then*
> *there was the time we were first to arrive. The police*
> *on the gate couldn't let us in, but said that if we went*
> *down the track and found an unlocked gate, he couldn't*
> *do anything about it... so we did, and off he went, and*
> *we cut the wire for everyone else." Andy.*

Police lend a helping hand

The festival never happened within the sacred area - tents, stages, vehicles, all gathered in the fields opposite the monument, and people went on foot to celebrate appropriately.

"The 'Peace Convoy' really began in '81 when we went from 'Henge to Greenham Common to support the women camping there." Andy.

The 'convoy' leaving Stonehenge

A group went beforehand to check out the site, then everyone painted up their vehicles, and a core of about 120 snaked away from Wiltshire.
"It was all peaceful. When we met a roadblock, we'd

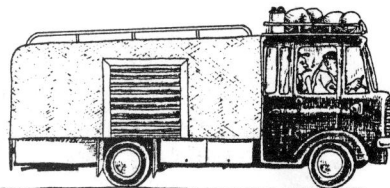

stop, get out, and just lift the cars out the way, with
the police inside..." Andy.

The community's strength was its sense of unity; a tribe united in striving for a better world, and employing non-violent means to attain it. It's from this point that the scene seemed to develop. Glastonbury Festival became increasingly commercialised, the 'peace convoy' started receiving media attention, and everything snowballed.

Those who didn't want to pay for festivals were drawn to the free gatherings. Other groups from society were attracted to the scene, including the obvious anarchists, and there were a number of the criminal element joining the permanent Travellers, possibly to avoid detection. Hard drugs first became a problem in '82; and in addition there were some people who were just plain mad! But the 'peace convoy' retained its collection of brightly-painted vehicles and a much more idealistic group of Travellers. Confrontations with the police were almost a game.

"They harassed us for miles, till in the end, we all
packed up for a smoke and a brew, 'til they got
bored." Mush.

Other groups, such as the Tibetans and the Mutants, travelled in smaller convoys, and everyone tended to specialise in some skill or another.

"What everyone forgets- well, it wasn't just a rock
festival, there was everything - cabaret, theatre,
circus, kids' entertainment, the lot. It was a whole
experience." Andy.

Winter park-ups were not subject to the stringent legislation of today, so green lanes and common land could be used. Benders were practical homes, and several people could still share a vehicle.

"One bloke used to have everything. We'd load up the truck;
then jam in four sleepers as uprights at the corners; then pile
in loads more tat, and rope it all round, then sling
a tarp on top... he used to have so much, he'd give
anyone new a kettle, or an axe, or whatever. That
way, of course, he could always blag a brew or
some kindling, too , 'cos we'd kind of owe it
to him." Mush.

Throughout 1983, police harassment had grown. Large official presences appeared at many gatherings, including Inglestone Common and Sizewell. In the spring of 1984, police action became heavier. When several Travellers parked up in Fargo woods after Shaftesbury Grove in April, riot police appeared in coachloads to move everyone on. Benders and tat were burned while helicopters circled overhead.

"We all met up at 'The Mount', between Salisbury and Winchester
and were together again within 24hrs." Gwen.

Similarly, police trashed a coachload of protesters at Boscombe Down. This was repeated in small instances all over the place.

"If we'd known in '76, the reality of '84, we'd never have
believed it." Andy.

Druid ceremony at Stonehenge

The last ever Stonehenge Peoples' Free Festival took place throughout June, 1984. It was not a haphazard conglomeration of people trying to 'get by', but an event controlled by the long-term Travellers who also wanted to maintain a healthy environment.

> *"What people don't realise is that it was all organised*
> *Money was collected from traders for the rubbish crew,*
> *who went round 3 times a day; there was a security*
> *squad, and cash went from the dealers to pay St. Johns*
> *and stuff." Andy.*

From June 1st onwards, the party grew, until it is estimated that well over 30,000 were in attendance.

> *"The site seemed well-organised with a trackway system*
> *laid out, toilets and standpipes... alcohol, food and crafts*
> *and of course drugs, were on sale. Bands played all over*
> *the site almost 24hrs a day! First Aid, Samaritans and*
> *Lost Children tents were on site... it was a spontaneous*
> *experiment in human trust and co-operation.. to live an*
> *alternative without the State." John Harrison.*

It was not all good, of course. There was crime on site - inevitable with those numbers, so many of whom were punters, out to spend money and party. Over 65 stolen cars were abandoned there afterwards, and others were burned out. The police turned a blind eye to pretty well everything, and the tourists gawped from their coaches as they paid for a controlled walk in the vicinity of the Stones, kept well away from the monument by fences.

> *"I arrived on June 3rd on the back of a trials bike with*
> *one bag of possessions, and saw the 'Henge for the first*
> *time - a magnificent monument with a few hundred*
> *people on the grass across the road, setting up along the*
> *drags. It evolved really quickly, and the month is a haze*

of images... swimming in the river at Amesbury....
Hawkwind and the Enid on stage... siphoning petrol
to blag bike rides... nights by the fire, days lying
in the sun....Pete's sagging bender leaking in the rain...
a sense of total freedom, timeless energy... and solstice
morning; the chill of pre-down darkness, walking to the
stones, chanting, dancing - the sun rising majestically
above the Heel stone while music echoed around. "
                                                        Fiona.

"There were several thousand people on site for a month
One of the reasons for this must be that the number of
free festivals was decreasing, whilst the demand for
them was certainly not. "
                          Don Aitken, Festival Eye '90.

Robert Calvert:
The Captain

I focussed the magnifying glass
That brought the downfall of Icarus.

Balloons were easy; a simple pin.
Or a knife in the case of the Zeppelin.

That blade was the cause of many a prang
In the early days of stick and string.

I am the gremlin. I was there.
Making mischief in the air.

And always will be, wherever man
Flies in the face of Creation's plan.

Whatever the experience, Stonehenge had become massive, and the authorities could no longer tolerate such successful subversive organisation. Groups moved off to pass the summer in smaller gatherings, and one convoy travelled north to Cumbria and Yorkshire. As August progressed, it splintered and snaked across the country.

Nostell Priory.

The police in northern England had been fired up by the force used to quash the miners' strike. Their action at Nostell Priory was reported by the media, though it was against a relatively small number of the total travelling population. Over the August Bank Holiday a commercial event took place, with a fringe free festival in the car parks. Many Travellers noticed new faces there, some of whom were dealing drugs heavily.

"One guy, he'd come back from India and asked
me who they were. He challenged some of them, but got
nowhere - afterwards, we reckoned some were
undercover. "   *Phil.*

Sunrise in the Morning

Want to see the sunrise in the morning
Join the folks that gather there
Got to brace that broad horizon
Touch the Stones' ancient despair
When you've walked down that road
And felt your worries unload.
Or run down the same road
As the trouble explodes
And the law takes its course

But the Stones are still standing
Alone, undemanding
For they care not for time
In the ancient cosmic rhyme
They endure the ages
And serve to remind
'Til the age when the Saracens
Are washed by the brine

Want to see the smiles on peoples' faces
Join the rituals happening there
There will be dancing and singing forever
At this year's solstice fair
So, if you've partied on the main drag,
Or crawled up Easy Street,
Or veged out there in Tent Land,
'Til you no longer find your feet.
The sheer spectacle of Albion
Without which the year isn't complete.

But the stones......
Want to see the spirit of the people
In its undivided form.
Want to see the extremes and has-beens
That make a mockery of the norm.
Naked chaos in the glorious sun,
The moon and the music, the dogs and the done,
The trucks and the horses, the freaks and the fun,
One love, one chalice
To an age when time began.

CG

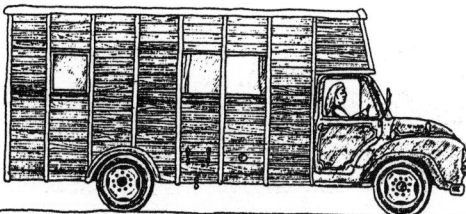

On the Bank Holiday Monday, police raided the site, catching people unawares, and arresting everyone that was present. The minority who escaped took drastic measures, such as lying along prop shafts.

> *"It was ridiculous. How can over 200 people*
> *all be commiting an offence in the middle*
> *of the morning?"   Phil*

Children were locked up with their parents to await charges.

> *"There were these 2 little toddlers racing at the*
> *walls and shouting at the tops of their voices." Gwen.*

When released, Travellers returned to find that vehicles had been ransacked, possessions scattered, and benders burned. Collecting them, they limped away to other gatherings.

Molesworth.

Throughout the early '80s, a series of peace camps and green gatherings had been established to highlight Government policies. One of these was at Molesworth, where C.N.D. supporters and Travellers had set up a camp which became known as 'Rainbow Village'.

> *"A community of 100 or more beautiful souls."*
> *Bruce Garrard.*

On February 5th, 1985, eviction was powerfully enforced.

> *"It was a beautiful evening..... then we saw it,*
> *all along the horizon to the North, 500 pairs*
> *of headlights."   Brig.*

Although local police were present, it was the army who gave instructions over the load-hailer: 1hr to pack up several months' life, and leave. The deadline was extended to the morning, but then they announced that:

> *"If those remaining do not leave voluntarily, the*
> *army will clear the site and use the minimum force*
> *necessary."*

How much was that?

1,500 Royal Engineers busily erected a double temporary fence of coiled razorwire around the entire 7 and a half mile base perimeter. It was:

> *"the largest single Royal Engineer operation*
> *since the Rhine Crossing in 1944." Daily Telegraph.*

At about 8.00 a.m., contractors moved in to tow or shove away buses and caravans that had not been moved.

> *"More and more fires were being lit. My woodpile*
> *went on a bonfire, and everything I couldn't manage*
> *to take."   Bruce Garrard.*

In the middle of the morning, the media watched Michael Heseltine arrive by helicopter in his combat gear; but he left before final inhabitants had been pushed off the land.

> *"By 2 p.m. their initial one hour to get off had stretched to fifteen;*
> *we'd kept our dignity, and avoided any kind of violent confrontation,*
> *and managed to save our homes and practically all our*

*equipment....most of all we knew that we had pushed Heseltine
into his biggest blunder ever."   Brig.*

**People had a vision for transforming
this land into a place of positive Hope &
Usefulness for Humanity. In the space
of 48 hours, the Government has used
the full force of the military & police to
destroy that vision & turned it into
a place of evil, a symbol of death &
destruction. Its only purpose to threaten
the survival of the planet.**
Rainbow Village. Molesworth February 1985

And onwards to the Beanfield......

During the early months of 1985, small groups continued to gather, especially in the South and South-West of England.

Movement of convoys was haphazard at times :

> *"Spider and Pikey were up front, and wouldn't tell any of us where
> we were headed. They reckoned that way the pigs wouldn't know.
> So we all sit at the back waiting and waiting, and when I walk down, there's
> Diane bonking in her truck. The front half had gone on , and she's bonking,
> at a time like that...."   Phil.*

On May 31st, several hundred headed east towards Wiltshire for the annual Stonehenge People's Free Festival. They stayed overnight in Savernake Forest. However, a whole series of authorities had conspired to prevent this twelfth festival from happening at all.

 Although a popular rumour on the road is that once an event has happened twelve times, it cannot be halted ever; there are many other excuses for what later became known as the 'Battle of the Beanfield.' The National Trust and English Heritage issued a poster claiming that land of archaeological interest was threatened by the festival. This is hardly backed up by the heavy M.o.D. use of such land all over Salisbury Plain!

Also, Stonehenge is regarded as a tourist attraction by the authorities, rather than the sacred site for cultural celebration which is the Travellers' vision. So an influx of thousands of 'deviants' throughout June was not regarded as acceptable or economically viable. Other

excuses were added, such as witchcraft being conducted on the site, or the threat to nuclear convoys if they had to pass along the A303. But, basically it would seem that Margaret Thatcher's personal threat to the Travellers to:

> _"...make their lives as difficult as possible..."_

was planned efficiently, with the precision of the exercises at Nostell Priory and Molesworth; though on this occasion police had not bargained on public outrage at their abusive physical tactics.

Beanfield

Though popularly recalled as the 'Battle of the Beanfield,' it was, more accurately a cowardly attack by armed men on family groups including many women and children.

June 1st 1985 was a sunny Saturday morning, and the long convoy of vehicles travelled slowly towards Stonehenge, followed by a police helicopter. Encountering a road block seven miles from Stonehenge - still outside the four and a half mile exclusion zone that had been imposed - the lead vehicles turned down a narrow road. There was another road block on the next road, and police, clad in riot gear, moved into position at both front and rear of the convoy.

As police attacked vehicles at both ends, smashing windows with truncheons and dragging people through the debris; the vehicles in the centre of the column smashed their way through fences into neighbouring fields. The police were wearing heavy overalls with no identity numbers. They were employing massive force against women and children, as well as the men they encountered. They were protected physically , and from recognition, by visored helmets and two shields. After initial arrests, it seemed that there was to be a peaceful solution. Police communicated into radios, while Travellers brewed up, and looked warily around them.

> _"....it seemed like a trap that had been well planned.....a lot_
> _of us just wanted to get in our vehicles and leave peacefully,_
> _but that was not being allowed."_   Tash.

Negotiations were impossible - the police refused to talk; and suddenly, at about 7 o'clock in the evening, the police charged. Travellers started up vehicles if they could, and drove frantically into the neighbouring beanfield to escape the squads of indiscriminately attacking men.

> _"I was struck by a brick thrown through the windscreen."_   Debbie.

> _"I shall never forget the screams of one woman who was holding_
> _up her little baby in a bus with smashed windows.....5 seconds later_
> _50 men with truncheons and shields just boiled into that bus."_
>   Earl of Cardigan.

> _"One of them hit me in the ribs with his truncheon..."_   Nell

> _"I was dragged out of the vehicle and two cops jumped on me_
> _and told me that if I moved they'd kill me."_   George.

The vehicles had no means of escape, and those circling in the beanfield slowly staggered to a halt as a posse of anonymous police smashed their way on board, destroying manically.

> *"I'd had my home trashed at Nostell Priory, and here was*
> *my fire engine again, being smashed up by 30 officers.*
> *They burned my home and made me watch."*   Phil.

By the end of the day, 520 people had been arrested - the largest mass arrest of civilians for centuries in the UK. Incarceration facilities were often appalling - little attention being made to offer food, drink or more than the most basic of medical attention. Many of the children were taken into care in the middle of the night, having witnessed the traumatic destruction of their homes, and beating of parents and friends.

> *"She said the law of the land......if you don't sign this piece*
> *of paper placing them voluntarily into care, then we will have*
> *to place them forcibly into care and then it will be harder for*
> *you to get them back again."*   Sheila.

Some animals were destroyed or beaten. All the vehicles had been smashed badly, and many had been completely gutted. The riot police were prepared for aggressive action, and those Travellers who escaped into surrounding woodlands were met and detained by members of the local constabulary sickened by the violence.

> *"All around the country for a while after that we'd meet local*
> *police who'd apologise and say they wanted nothing to do*
> *with it all."* Gwen.

Journalists witnessing the Beanfield were shocked :

> *"This was the weekend when Belfast type scenes came*
> *to Marlborough...the sight of police patrolling the town in*
> *threes and fours - strange policeman who could not answer*
> *requests for directions - became the norm. The only police*
> *vehicles to be seen had steel grills all round, ready for an*
> *impending something. That something turned out to be*
> *the bloodiest civilian battle the county had seen since the*
> *agricultural revolution, bloodier even than that."*
> *3/1/86. Gazette & Herald.*

Television viewers were astounded by scenes of police violence on an unprecedented level - and these were the censored films. The Earl of Cardigan was profoundly affected, and later gave evidence in court. Phil's case was heard a couple of years later at the Magistrates' Court in Salisbury. He was found not guilty on all charges, and, as his had been the test case, outstanding charges against all the others were also dropped.

In 1991, a number of Travellers fought for compensation at Winchester Crown Court. Emotive witnesses recalled events, backed up by film, and recorded police conversations.

> *"The jury wanted us to win, but the judge, he gave them really*
> *limited options. If just one person may have wanted to go on,*
> *we were all guilty. They got confused, but did award damages."*
> *Jill.*

The judge , however, recalled all compensation payments to cover court costs.

"Some of the jury were crying. They hadn't realised. The clerk hadn't explained to them. They didn't want to give us so much that the police appealed; but nobody told them all the costs could be taken away first."

Jill.

Stonehenge is more than a festival, it's a way of life, a celebration of a way of living all year round. For many, it's as much a part of the annual cycle as solstice is to summer.

is it really possible to stop the solstice sunrise?

Sheila, 1986.

Chapter Two:
A CHANGING CULTURE

1985
1986
1987
1988
1989
1990
1991
1992
1993
1994

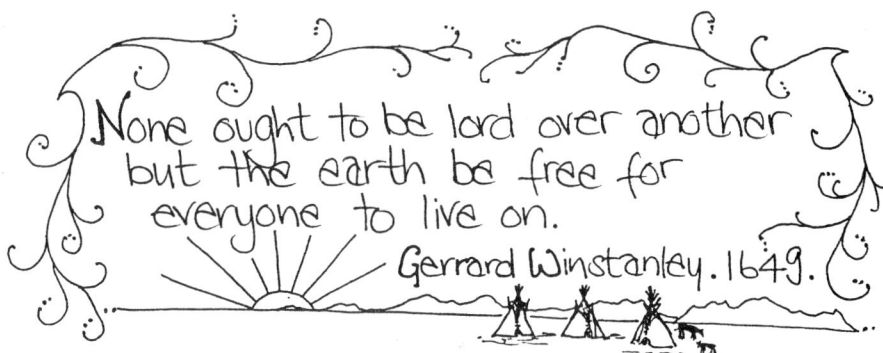

None ought to be lord over another but the earth be free for everyone to live on.
— Gerrard Winstanley. 1649.

The 'Peace Convoy' had been effectively smashed near Wakefield in 1984; the Rainbow Village had been hounded into small groups by spring 1985; those Travellers attempting to reach Stonehenge for the summer solstice had been viciously attacked. As a systematic destruction of a lifestyle, it could have been an effective campaign - yet spirits had not been crushed, and the culture has continued, evolved and grown.

This chapter focuses on the last decade, looking specifically on the summer events.
> *"Ideally you have a festival season during the summer and you have a kind of quiet period during the winter...you spend the winter living fairly quietly and cheaply somewhere out of the way, getting things together. When you go to the festivals you've got things to barter.....so hopefully you can afford to put a bit of money away in the bank, or a bit of capital to keep you going through the winter."*
> *Es.*

Whilst this statement is true of many Travellers, it must be emphasised that not everybody bothers with the whole, or even any, of the festival circuit. Travelling is a whole year occupation, which is discussed in Chapter 3. This chapter mostly attempts to give a different view of those events which the media has brought to the attention of the general public each summer; having ignored us all winter. Festivals and gatherings are an important focus for discussion and conversation, but must remain within the context of a massive range of different national experience.

Broadly speaking, Travellers celebrate a number of 'special' times throughout the year, either on a small local scale, or at a major national gathering. Individual celebrations are eclipsed by media emphasis on major events, but they are an important focus. There are some events we have missed out, like the Elephant Fair, not because they are unimportant, but because we want to re-tell stories the media misrepresented.

Apart from the full moon, the following seasonal cycle is commonly followed:

> *Spring equinox*
> *May day*
> *Beltane*
> *Summer solstice*
> *Summer parties*
> *August bank holiday*
> *Autumn equinox*
> *Winter solstice*

There are also numerous local commercial fairs and events; horse fairs such as Appleby; steam rallies; bike shows; narrowboat rallies and small gatherings at ancient monuments and places of particular power, which many Travellers do attend. And then there are some who just get on with living.

1985

After the trashing at the Beanfield, those arrested were allowed to collect their damaged vehicles from the land, and limped to Savernake Forest for a brief period of recovery. Many went on to Westbury, an ancient hill fort where :

> *"......at last the festival did get under way.....in spite of being in a*
> *state of siege for much of the time; police sealed off lanes and prevented*
> *people who left site from returning."*   Sheila

Everybody split up , and found their own smaller groups in which to recover.

> *"The tribes were scattered, the festival, the rainbow and the*
> *solstice were celebrated in our hearts, not around the stones."*
> *Chris.*

Those who travelled North held festivals in Cumbria, Norfolk, Yorkshire and Wales; on sites which had previously been used successfully. Gradually, the massive damage was repaired, lives rebuilt and money made. Some retreated to Greenlands Farm, near Glastonbury, a Christian community founded by Alison Collyer and partially administered by the Paddington Farm Trust. Local debate, fuelled by media distortion, led to High Court action disputing the legality of a 'properly supervised camp.' By early January '86, everybody had moved off to Cheddar, Frome and the Quantock hills, leaving Allison Collyer ill as a result of the pressure - not from Travellers, but from local residents.

Some town councillors collected £700 to buy the infamous 'hippy wrecker' -a tow truck with winch - to safeguard themselves against future 'invasions'. Its illegality was pointed out by police, and it has hardly been used. Glastonbury town however, remains a New Age focal point, as the shops and cafes thriving on this reputation clearly indicate. There are many locals who uphold alternative lifestyles - albeit in a somewhat 'sanitised' and idealistic manner.

1986

Small groups of Travellers spent the early months doing different things and getting different reactions or hassles all over the place. The Stonehenge '86 campaign requested the use of a disused airfield, but permission was refused. Wiltshire County Council stated that :

> *"In view of the threats of violence and demonstrations, it is clearly*

impossible to give access to the stones this year. "

By May, razor wire had been erected round the monument; a 5 mile exclusion zone for vehicles and a 1 mile exclusion zone for pedestrians was announced; and felled trees blocked all but one access point to Savernake Forest.

Pandora's Box

When Pandora's box was opened,
  Babylon began to sing
There'll be hate for the government
  and sorrow for the king
Vengeance for his lord
  and deceit for his lady
For the travelling people
  there was just a lot of maybes
There was guilt for the government
  and sorrow for the police
And for the travelling people,
  there was nothing left but hope for peace.

So you can open your box and let all your horrors fly
Your jealousy, your hatred and your greed
All we have is hope and faith in Mother Earth
We've found this is all we really need.

They hounded us and pushed us
  slowly down the road
Out of the sunshine
  and into the cold
They banned us from our ancient site
  with no place to roam
So we headed for the forest
  where we tried to have some fun
Some singing and some dancing,
  some laughter and some games,
For we knew that in our lives
  everything had come to change.

So you can ....

That was early Monday morning
  when the police came in
Looking for a fight,
  they were trying to cause a scene
So all our people stood there
  and we asked them - what's the fuss?
You want to take our homes again -
  every trailer, van and bus?
Well, they burned down all the benders
  and they took our tat away
But we still have the spirit
  and this is what we have to say

So you can ....

So our people started walking
  slowly down the road
Many were arrested -
  for what, we were not told
The more you try to push us,
  the stronger we become
Although they say it's finished now -
  you know it's just begun
For there's guilt for the government
  and sorrow for the police
And for the travelling people
  there was nothing left but hope for peace

So you can open your box and let all your horrors fly
Your jealousy, your hatred and your greed
All we have is hope and faith in Mother Earth
We've found this is all we really need.

a traveller.

Yet in mid-May, 200 people converged at Stonehenge, and 380 police moved them off. They were shunted around southern England until they reluctantly pulled up in a farmer's grass field. Les Atwell, the farmer, suffered an angina attack, which was gleefully reported by the media, disregarding the desperation of Travellers with no other place to go. A High Court order forced them off the farm land 7 days later, and 'Today' newspaper offered to pay Mr. Atwell's costs. Movement was halted on the Dorset border by police in riot gear - without identity numbers. This was happening to small groups all over the southern counties, and on June 2nd, a convoy desperate for fuel and repairs, moved on to a disused airfield near Stoney Cross. Holiday-makers nearby were moved because of a 'health risk'; and the chief constable of Hampshire was heckled off site. The media was concerned :

"They are a bunch of lazy, ill-mannered drop-outs...."
Manchester Evening News. 4/6/86

The Guardian 30/5/86

(about the Travellers)............"they sound as if they just have to be good people. Partly it's the rotten treatment they got from the police at Stonehenge last year - nobody deserves that. Partly it's the romance (however ill-founded) of their life on the road, under the stars, free from authority. Partly it's the sense that they are in some however absurd way, the lost tribe of the deserted village, the resurrected victims of the enclosure of the common land that devastated the lives of uncountable numbers of all our forebearers, the spiritual heirs and witnesses of Gerrard Winstanley and all the deluded and humiliated utopians and millenians through our history who have tried to show by example - and in the teeth of derision and persecution - that there is a life that can be lived free from the State, money and the nuclear family."

On June 9th, 'Operation Daybreak' was launched to enforce the High Court order of the previous day. 440 police encircled the site at dawn, and arrested the people, then impounded 129 vehicles on which files were held. Only 2 vehicles were allowed to leave; so, loaded with women, children and animals, they headed to Worthy Farm. The police had learned from the Beanfield criticisms, and provided a coach to Calshot reception area for food, drinks and transport passes - ignoring the fact that for many, their homes were in Nursling vehicle pound. Over 250 set off to walk through the drizzle, along the A31 towards Somerset. Some sympathetic landlords gave overnight stopping points, and:

"We were inundated with supplies." Dawn.

90 miles on, they reached Pilton, and were joined by those who had faced charges at a special Magistrates' Court in Southampton.

Glastonbury

This festival has grown constantly from 1986 onwards, and whilst an admission charge is required, it is not a commercial festival run by promoters as such. Michael Eavis, whose main income still comes from farming, oversees the organisation of the event, and has to cover all the costs, as well as choosing to make generous charitable donations. He has had to adapt to meet legal and financial restrictions, but welcomed Travellers for a number of years.

On 18th June, at Worthy Farm, Michael Eavis was forced to make a show of evicting the refugees in order to comply with legal regulations.

"Today a 'convoy' of so many vehicles will leave site, hopefully to return as soon as possible." Bruce.

Many Travellers celebrated the solstice at Pilton - the 'muddy year', bathed in of oceans of mud!

Stonehenge

Wiltshire police allowed about 200 people to walk to the monument for a brief solstice celebration.

"Security guards with dogs were the only sentient beings on those sacred grounds." Richie.

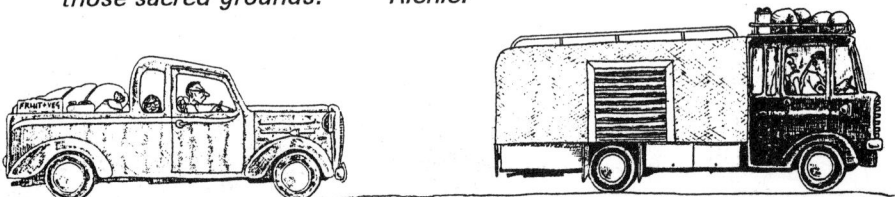

Nursling

Those Travellers whose homes had been impounded spent many weeks battling against time and police pressure, to rebuild them. Not only did vehicles have to pass a garage M.O.T., but also a rigorous police inspection - and all work had to be completed during the hours when access was allowed to the pound.

> *"Lots of vehicles got weighed in by the pigs one night. There was a storm, so we couldn't hear them take them away."*   Phil.

The Public Order Act, limiting sites to twelve vehicles or less; and other social pressures, resulted in smaller units and park-ups. Some people moved to Wales, Ireland, Spain and Portugal, where land prices subsequently rose. Others continued to campaign peacefully at Menwith Hill and such like. Others established alternative communities like the Weirdzone - as Wheatstone became known. Others just carried on living in smaller groups. In a way, the government action was counter-productive. Few people totally left the road, and although the 'peace convoy' was effectively de-commissioned, a whole new group of Travellers joined the scene.

1987

Avon Free	Cantlin Stone
Forest Fayre	Happy Daze
Glastonbury	Ribblehead
Rollright	Nenthead
Elephant Fair	

Many diverse projects came together in 1987, with small functioning co-operatives and companies being established for circuses, stages, cafés etc.

Rollright

A solstice party was held at the Rollright Stones in Oxfordshire. It was wet and muddy, and on the final day, Douglas Hurd visited the site. After his much quoted comments about 'medieval brigands' the previous year, he was met by angry Travellers who had been blockaded in by manure dumped by an angry farmer, and was pelted with the muck.

> *"....while everyone shouted 'Hello, Mr. Turd!' "*   Herring.

Glastonbury

The festival had grown rapidly, attracting punters who had previously gone to Stonehenge, as well as Travellers preferring to trade legally rather than face arrest yet again. The latter made a colourful contribution to the event, with wagons and horses, tipis and benders; as well as skilful acts, and alternative attractions such as the Mutoid Waste Company's 'Carhenge'; 'Archaos;' and Wango Riley's Travelling Stage.'

In some ways, it was regarded as one of the worst festivals ever, with conflict on site between urban drug gangs and Travellers - Michael Eavis lost many of his original, good, site crew. He said:

> *"It was wearing us down, the constant unpleasantness."*

Carhenge at Pilton

*Live life in a gutter,
Or somewhere sublime,
You can influence fate,
Whilst you're biding
your time,
Out in the elements,
Under the sky.
You can't understand
Till you give it a try.*

1988

Barbary Castle	Cissbury Ring
Stonehenge equinox	Ribblehead
Wyke Tip	Aktivator
Stonehenge	Bilbo Baggins
Clun	Stonehenge winter solstice.

Glastonbury

The festival was not held, maybe as a result of the vast numbers in '87; way beyond security control.

Stonehenge

Several thousand people had gathered in Cholderton Woods by June 20th, and were subjected to the 5 mile exclusion zone around the monument.

> *"There was a site meeting in the afternoon; we partied at night,
> bands played, and everyone set off at midnight to walk to the Stones."*
>   *Herring.*

Police herded walkers into a penned-off section of road where they ranked 5-deep along the fences. Ritual chanting and conch blowing was accompanied by continuous helicopter whirring. Spotlights cut through the darkness as everybody sat on the road.

> *"People got frustrated squashed along the roadway. Harassment,
> provocation and insults from the police, then a few missiles were
> thrown."*   *John Harrison.*

Tension grew , and the chants became angry :

> *"The stones are ours
> And that's a fact,
> So fuck your
> Public Order Act."*

The police baton-charged at dawn in:

> *"I believe, some sort of 'police-riot'.....cynically decided well in advance by senior officers....this charge was....indiscriminate and terroristic, hitting at random with clubs, shields, boots and body armour on arms and legs."*
>
> Ian Lee. Alternative News Digest. '88.

A front line of police trapped everybody in the road end, and 'snatch squads' were sent into the middle;

> *"...dragging out people , kicking and screaming.....women, kids in pushchairs, toddlers; hysterical and terrified."* Herring.

NOSTALGIA TRIP

Well I just got back from Stonehenge
Saw the people being turned away
Some were hurt
Pride trailing in the dirt
But that's not what the media say
Then hounded back to site
From where they came the previous night
To see the first new hope of solstice light
Just as the monument was then
As some monolithic hen
As sure as those who had forgotten
Will doubtless forget again
Those who simply can't refrain
Return again to face the pain
In the time it takes a thousand songs
We humans come to right our wrongs

When the National Trust builds a Trust House Hotel
And a petrol station as well
Three lanes either side
With easy access to the plastic cafe and the fun rides
As travellers drive out of the dip
They'll see a sign saying
'Stonehenge Nostalgia Trip'

CG

The media concentrated on the police reaction to crowd violence, ignoring;

> *"...the presence of plain-clothes police dressed as hippies amongst the crowd."*
>
> Ian Hill.

67 arrests were made; 37 people later faced charges. After this long walk, pitched battle and hard trudge back to Cholderton, Travellers had one hour to clear the site.

> *"1,000 men lined a nearby road ready to evict them unless*
> *they complied with the order."*   Daily Telegraph. 22/6/88.

Several accidents and at least one fatality ensued, due to exhaustion. Clouds obscured the sunrise.

080888

Druids

A gathering of several hundred took place at Glastonbury Tor to celebrate this date.

Aktivator

Held during September in Gloucestershire, this was organised by the T.S.C. to raise funds for the Skool Bus (see Chapter.4) Events included a truck tug-of-war, and over £2,000 was raised. At one point during the event, Sid turned on the hoses on his fire engine to pacify a few people who were getting too loud at the bar!

Bilbo Baggins

A smaller event in October gave trade to the festival stages, bands and other performers. It

was held;

> "......by hippies, for hippies, and loads of Travellers turned up."
> *Herring.*

But again, it raised over £2,000.

1989

Equinox
White Horse
Inglestone
Strawberry Fayre

Village Idiots, Watling
Camelford
Ribblehead
Bally Hope Common

Glastonbury	Frodo Baggins
Holden Hill	Happy daze
Treworgey	Equinox
Clun	Solstice

Stonehenge

There were many small sites in the area such as Figsbury and Amesbury. 800 police were deployed to arrest anyone attempting to walk within the exclusion zone - 261 were arrested, including some locals.

> *"Quite a few other people were....also hiding in the fields, woods and on the barrows, and we could see them all running away."*
>
> *John Harrison.*

Meanwhile, Alex Rosenberger was arrested at Salisbury Cathedral for his peaceful protest against such human rights infringements.

Glastonbury

High fencing and imported security marked a new era for this event, though a fringe festival took place outside the perimeter. Despite the threat of fines, Michael Eavis did not enforce eviction, and once the main event was over, the solstice was celebrated. Wango Riley's stage presented bands all night, whilst chanting and acoustic music sounded from those on the green fields of the official festival. Between, lay only the empty littered valley.

> *"It was a marvellous year."*   *Michael Eavis.*

Autumn Equinox '89

Treworgey Tree Fayre

Held at the end of July, this event in Cornwall escalated beyond the plans of the organisers. Many Travellers arrived straight from Pilton, and found a very varied landscape - a high, dry dust trap to which they were directed; while the paying event was in a marshy dip. Toilet facilities were woefully inadequate, as were the water supplies, and many people were quite ill. Official security was badly organised and when they were not paid their promised fee, it led to a raid on the farm and a pitched battle with Travellers protecting the house. In the end the 'security' people were paid, and left site. Attended by about 50,000, this was the nearest in atmosphere to the Stonehenge People's Free Festival.

Frodo Baggins

Another T.S.C. benefit held at Clyro Court. Bands played on Wango Riley's Stage and inside the building, while children explored the Skool Bus. A lot of Travellers turned up, and most paid to park up - benefiting the Skool Bus further.

all profits to Travellers School
reg. no. 327731

and the Travellers Aid Trust
reg. no. 299463

The Mending of the Ways

FRODO BAGGINS' 123rd BIRTHDAY PARTY

£7.50 on the gate

£5.00 in costume

ON WANGO RILEYS TRAVELLING STAGE:

HAWKWIND
AGENT BEARTRAP
HIPPY SLAGS, CRAFTY JACK
JOHN PERKINS & KESHEV SATHE:
INDIAN CLASSICAL MUSIC
FRUMNIKMOL'M'LOM, & SURPRISE GUESTS

DANCE HALL:
7 KEVINS
CONNECTING ROUTES
Radical Dance Faction
Sons of Spock
Another Green World
STALLS

CABARET:
FLYING PATROL GROUP
WHITE LEAVED OAK
CLICK BACK
Rainbow Minstrels
Puppet Shows
CIRCUS & THEATRE

SKOOL BUS
CHILDRENS ACTIVITIES
ONE WORLD FILMS
SATURDAY 16TH SEPTEMBER
from 2.00 pm till late at:
CLYRO COURT
off A438 Brecon → Hereford road nr. Hay
BAR   FOOD

1990

Equinox	Morton
Poll Tax demo	Telecombe Cliffs
Hungerford Common	Clapham common
Inglestone	Camelford
Glastonbury	Equinox

Stonehenge

There were small gatherings for both equinoxes, but little emphasis on the solstice - despite massive police operations again.

Inglestone

Police roadblocks stopped and searched many vehicles on the way to the common, and for several hours the rumours of eviction persisted. By the evening however, quite a large event had been established around Wango Riley's, the rave tents and the Skool Bus.

Glastonbury

Travellers had been offered access to fields bordering the paying festival, but arrived early to find the gates still closed. Some were shunted off to another site 4 miles away, while others queued for hours while the entrance was cleared. Driving onto a sloping field in the dark while it's raining is not easy, and many vehicles were damaged. Next morning the remainder trailed in, most with burned out clutches or no fuel from the prolonged wait. Wango's was set up, along with the rave tents, cafés, bars and other stalls; and punters poured between the official and fringe events. Rumours of the hard-core security reached Travellers, with complaints of corruption, sexism and attacks.

On the day after the main festival, Travellers and litter-pickers went tatting - collecting abandoned possessions such as tents, as well as the mountains of perishable food left by traders.

Hello

Micheal Eavis Owns This Farm he has a bald head and a grey beard and he Owns lots of Cows

Kali

"One bloke was driving a green truck through fences, and pinched the Church tent. He was obviously drunk and his behaviour was out of order. Security were sent down because of the threat to children - he admitted he was drunk, but unfortunately, Security cracked his windscreen before police arrested him and took him away. The lorry was towed to the site compound, but one of the children shouted, 'I'm going to get the posse.' "   Michael Eavis

The story that reached the Travellers was that Security had forced a Traveller off the road and out of his landrover, then;

> *"...twatted him, fracturing his skull and hospitalising him."* Herring.

A pitched battle ensued as Travellers armed with lumps of wood, axes and other implements in daily use lined up on the hill to face a barrage of petrol bombs hurled by Security. At least one Portakabin was fired, and many vehicles were damaged as the outnumbered Security backed towards farm buildings. Once the situation was temporarily calmed, Security were removed from site.

> *"The police wanted to prosecute the security firm for incitement to riot, and came up asking people to testify."* Herring.

Travellers staying to work moved down to the lower fields, gathering for safety. The incident was blown out of proportion:

> *"...as a form of manipulation. All the problems of the festival were off-loaded onto us, and the event seems to have been sanitised by excluding the 'convoy.' "* Roddy.

After the 'riots' and fight with security staff, everyone was sat round the fires telling tales of the day's excitement and their heroic deeds. My mate, Stewart, was full of himself and told how he was in the 'front line' and had put a telegraph pole through the windscreen of one of the security vehicles - everyone was impressed, until we heard another Traveller telling the tale of how he'd got in one of the security landrovers and tried to ram the police. Some idiot had nearly killed him with a wooden pole inches from his head, thru the windscreen.   Es.

Morton

Many rigs travelled north for an unprecedented event at Morton Lighthouse. The colourful stages and performers attracted a massive number of local punters, relatively 'straight', who had never seen such a gathering. The atmosphere was carnival-like as settled grandparents and toddlers mixed with the Travellers.

Equinox

This was the last time that vehicles have been allowed near the Stones. Several parked on a green lane opposite the monument, which was blocked by the council with grit. The tense atmosphere was not alleviated by the presence of bullet-vested police; and a hit-and-run incident, where the victim's foot was practically severed. The vehicle somehow evaded the blocks set up to halt us. A few weeks later, I.R.A. suspects were caught near the monument, and the massive security was more understandable.

TAKE only pictures
LEAVE only footprints
KILL only time
Mark Vjuyan Jones

Poll Tax Demo

Whilst not directly a Traveller event, the Trafalgar Square demonstration against the introduction of the Government's infamous, Community Charge, aka the Poll Tax, was attended by a number of Travellers and many other people who viewed the new tax as socially unjust. The police handling of the demonstration was heavily criticised at the time as being brutal and an over-reaction, and in many ways the event was reminiscent of the police activity at the Beanfield and in the Miners' Strike.

Bert at the Poll Tax demo '90

1991

Chipping Sodbury	Morton
Forest Fayre	Deeside
Rats Run	Bala
Peasdown St John	Trecastle
Abbey Foregate	Clapham Common

Glastonbury

The festival was not held, probably as a result of the skirmishes in '90.

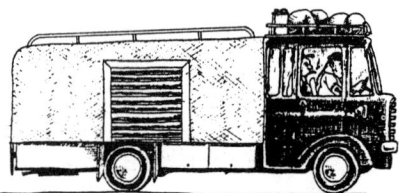

Peasdown St. John

Held on a small farm site near Bath, this attracted hundreds of Travellers. Stages were improvised, so live bands performed, and raves took place. There was a positive atmosphere despite some harassment.

Rats Run

Evicted from Stockbridge Common in Hampshire, a group of Travellers moved onto a green lane just a couple of miles away. The festival was blockaded, so punters had to abandon vehicles on verges and walk, but the atmosphere was good until police refused food and water runs. The dispersal was dismal.

Morton

Officials opposed a repeat of the '90 event, and word reached site that social services and local hospitals were on standby for the following morning.

> "......................the evening before the 1991 eviction, an ambulance worker came to the site and warned us that hundreds of staff and ambulances were on standby for the next morning at Arrowe Park Hospital. Also a social worker came to tell us that they were on standby to take the children. The next morning a helicopter circled the site announcing: "Leave now and you will not be hurt." Fuel tanks were brought on and everybody's tanks were filled up with free fuel. The first riot van arrived as this was happening and within a few minutes the whole common was lined with vans and pigs. The tow trucks and pigs started moving in, so people started to pull off. I got into the road and found I had no brakes, so I pulled over and told the pigs I had to wait for help. Instead I got a police escort along the motorway and into Wales. Once over the border, my escort disappeared and I was left on the Welsh hills with a lorry, a trailer, my son and no brakes!"
>
> Liz.

Winter

By the winter of '91, Travellers had begun to establish large winter sites of about 200 vehicles, with bars, cafes and bands. Party atmospheres continued all year round, and traders could keep making money. The Avon C.C. policy of non-harassment meant that safe unauthorised sites were available in that region; and some , such as Hanham, became authorised and gained basic services. But it meant that many people became stuck in and around Bristol, because it was a relative haven.

1992

Castlemorton
Lechlade
Strawberry Fayre
Forest Fayre

Glastonbury/Laxton airfield
Ashbourne airfield
Kerry
Otterbourne/Romsey

Castlemorton

With all areas around Inglestone protected by exclusion zones, a sudden influx of Travellers in Worcestershire resulted in police confusion, and Castlemorton Common became a site.
Word spread, not only by the grapevine, but thanks to media coverage, and 20,000 people converged. Police roadblocks were organised to prevent further arrivals from roads between Gloucester, Malvern and Upton. They also advised shopkeepers and publicans not to serve 'hippies or Travellers.' Although the media emphasised the filthy squalor, in reality several hundred Travellers remained to clear up, and:

>"...one local said he'd never seen the common so clean." Herring.

Much media attention was focused on the confiscation of rave equipment, particularly that belonging to Spiral Tribe.

>"Spiral Bribe mouthed off, caused loads of shit, and were then too scared to leave site, hiding in other people's rigs. Once off the site, they continued their bullshit to the media, and so got charged with organising. Serves them right."
>Herring.

Glastonbury

A 10' fence encircled the site, and an exclusion zone was enforced. Although many Travellers were employed as site crew, others expecting access, were escorted out of the county with fuel provided by Michael Eavis. After five years of trying to accommodate Travellers, he had had enough. (He has campaigned unsuccessfully for years to establish an alternative site for the Stonehenge festival, but still has to make plans for those who turn up at his event - with a significant change of atmosphere as anarchy has been swept away.)

The event was *"one of the best ever,"* Michael Eavis said afterwards, and a small stone circle had been erected in the sacred field; which was dedicated at sunrise on the solstice. A very successful alternative free event was held at Laxton airfield.

Kerry

This was a pleasant festival on a peaceful agricultural site in Wales, until the D.S.S. and media combined to provide the 'Hippy scroungers' story.

Media circus at Kerry

> *"They brought B.1.s up to the site to stop an influx of Travellers into Newtown. A media circus ensued, and bored police had a chance to show off. Hardly any one actually signed on, fearing a trap, and details going on to intelligence files. Next day the papers were full of it, though housedwellers cost the State at least twice as much in benefit."*
>
> *Herring.*

Travellers still had to collect giros and cash them in town, as well as completing shopping!

Otterbourne

Hants and Thames Valley orchestrated an anti-festival operation, so Torpedo Town Festival was split into two sites, with heavy policing at each. There were battles at 'Chivers' in Romsey; and at Otterbourne the incinerator went up in flames on the Saturday night.

> *"No one on site would have fired a building so close to so many vehicles. Naturally we got the blame."* Herring

There was 24 hour occupation of the site by riot police in un-numbered black boiler suits, with riot shields, helmets, batons and tear gas. The atmosphere was ominous, especially with the Skool Bus and many children on site.

1993

Coombe Farm	Midlands
Forest Fayre	Phoenix
M 5	Wales
Glastonbury	Norfolk

Coombe Farm

Beltane was celebrated at an established site in Staffordshire; where over 200 rigs congregated. But police from three constabularies enforced a P.O. order in full riot gear, and for the first time, communications were blocked, and small convoys could not meet up.

> "...........At around 11 a.m., the bailiffs turned up - backed by hundreds of riot police and tow trucks. Behind them came the media. As the bailiff read out the notice, surrounded by film crews, he was hit in face by a strategically aimed piece of horse shit. The flying turd was the catalyst for the the riot pigs and tow trucks to move in...............We tried to wait on the road, but the pigs were having none of it and we started off on a three day journey to nowhere. We were continuously lied to by 3 police forces (Oxfordshire, Warwickshire and Staffordshire) and shunted between three counties...........I read the papers at the end of the weekend and it reportedly cost £250,000 for the police operation to keep us on the road for three days." Liz

Forest Fayre

The Forest Fayre , organised by the Rainbow Circle, provided a party haven after the dismal non-event for Beltane.

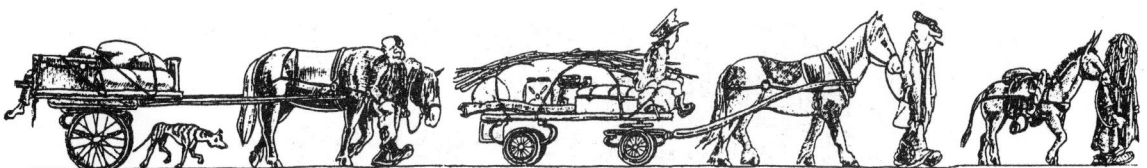

"It was well attended, a big site presence, and despite a 'lights out and pumpkins at midnight' policy, not much trouble. The rain was a pain, but not a washout."   Herring.

M5

Exclusion orders for Castlemorton Common were served on sites 100 miles from it. With no word of a specific location, vehicles congregated at Strensham and Gordano services on the M5.

"We were forced on to the motorway, where we didn't want to be. Bank holiday traffic which wanted to be there, wasn't allowed on. Then the entrances and exits to the services were blocked, so that we could not join up. As usual, Travellers were blamed for the resulting chaos."
Roddy.

The operations cost a rumoured £500,000. Arrests were made, but a clerk of the court happened to be at the services, and all charges were thrown out.

Small sites

Due to the police crackdown on free festival sites and the chronic lack of park ups, there were numerous battles to leave or join laybys in the west country. At Milverton and Ivythorne, people were denied access to water, painting desperate messages on their rigs for mercy from passers by.

Glastonbury.

Heavily promoted by Radio 1, and with a second music stage, the atmosphere had changed. The areas were separated, rather than incorporating many attractions; no animals were admitted; few Travellers attended, other than site crew. It had become very much a music event, although the sense of cabaret remained. Traders on the green fields noticed a shift in emphasis, with young punters only visiting raves and foodstalls.

Phoenix

Very much a rock festival, there was, nevertheless, a big Traveller presence in the Stratford area. Heavy policing and security meant that those who attended did so without their rigs. Yet the battle between youths on the rampage against heavy-handed security was reportedly much more ferocious and indiscriminate than at Pilton in 1990.

Strawberry Fayre

Once again, the unofficial site squeezed under the bridge at Cambridge, and even those with pitches on the official site joined the punters that swarmed over at midnight.

1994
Glastonbury
Phoenix
Forest Fayre

Isle of Wight
Strawberry Fayre etc

Stonehenge

Although it gets relatively little media coverage, the Stonehenge Campaign continues. English Heritage usually allow access for Druids and holders of a limited number of tickets for summer solstice. The exclusion zone is still enforced. Summer 1994 will mark 10 years since we were last there .

English Heritage
Historic Properties South West Region
Stonehenge Nr Amesbury Wiltshire SP4 7DE Telephone 0980 623108

11th March 1994

Dear Sir/Madam.

As with previous years English Heritage will not be allowing out of hours access to the Stonehenge Monument over the Summer Solstice period. The site will be open to visitors during normal opening hours.

I hope that this information is of help to you.

Yours sincerely,

Sharan White.
General Manager
Stonehenge.

WILTSHIRE   CONSTABULARY

DIVISIONAL HEADQUARTERS,
Wilton Road, Salisbury,
Wiltshire, SP2 7HR.
Telephone: 0722 411444
Extension: 413
Telex via 44206
Fax: 0722 435291 (24 hours)

Reply contact name is: Inspector Shearing   Your Ref:

Date: 11th March 1994   Our Ref: AS/SAP

Dear Miss Earle,

In reply to your letter concerning persons attending Stonehenge this Summer, by which I presume you mean around the Summer Solstice period, I have reproduced for you below. the details of our press release issued on 4th March, 1994 by the Chief Constable of Wiltshire:

"At a meeting held at Police Headquarters, Devizes, today (4th March, 1994) the Chief Constable of Wiltshire, W.R. Girven, Esq., O St J. QPM, LL.B. FBIM, discussed the outline of plans being made for policing the Summer Solstice at Stonehenge, with representatives from English Heritage, National Trust, Police Authority, County Solicitor, Salisbury District Council, Amesbury Town Council, National Parents' Union and the County Landowners' Association.

Representatives expressed concern over the incidents of disorder involving travellers and illegal trespass in other parts of the country in 1993 and there was support for the successful policing policy in Wiltshire over recent years.

English Heritage made it clear that there will be no change in their policy relating to the Summer Solstice and they will not allow special access to the monument for the 1994 celebration.

The Wiltshire Constabulary will continue to commit resources to prevent disorder and illegal trespass this year and amongst other plans, the Chief Constable will apply to Salisbury District Council for order under Section 13, Public Order Act, banning procession in the area of Stonehenge for the Solstice period."

I hope this information is of assistance to you, and if I can be of any further help, please do not hesitate to contact me.

Yours sincerely,

A. SHEARING
Inspector

Glastonbury-Phoenix

These events are planned again, and the emphasis remains on music and alternative culture - without Travellers. Glastonbury, in paticular, still seeks to promote that original atmosphere of cabaret and entertainment for all the family, with varied attractions in each field.

Protest Sites

As a section of the Traveller movement in the early '80s focused on anti-nuclear campaigns; there is an increasing interest in opposing dramatic road development schemes swathing through the last remnants of countryside, and ancient sites.

At Winchester, Travellers took a local site, then a tribe called the Dongas moved benders and tipis onto the threatened land. The final showdown was brutal, as local campaigners joined site

inhabitants in a futile attempt to stop the bulldozers. New campaigners are joining the Travellers who are fighting in this way.

Ireland and Europe

Many long-term Travellers have moved overseas in order to avoid conflict. With less oppressive legislation, and greater scope for moving around and making money, it is an attractive proposition.

> *"When you're trying to run a business which involves going away,*
> *not knowing if you can return to your 'safe' site is a major problem.*
> *We feel we have no option but to go to Ireland."*   Lizzie.

As we write, in March, most big party rigs and circus groups are going abroad to the embryonic 'Free Scene.' Others are frantically seeking legal pitches at commercial events. Most people have spent the last year desperately fighting evictions and judicial reviews, just to secure a place to live.

> *"There is mounting terror at the implications of the 'Criminal Injustice Bill' "*
> Fiona.

This means that plans for parties simply do not feature. Those who choose, or have no option, to stay in the U.K. will band together for safety. 1994 will probably resemble the ferocious pitched battles witnessed in the pre-'68 Criminal Justice Act era.

> *"There will be repeats of the war for sites fought by gypsies before*
> *the C.J.A. '68, only fiercer and longer, as so many more people are on the*
> *road."*
>
> *Peter Mercer, Gypsy Council.*

Travellers can only hope that groups such as the L.C.T.R., F.F.T., Liberty and suchlike, which are working towards a peaceful solution, will be successful. Support is also expressed in many free information networks, and commercially published music or biker magazines.

> *"We support the Travellers, (creators of the festival scene) and*
> *their plight against the government and the intimidation and*
> *violence inflicted upon them by the police force."*
> *Musicians Network '93.*

> **The culture is strong, and though it has developed and changed over the last two decades, it should not be crushed simply because it seeks to be different.**

GLOSSARY

A-frame: 'A' shaped frame on a caravan which hitches it up to a vehicle.

Bender: dome shaped shelter constructed of flexible poles covered with a tarpaulin.

Blag: to gain something through articulate argument or persuasion.

Blat: a short journey, usually for pleasure.

Blat motor: small vehicle used for chores and visits - may be communally owned.

Blim: small, e.g. blim bus is a small bus.

Blue meanies: traffic police.

Breadhead: someone concerned only with making money.

Brew: tea. or strong lager.

Brew crew: see 'crusties'.

Brewed up: made tea or very drunk

Bucketing: collecting money

Burner: wood burning stove

Bus: coach.

Butts: water containers.

Cheesy quavers: see 'ravers'.

Convoy: line of vehicles travelling together.

Cosmic: often derogatory, refers to the spiritual illusions of universal consciousness.

Crusties: West-country originated; generally filthy, obnoxious and indulging in drugs or drink; financed by begging and DSS payments; often live in squats rather than on site.

Cushty (or Kushti): good. (taken from Romani language.)

Crystals: used in New Age healing techniques, believed to focus cosmic energy.

Decker: double decker bus.

Diddish: describing something associated with traditional Travellers. (possibly degrading).

Drag: route through a site.

Drongo: see 'crusties'.

E-heads: punters enjoying ecstasy.

Equinox: late March/September; point at which day and night are of equal length.

Fascists: police.

The Feds: police.

Festival: generally a commercial event though previously there was a strong tradition of free celebrations.

Filth: police.

Flat-bed: the flat base of a truck behind the cab.

Gathering: large group of people meeting to celebrate.

Gennie: generator.

Geodesic dome: prefabricated structure of metal bars forming a grid of polygons, on which plastic or tarp is stretched.

Giro: cheque from DSS.

Greenies: those with strong ecological or environmental beliefs.

Gypsy: traditional Traveller.

Hippies: bohemian liberals, especially from mid-60s to mid-80s, associated with drug use and 'free love' philosophies.

Hippy rumours: 'Chinese whispers' - stories distorted by oral retelling.

Kindling: small twigs or sticks of dry wood to start a fire.

Lunch out (or out to lunch): incapable of concentration and completing all tasks with competence.

Luton: box-type structure of a van or truck over the cab.

Main drag: main route.

New Age: originally an astrological reference to 'Age of Aquarius' - now used as a general term for new consciousness and spirituality.

Nylon nightmare: tent.

Old Bill: police.

Orbital: person who lives permanently in the vicinity of one settlement.

Park up: small place to stop, usually temporary.

Party animals: people who enjoy frequent parties.

Peace convoy: group of vehicles which travelled together through early '80s, from free festivals to camps, etc.

Pigs: police.

Pilton: site of Glastonbury Festival.

Punter: paying person at commercial event; non-traveller at unauthorised event; generally associated with having money to spend.

Raver: one who attends a rave.

Raves: mobile underground mass celebrations attracting the 'Acid House' subculture.

Rig: someone's living vehicle, or combination of vehicles.

Rom: Romany Traveller.

Script: prescription, usually for methadone.

Section 39: so-called 'hippy clause' of P.O.A.

Silly Season: police reference to summer festivals.

Site: area on which a group of travellers live. It may be authorised or unauthorised (which means that eviction may be forthcoming).

Skip run: collecting food and other rejected products from rubbish skips.

The Social: D.S.S. office.

Sorted: good.

Squatting: homeless people occupying unused property, without permission or payment of a rent.

The Stones: Stonehenge monument.

Straight: house dweller.

Summer Solstice: longest day, 21st June.

Tarot: fortune telling based on original set of 22 picture cards.

Tarp: abbreviation of a tarpaulin.

Tat: possessions.

Tatting: collecting discarded items for use or sale.

Tatting down: clearing all possessions away prior to moving on.

Techno: progressive electronic music characterised by a frenzied rhythm and futuristic noises.

Tipi: conical shaped structure of poles and canvas, based on native American homes.

Tow: pull something behind a vehicle or truck.

Trader: commercial tradesperson.

Transit site: site on which temporary residence is allowed.

Trashing: beating up and destruction, generally by police.

Travellers: people of a nomadic lifestyle, usually termed 'New Age Travellers' by the media.

Veg out: relaxed, unconcerned state

Vigies: vigilantes.

Wagon: horse drawn caravan.

Water run going to collect water.

Weigh-in: scrap vehicles - based on value of weight of metal.

Wicked: term of great appreciation.

Wooding: collecting wood.

Wood run going to collect wood.

Winter Solstice: shortest day, 21st December.

Chapter Three:
Life on the road

> We are the new people,
> We are the old people,
> We are the same people,
> Stronger everyday.

Life on the road is not easy. Basic daily needs have to be maintained in the face of increasingly oppressive laws. The diversity of people makes it impossible to even attempt some kind of all-encompassing explanation. This chapter tries to answer some of the popular questions asked by individuals, and address some of the myths promoted by the media.

The best way, of course, is to be there; be part of it - this metamorphic community.

At home

Who lives on the road?

This is like asking, "Who lives in Newark or Crewe, or Thirsk...or wherever?" There are people of all classes, creeds and colours; representatives of every skill, trade and profession; realists and idealists; families, couples and single people; workers and the unemployed. There are Travellers with postgraduate qualifications and others whose parents are Romanies. Some have severe psychiatric and/or drug problems, while others are respected members of their chosen professions.

Demographically, the Traveller community has a high proportion of young adults and young children. Yet the seasonal and annual totals alter so frequently that there is no accurate final assessment. The definition of a 'Traveller' is so open to interpretation that probably the fairest suggestion is that of:

.......someone who has the means of living a nomadic lifestyle.

There is no minimum monthly mileage, nor a set period of time which someone has to travel for, that qualifies a person to be a Traveller. There is not a totally common dress code, musical preference, or philosophy. In fact, the only statement that expresses the feelings of every Traveller is:

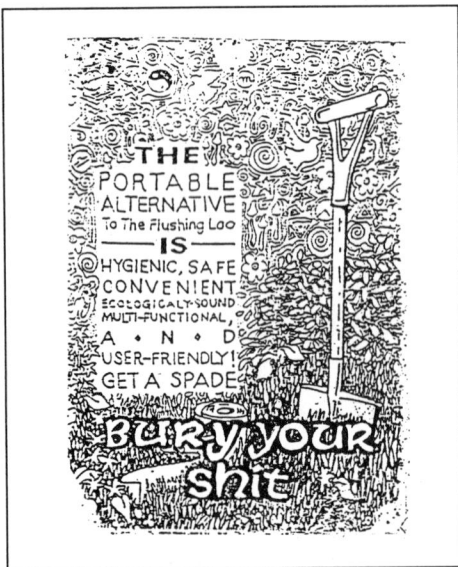

THE PORTABLE ALTERNATIVE To The Flushing Loo —IS— HYGIENIC, SAFE CONVENIENT ECOLOGICALY-SOUND MULTI-FUNCTIONAL, • A • N • D • USER-FRIENDLY! GET A SPADE BURY YOUR shit

This is almost a slogan, anthem or mission statement for Travellers. At the basic level, it means take a spade and bury your excrement. It also means more - leaving no scrap and other debris when moving on.

There is no clear hierarchy amongst Travellers, although those with most experience can help those new to the road. The lack of an official 'leader' on site often confuses authority; named people fighting for a judicial review or enquiry become a natural focus for attention; those owning stages, sound systems or marquees are more noticeable than those without.

Most people live nomadically throughout the year. Some move throughout Europe and Britain. Some remain within one country, or orbiting around one town, maybe heading away for short times at intervals. Some never move from a secure piece of land. There are part-time Travellers who have access to houses, but also have a bus, bender, van etc.. This is especially true in the summer months for the festival season.

Then there are punters and ravers who spill onto the scene for parties and festivals each summer. Who is and who is not a Traveller is a preoccupation with the media.

On the Road.

He's always been a roamer,
A van he calls his home.
He's travelled many highways
And often lived alone.
He's seen a lot of sorrow,
But never had regrets.
Remember all the good times,
The bad times he'll forget.
He's made a fair few enemies,
But he's got a lot of friends.
Never has he worried
What the next day sends.
Tommorrow will take care of itself,
He'll take care of today.
If he finds another highway
Then he'll be on his way.   –JENNi–

Many squatters and high profile young street people, epitomised as 'Crusties' or 'Smellies' in the press, are written about as Travellers - yet the reality is that they live in a flat or house. Others who live nomadically, appear at work or college everyday, and because they do not advertise their lifestyle, are never classified as Travellers.

"I didn't pay poll tax or council tax, have no fixed abode, lived on a narrow boat for a couple of years, but work for all sorts of employers, including the Department of the Environment!" Alan.

It is often other people who feel the need to brand them as 'Travellers'. Being a Traveller is almost a state of mind:

"He doesn't think with his head, he feels with his heart."
The Guardian.....describing Phil.

You cannot immediately recognise a Traveller - there is no separate language or code, no initiation rite. And simply because of this, the media is particularly misleading in its representation of Travellers as a homogenous group. That sense of belonging just happens naturally in some circumstances, perhaps as a result of harassment. Then, a large group of individuals can, quite genuinely, develop a strong sense of unity and at least for a short time become a family, community or tribe.

Many Travellers are known by first name only or by a nickname. The formal address of conventional Society is abandoned in such close living conditions. There are people we've known for years whose 'official' name we'll never know. Not because of any secrecy, but because it seems an irrelevance. Names become absorbed over time, rather than being a focal point for a first meeting - nicknames are common, their origins often obscured by time. They are as obvious or vague as those amongst all groups of people. Second or third generation Travellers may have names reflecting their new culture - related to nature or legend, or spelled alternatively. Full names seem irrelevant labels and represent for many a life they've left behind.

Much is made by the media of dress code, but in reality, the way of life sets certain constraints:

- boots are comfortable and practical
- huge woollen jumpers are warm
- there is limited wardrobe space
- leggings or trousers are hard-wearing
- dark colours are utilitarian

Parties offer the chance to be brightly coloured and wildly impractical. But it's all generalisation. People have individual style, dictated by living and working environments. Caricatures focus on the crusty image, rather than any other, because it emphasises dirt and deviancy rather than conformity. Travellers are a modern day folk-devil largely because of their images in the media. This is accompanied by a fear and loathing which the unwashed, unkempt, drug-taking, thieving, dole-scrounging stereotype provokes.

The 'Grunge' look became a predominant teenage fashion in recent years, with layers of skirts over leggings, shirts over vests and baggy jumpers over the whole ensemble. Dingy colours and natural materials epitomised this look. Doc Marten boots have also become phenomenally popular throughout the teenage population. All of these are reflections of the basic Traveller wardrobe. However, the fashion chain 'Top Shop' went one step further when it presented a catalogue entitled 'Travellers.' A barefoot, cross-legged, heavily made up model gazes wistfully at the reader from the cover; and a series of five double-page spreads present a number of fairly impractical outfits modelled by three immaculate young women. They gallivant through idyllic meadows with two denim-clad, clean shaven, long-haired 'hunks' and a white camper van. Captions tell the reader:

"There's only one rule...feel free!"
"On the nature trail...the spirit is true gypsy"
"For the great outdoors, take the rough with the smooth."

On the back cover they are *"Homeward Bound"* - still fresh, clean and uncrumpled!
It is interesting that this chain cashed in on teenage fascination with alternatives, even though the representation was romanticised and sanitised. The catalogue certainly caused amusement on site!

However, many of the ethnic jewellery styles currently regaining mainstream popularity, have been popular amongst Travellers for years. Beads and friendship bracelets are made on site and there are a multitude of crafts people using a wide range of natural materials.

> "I am the highway and a peregrine and all the sails that ever went to sea."
> ......The first thing people think of when they hear the word 'peregrine' is falcon. But there are other meanings of the word.....one is 'foreigner, alien'. A second is 'roving or wandering, migratory.' The Latin peregrinus, which is the root of the word, means a stranger."
>
> Robert James Waller

Music at home

The musical taste of Travellers is wide-ranging. There are usually a number of acoustic guitars, bodhrans, fiddles and penny whistles on site and some good singers. Apart from personal entertainment, busking can be a profitable pastime. There are still acoustic music festivals and small gatherings where everyone has an instrument. There are chants of celebration and protest, echoing and interspersed with ancient songs:

> Make me at one with the infinite sun
> Forever and ever and ever
> Make me in tune with the luminous moon
> Forever and ever and ever
> Ku-Wa-Te, Le-No, Le-No, Ma-Ho-Te
> I-Ano, I-Ano, I-Ano.   *Native American.*

Sharing songs and dances at a sacred site is a powerful, emotive experience; particularly as the sun rises, tom-toms beat and horns echo around. It is a retreat to primitive, tribal celebration; an awareness of nature and the ancient monuments built by previous civilisations.

> Air my breath
>   and fire my spirit
> Earth my body
>   water my blood.
>   *Chant*

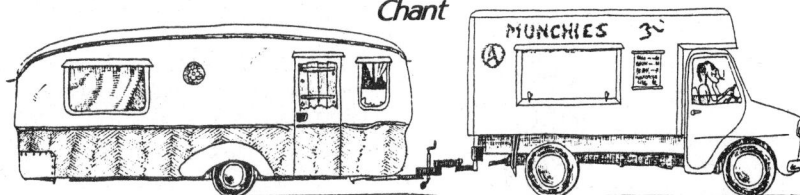

Throughout the eighties, stages were set up at free festivals for live band performances and jam sessions. Commercial events like Reading, Cambridge and Glastonbury provide high quality sounds from famous bands in a festival atmosphere - but at a cost which excludes many Travellers. There are still lots of live bands on the Traveller circuit; rock, punk and techno. These may perform at smaller events, such as Treworgey or Strawberry Fayre, where fringe or free events run alongside, or outside the main event. Their songs may reflect events in Traveller culture:

> ***Time Bomb by Kuru*...................**
> *The only real people you've ever seen*
> *Are the poor people crushed underneath your feet*
> *High class entrepreneur,*
> *Behold your future executioners.*

Some popular chart bands imitate Traveller culture by building their image and lyrics around infamous events in its history and the lifestyle in general:

> ***Down the 303 at the***
> ***end of the road***
> ***Flashing lights - exclusion***
> ***zones***
> ***And it made me think, it's***
> ***not just the stones***
> ***That they're guarding.***

> **the levellers**

The hypnotic beats of music from sound systems such as Spiral Tribe, the Orb, Bedlam and Circus Warp have exerted a powerful influence on a number of Travellers. Many see their move to becoming a Traveller as a direct result of involvement in club, squat and warehouse parties. The rave scene is usually accounted as having been born in Ibiza, imported into clubs in London and Madchester (as Manchester is known) and then exported to sites all round the country, but particularly in the orbit of the M25. The 'Freedom to Party' campaign mushroomed (no psilocybin pun intended!) and sound systems started to become a feature of festivals following the so-called, second Summer of Love in 1988. As Alex Rosenburger wrote in an article entitled 'Rave On' in the 1990 Festival Eye:

> *"Nothing messes up the scene the way money seems to,*
> *which goes some way to explaining why ravers are looking*
> *more to festivals as venues this summer."*

This was seen to be true in the period through to 1994 with larger and larger sound system rigs appearing at gatherings of all kinds. For some, the music itself is a kind of drug and reason for being. For other Travellers, the addition of ravers onto the already hassleful travelling scene is an added aggravation with conflicts of culture, and even more interest from police and authorities.

At Castlemorton Common Festival in May 1992, Spiral Tribe played 24 hours a day. Jackie Nike, writing in Labour Campaign for Travellers' Rights Newsletter, said:

> *"During the event Spiral Tribe refused to turn their music down*
> *when asked by Travellers after three days of insistent drum beat.*
> *A Tribe DJ said "I've come here to party and I'm not going to*
> *stop partying 'til I leave - I've come here to get away from rules."*
> *To this the Traveller replied, "That's cool, but anarchy doesn't*
> *work unless you think about it." "*

Following the Castlemorton gig, thirteen members of Spiral Tribe were arrested and seven charged with causing a public nuisance. Like a lot of the sounds rigs and so-called Traveller bands, sounds' members nearly all live in houses and are basically tourists or visitors on Traveller sites. The counter view is:

> *"There have been hippies going for years and years, but they've*
> *all stagnated, especially after the Beanfield. Everyone buggered*
> *off after that. No one dared bring a sound system into a field*
> *and just play for days and days. Sound systems have brought*
> *the Travellers back. The anti-rave cosmic hippies sit there and*
> *moan and groan about rave music, but people have forgotten the*
> *Travellers existed until now. That's one of the reasons they don't like it."*
> > *Simon from the Tribe in 'Travellers'*
> > *Lowe & Shaw. Fourth Estate. 1993.*

We don't agree with Simon, but there you go, it's a (fairly) free Society!

At most big gatherings there will be sounds of all kinds, at all times; and on site, individuals rely heavily on radios and favourite cassettes for music. But there is no common bond, other than the love of music.

Whilst it may seem that all Travellers are anarchic, anti-social dropouts, there are no such limitations. Everyone is different. With no corporate music, dress-code or belief; no single geographic location; no ethnic or social majority; no central philosophy. The term 'Traveller' is as all-encompassing, as wide or narrow, as the person using it.

Why do people live on the road?

Again, there are as many answers to this question as there are Travellers themselves. Some have no clear cut reason, while others were triggered by circumstance. Generally, the reasons are less relevant than the lifestyle itself; and it is a question rarely asked by fellow-Travellers, but constantly forwarded by the rest of Society.

> *"Me and my sister spent our late teens/early twenties attending*
> *the famous 'Warehouse parties' in Blackburn and the north-east.*
> *This in turn led us to look for something 'more'. Hence,*
> *we are both now Travellers. There was a feeling of unity and*
> *challenge to the status-quo - to us anyway - which was killed off*
> *by regulation and the later commercialisation of the rave scene."*
> > *Jackie*

There are inevitably an increasing number of young adults who were born on the road during

the seventies. They, like the traditional Gypsies/Romanies are continuing the lifestyles of parents and friends; and some are now bringing up third and fourth generations. This has interesting repercussions when the legal interpretation of a 'Gypsy', who has rights under certain laws, may be:

"One of a second or further generation of nomadic lifestyle."

On the whole, however, most Travellers have come from a settled existence to a nomadic one.

"I had no real motivating factor - I met a lot of Travellers in
Southampton in the early eighties and went to Stonehenge
in '84. I moved into a bus with a friend in '88, then got a trailer,
then a truck. I am very aware of the advantages - I can move
to where work is available, without worrying about accommodation;
I am responsible for my effect on the planet; I can't live happily
in urban areas; I have time, space and friends....I could go on... "
Fiona

In some cases, as above, there are no clear-cut reasons, but lots of advantages learned over time. People whose friends are, or become, Travellers may be drawn to join them. Several towns and cities have a core of orbitals, whose lifestyle is appealing. Similarly, a house dweller may start a relationship with a Traveller and join that partner.

"I couldn't pay the mortgage on a flat in Essex and decided
that living afloat and travelling on the canals and rivers would
be an adventure. It was!"   *Alan.*

There are a multitude of positive ecological and environmental issues which persuaded some people to live nomadically, some political. The opposition to nuclear weaponry and its power, led protesters leaving their homes and moving onto, or around, bases; in particular Greenham Common and Molesworth. Although the cold-war threat has receded, political reasons for living nomadically still exist. The police action of 1985 culminating at the Beanfield, brought many new people onto the scene. Some who believed in anarchy or in the rights to question authority, replaced others who believed stongly in a pacifist role. Legislation, such as the Public Order Act 1986, stirred people to defend basic human rights - as is happening now, with the Criminal Justice Bill. Likewise, the 1990 introduction of the Poll Tax, gave an impetus to some Travellers to try living away from houses.

Other positive reasons include the reaction against the constant consumerism of Society today. The clutter of possessions and their supposed value can be left behind. The importance of money reduces and other qualities become more relevant. People need much less space and some Travellers believe that a nomadic existence is that which the planet can sustain most successfully.

Slushy, sloppy, runny mud
oozing, wet, sticky mud
when i slip and fall on my bum
i can't get up until i'm done

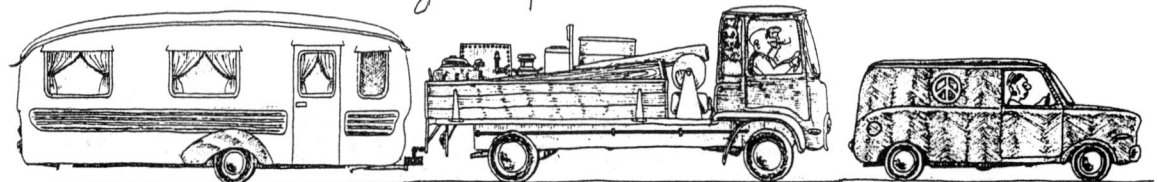

Reflecting that, another reason is to be closer to the earth, and nature. Sealed in houses, individuals are removed from plants and weather, air and animals. A Traveller has to take note of surroundings, and some do their best to live in harmony with the earth. Some people just cannot cope with the isolation and corruption of city life, and move to rural areas instead; recognising the security and freedom of close-knit Travelling communities. Others believe strongly in the right to live nomadically.

> *"..............life on the road started seriously for me and Elouise in the summer of 1982. Feeling ambitious and wanting a 'life', we took up travelling with the man who we were to spend the next eleven and a half years with.*
> *In the summer of 1986, I conceived Rohan, so I bought a truck, and converted it into our new home. He was born in February 1987 on a Gypsy transit camp near Swindon."*
>
> *Sharon.*

There are also a lot of negative reasons for travelling, negative in the sense of getting away from something, rather than actively opting to participate. The current housing crisis is a major factor in many peoples' decisions. With the recent changes in the law regarding squatters, it is possible that more will be forced onto the road. High rents and constant bills can be traded for a cheap mobile home and few bills. In some cases, the accommodation available is so poor that it does not seem worth paying. £50 p.w. for a room in a shared house, which compares unfavourably with a £200 trailer.

The Government's 'back to basics' campaign makes housing unavailable to young people, forcing them to live with friends and relatives... or wherever they can. The high level of unemployment has influenced many to become nomadic. In some cases, it is to look for work and be able to live wherever the work is; in others, rented accommodation is unavailable to those with limited finances.

There are people trying to escape painful personal situations. Pregnancy may force a young woman away from a settled home; a man may leave his family - with few possessions to take away; abuse by parents or partners may drive people away from their home. There are also those released from prisons, children's' homes and other institutions, who wish to make new lives for themselves, away from their history. The Traveller scene is receptive, judging on present attitudes and behaviour, rather than the past. Frequently, there are acts of random kindness that give individuals the time and space to develop.

> "......The freedom. The fact of having people around you all the time, the community, it's like a family really........The Jamie Bulger case made me think. There were so many witnesses who saw the little boy being taken away and just thought it was none of my business, nothing to do with me. I was thinking that on site, well, a lot of people may be miserable for a day or two or whatever, sit in their trailer, but the thought of a lad not having anything to eat, or coming to harm, or whatever, it couldn't happen, because everything is everyone's business all the time. It's a pain when you want privacy, people talking at you, but the advantages outweigh the cons........"
>
> "When you are on the road you make the most effort to get on with someone, say if you haven't seen someone for a few months and they pull on, well because of all the coming and going, you always make the most of your time with people; people are more direct and upfront about their feelings, giving each other hugs, more affection and concern, because you know at any point your friends could move away or you might not see them for years or ever again. It's not claustrophobic like villages, but a supportive network wherever you go."   Es.

The quality of life on the road is a major factor in its favour. Whilst necessities are harder to obtain, luxuries are enormously appreciated. It is the experience of actually living, rather than existing within a rat race. Everyone is master to themselves, making conscious decisions and taking responsibility for their own lives. People may want a positive lifestyle for children, within a caring community. Others may want to escape the financial trap of house-dwelling and live more independently. Young people may be drawn into the scene after attending a rave or gathering. The exciting atmosphere is attractive, but the appeal may be swiftly lost after a spell of bad weather or broken engines!

Everyone is there for a different reason; romantic; raves; pissed-off; looking for something; alienated; non-conformity; nowhere to go; searching to belong; freedom; independence; escape; drugs and parties; self-awareness; anti-materialism...and so on. Travelling is the ideal way to meet new people...and for some, the only reason for being on the road is:

> **"It seemed like a good idea at the time."**

How do Travellers live?

There are four basic necessities for survival:

shelter, warmth, food, water;

and one great luxury:

company.

Whilst Travellers have to constantly consider the above and ensure these needs are met, they can also create comfort and luxury with relative ease.

Shelter.

Traveller homes are as idiosyncratic as their owners. There is no formula to follow and individuals stamp their place with a unique style. Just as a settled person may occupy dwellings as diverse as flats and cottages, terraces and mansions; so there are a vast array of homes available to Travellers. Mobility and economy are the major considerations.

Tipis, benders and tents.

A tipi is usually associated with native Americans. A cone of poles is surrounded with a cover of hides or canvas. It must be built with precision, but it is a strong and quite spiritual structure.

> *"The tipi is much better to live in; always clean,*
> *warm in winter, cool in summer; easy to move.*
> *The white man builds big house, cost much money, like*
> *big cage, shut out sun, can never move."*
> *Chief Flying Hawk, Sioux.*

There are places most obviously Talley in Wales, where groups of people live in tipis. They are rarely seen on most sites, however, though a circle of tipis is often seen at free festivals. A well - made tipi canvas is quite expensive and the poles are also valuable.

A bender is a dome of supple poles, usually hazel, over which canvas is stretched. It can be of any height and circumference, depending on the size of the tarpaulin. Canvas is better, but plastic is inadequate. Blankets are often hung internally from the woven poles. They are natural, traditional structures of Scottish Tinker origin called barricades, whose simplicity is in their strength. Easily warmed or cooled, their principle disadvantage today is that constant harassment necessitates the ability to move quickly. Valuable poles and canvases need to be transported and sometimes there is hardly time to finish building before eviction threats begin.

Tents are commonly used by weekenders - ravers, traders, punters etc. Known as 'Nylon Nightmares,' they are too small, inflammable and unstable for constant use. A few Travellers have tents and marquees for business, or for the children to play in; but generally, tents are confined to the big gatherings and festivals.

By Melody Kin

Caravans.

The advantages of a towed space are; that you can use your towing vehicle without tatting down each time you move; if your vehicle breaks down, someone else can tow you; and they are usually easy to sell or exchange. They do have their disadvantages too, of course. The 'A' frame can snap, the axle may buckle, or the lights fail. They also suffer from bad condensation. Ranging from 10 foot holiday caravans to long chrome trailers, up to huge showman's wagons; their only common feature is the towbar.

The little caravans can be bought cheaply from families and farmers and may be quickly adapted for permanent use. They are often re-painted and may have a couple of windows blanked out. They are easy to live in, but were never really built for inhabitation 365 days a year, or constant dragging across bumpy fields, so can quickly deteriorate. Best of all, a small van or car can tow them easily. Some of the older Carlight caravans, with Molycroft roofs and elegant cupboards are much tougher. They are more spacious, as are the chrome Vickers trailers associated with Romanies. These are specifically built for Traveller use and are increasingly popular. They do, however, need a bigger vehicle to tow them. Showmen's wagons are heavy and impressive - traditionally associated with fairgrounds and circuses, as their name suggests.

> *"In the bedroom were bunks or a large bed. The living room*
> *would have an open fire and a built-in sofa on the other*
> *side...In the kitchen there would be a large, black enamelled*
> *stove and plenty of cupboard space...the wooden panelling*
> *was often mahogany or teak...usually there would be velvet*
> *curtains and often one or two large engraved mirrors."*
> *Duncan Dallas 'The Travelling People'. Macmillan .1977.*

As these traditional travellers have bought more luxurious modern wagons, so some newer Travellers have bought the old ones to renovate and use. Unlike the single-axle caravan, they are on a multi-wheeled base, high off the ground and need a powerful vehicle to tow them.

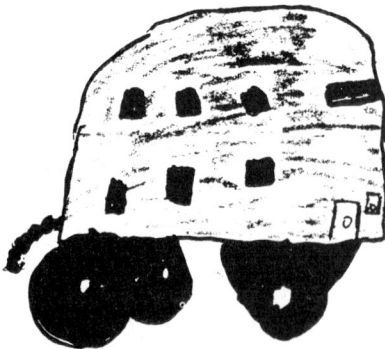

by
Ferbia

Buses and vans.

The media image of the 'Hippy Convoy' in the early eighties was very much that of the multi-coloured buses and converted old Bedfords and Leylands. Today, there are modern coaches, double deckers, ambulances and vans.

Coaches range in length and style. From a blim bus to a 52 foot twin-steer, they are convertible in a multitude of ways. Most people replace several windows with board in order to build shelves or cupboards. The whacky paint jobs still exist, but lots of people retain the anonymity of their vehicle's company colours.

Double deckers have the advantage of increased space on two floors and being easily adapted for living, storage or cafes. Their obvious problem is that of planning routes which avoid low bridges or overhanging trees.

Ambulances are more popular conversions. Cheaper to run than buses, and well insulated, they can be comfortable homes. There are usually an assortment of transit-type vans on site, either bought as campers or converted. Those with a Luton-box over the cab are particularly spacious. Whilst being convenient and self-contained on the move, a bus can be awkward as the only means of transport. Owners may have a blat motor or a bicycle for daily use. Also, if the engine packs in, it's your home at the side of the road.

Trucks.

From pantechnicon lorries to wooden horse boxes, to commercial trucks, they are very popular. They have much greater height than buses, and windows can be cut wherever required. They can also transport livestock, motorcycles or working equipment. Their principal advantage over buses is that they are often less conspicuous parked in an urban lorry park, or behind a farm for a few weeks. Otherwise, the problems and benefits are much the same.

Of course, you can always combine the lot!

Horse-drawn.

The romantic image of Gypsies in bow top, open lot, Reading or ledge wagons, drawn by coloured cobs has never been fully dispelled, as the popularity of rural horse-drawn holidays proves, especially in the south of Ireland. But the horse-drawn is one of the hardest ways of living. Tat space is very limited and the weight has to be kept down. Many of the daily chores are outdoors which is tough in winter. There are a substantial number of Travellers now using horsepower. They move at a slower pace and need grazing places and plentiful water supplies. Horses have to be fit, healthy and regularly shod for road work. They are often more tolerated by house-dwellers, who regard them as less threatening than Travellers in vehicles. Most of all, this form of transport is environmentally and ecologically sound.

> **"I'm not going to change my horses for a motor wagon...I want my lads to live the same way as me. It's the best kind of life."**
>
> *Cocker, quoted in 'A Romany Summer,'*
> *Barry Cockcroft (Dent. 1979)*

Boats.

Increasingly, a number of Travellers live in a variety of water-based homes. Water is a potentially lethal force and Travellers living on boats lead quite a hard life with floods, vandals and officials all making life "interesting!" The boats themselves range from fibreglass cabin cruisers, rudely called 'tupperware' boats, up to sailing yachts and traditional 72 foot narrowboats.

Some are fitted out with every comfort; others are a steel shell inside which people 'camp' and rough it. Cooking and heating is often from a traditional wood-burner and lighting can be provided by paraffin lamps or electric power from a generator or the boat's batteries. Finding moorings is a major hassle, since, increasingly, British Waterways Board and the Trusts which operate many of the rivers and canals, dislike permanent boat dwellers.

Is there a hierarchy dependent on type of home, as with houses?

Not really. We read one article which suggested that a double decker was the aspiration of all Travellers. Not true. Whilst early experiences may include living in many types of homes while the choice is limited by finances or ignorance, most people end up opting for the most comfortable for themselves. A vehicle may be restored and modified by an owner over many years; others change homes frequently.

Particular skills are needed for benders-building or horse care, for example, or for driving long, heavy rigs. Individuals can impose their own preferences on design furnishing and decoration, from sparse to luxurious. Houses cost constant money in mortgage repayments or rent bills; whilst most Traveller homes cost a flat rate. In both, there are costs of maintenance, repair or adaptation. Vehicle trade seems more brisk than the housing market at present, and while some people have to put up with anything initially, there is often the chance to move on to something else later.

Warmth.

One of the most common misconceptions about living on the road is that it is unbearably cold in winter. On the contrary, heating a compact space used for all aspects of living is much more efficient than warming several rooms. Few houses now have open fires or wood-burners, yet fire provides warmth. An adequate burner can be made from an empty gas bottle and a length of flexi-pipe. But there are many small stoves available, and a range provides oven space, as well as a hob and warmth.

In summer, an outdoor fire is a focus for evening gatherings and conversation. But small or large, indoor or out, the common requirement is wood. Lots of dead wood. With hundreds of trees still lying flat after the 1987 hurricanes, it seems that there should be plenty available.

It largely depends where you are. Friends of ours in Romsey, Hampshire, were threatened with prosecution for collecting wood from a verge because it belonged to a wealthy landowner. Dragging trunks or boughs from a copse may involve trespass. There is always media publicity about those who can't be bothered to participate in a wooding expedition with a flat-bed or van and who trash fences or sheds for firewood. They are a minority. As are those who destroy living trees. Creosote stinks, and green wood burns slowly, producing smoke rather than heat.

> *"Green wood won't burn and rotten wood burns in a flash*
> *with hardly any heat. So you need to search out sticks*
> *which have been dead long enough to season, but not*
> *so long that they're rotten...I feel it's very important not to*
> *'wood-out' an area completely, removing every last scrap of*
> *dead wood which supports ten times as much life as living*
> *wood...So it's very important for wildlife."*
> *Richard Whitefield. 'Tipi Living'. Unique Publications. 1987.*

Wooding is a daily chore; if not collecting a substantial woodpile, then axing, cutting or stacking. Kindling has to be gathered or chopped. The traditional saying that wood warms you three times is true; once when you collect it, once when you chop it and finally, when it burns.

A good fire, inside or out, is not merely a source of heat, but can be used for cooking. It is the focus of all benders, buses and so on. It is a healthy heat, without fumes, and stimulating to watch or feed. There are no hefty bills to worry about afterwards, and wooding keeps you fit.

Water.

This most essential facility is vital not only for survival but also for safe hygiene and sanitation. Yet it is the least available to Travellers at most times. Few authorities supply standpipes on un-authorised sites. Usually, Travellers are reliant on nearby garages or churchyards; but local opposition can be so great that a journey of a few miles is necessary. Some villages have common standpipes; others have their springs; but rivers, streams and livestock troughs are obviously potentially a health risk. We have used such water for animals and washing, but collected separate supplies for cooking and drinking.

Spa water is the safest drinking supply - or the use of a filter, commonly available in supermarkets. But practicality can over-ride constant consideration of safety. A household consume several hundred gallons daily. Travellers are forced to be economical with this resource, and waste it less, occasionally recycling when possible - for example, using water from boiling vegetables to mix with dried food for pets.

Sanitation concerns everyone and the filthy human defecation at festival sites is a focus for media attention. But as mentioned before, all full-time Travellers agree that to avoid health-hazards, excrement should be buried. Communal toilet trenches or individual pits are dug well away from vehicles and people, and covered over afterwards. The shovel is a crucial tool and in an effort to promote awareness amongst punters at festivals in 1990, the Travellers Aid Trust provided dozens of them - painted luminous pink to encourage use.

Another media myth is that of filthy squalor surrounding sites. We haven't the water for a daily deep bath, but it takes relatively little for an efficient strip wash. Admittedly, there are those who don't bother, but there is also the fact that ingrained dirt from living and working on vehicle sites, is impossible to shift without vast amounts of hot water.

The potential danger of a limited water supply is that regular handwashing between chores or tasks gets ignored. Sometimes showers are available at local swimming pools and sports centres - some even have baths. Sadly, public baths are being phased out. Washing clothes

can be an inconvenience. Drying space in winter is restricted and the advantage of launderettes provide is that they provide tumblers as well as efficient machines. But, they are less common than in the past, and may involve quite a long journey, as well as a supply of change - and some places won't admit Travellers anyway.

The lack of recognised sites with hard-standing means that many sites are muddy throughout the winter. Boots and clothes become caked rapidly and the general appearance of individuals and their homes can be that of dirt. Yet inside, it is so much easier to keep a small space clean than several rooms. Almost everyone removes footwear before going in. And in only an hour or so, all areas can be thoroughly cleaned.

Whatever, water is not wasted. A site may have a water-run, when all empty containers are taken for filling. But, unlike for housedwellers, it is a daily consideration; a chore that cannot be avoided.

Food.

Modern British Society has evolved a food supply reliant upon accepted retail outlets and Travellers are no different to anyone else in their need to buy basic foodstuffs. But the convenience frozen foods of most households are inappropriate for those who have limited or no cold storage. As a consequence, more tinned or dried foods are suitable, along with plenty of fresh vegetables and fruit - generally cheap and easy to store. Fresh meat cannot be kept long, so there are forced vegetarians, as well as those morally opposed to an omnivorous diet. Cereals, pasta, rice and pulses form the basis of meals for many Travellers, suggesting a healthier and more balanced diet.

End of Giro Stews   by Cori

STEP ONE : SEE WHAT'S IN THE SKIPS AT YOUR LOCAL SUPERMARKET.

Veggie Slop

4 handfuls green lentils   1½ tsp turmeric
1 large onion   1 Bayleaf
3-4 mushrooms   2 tsp coriander
1 carrot (grated)   1 tsp Cumin
1 medium potato   ½ tsp crushed dried
3 cloves Garlic   chillies.

Fry Onion & garlic with spices until onion is slightly browned. Add water & other veg & simmer for at least 2hrs. Mash & serve with chapattis.

Bone Soup

Any bones from butchers.   garlic, oxo or
1 Onion   marmite, whatever.
2 medium potatoes. Any other veg available.

Boil the bones for at least 3 hours. Remove bones and pick off any meat left on them. Fry onion and chuck in with the bits of meat and other veg cut into coarse chunks. Boil together for a further 30 mins & serve with chappattis.

∘∘∘∘∘ **Dole Pie** ∘∘∘∘∘∘∘∘∘∘∘∘∘∘∘∘∘∘∘∘∘∘∘

Boil some potatoes with or without skins.
Grate some cheese.
Chop an onion.

When potatoes are soft mash with cheese.
Add chopped onion

Wrap in tinfoil or put in metal container.
Cook on outside edge of open fire. 15 mins.

Alternatively:

Put mixture in flan dish and cook in an oven on medium for 20 mins.
Grate bread and cheese for crunchy topping.
Grate cheese and 1 beaten egg for fluffy top.

Great with baked beans!
Add tomatoes, mushrooms, corn, bacon, spam or peppers for different flavours.

by Jenni

Children tend to be less exposed to prepacked snacks and sweets. This could be because the location of a site, or the weekly trip to town necessitates bulk buying instead of daily shopping. Most Travellers can cook adequately, usually well, often using herbs and spices to enhance a meal. There do seem to be a high proportion of vegetarians and vegans, reflecting the outlook of those concerned about health or the environment.

Due to the nomadic lifestyle, it is rare for Travellers to grow their own fruit or vegetables, although most would like to do so. Many cultivate herb boxes. There would seem to be a high preference amongst many for organic produce, although the diversity in individuals makes such generalisations unreliable.

Those in rural areas may have livestock to subsidise bought produce. Apart from fowl to provide eggs and meat, goats provide milk. They are relatively easy to transport and care for. Then there is also the chance of game. Rabbiting is a tradition amongst Travellers and many keep a lurcher dog, but equally available in country areas are the rabbits and pheasants run down and left by the roadside. Although they may be unsuitable for human consumption, at times the dogs will devour them.

Another source of food for those on urban sites are the rubbish skips behind shops and supermarkets. Food past its sell-by date is chucked away when reduced prices have failed to shift it. Although a criminal offence of theft, raiding a skip can produce a mass of edible food.

Fresh fruit and vegetables, meat, dairy produce and broken packages are all there. It sounds repugnant, but most Travellers check the state of the food before eating it.

> *"One of the most delicious joints of lamb I have ever eaten*
> *came from a skip after a freezer failure and we've had a bus*
> *full of kids icing cakes for a competition."*   *Fiona.*

When a skip-run returns, the food will be distributed throughout the site - it's got to be eaten quickly. In retaliation to raids on skips, not only by Travellers, but also by settled people on low income, stores have devised a series of precautions. Some are locked, others have crushers, or some pour detergent over the produce. It's a horrendous waste of food that is often perfectly edible. Chemist skips have baby products and cosmetics; off-licences have corked wines or dented cans.

As with many house-dwellers, lots of Travellers are reliant on income support. This inevitably affects diet, but it is true to say that they are on the whole healthy. A combination of basic foodstuffs and outdoor life contributes to this.

Skip run

'Water, water everywhere
          nor any drop to drink,'
When it happens in 1990, it
          makes you stop and think.
The river's burst its banks,
Water floods storage tanks,
But "don't let the hippies have
          it - they're dirty and they stink."
Fiona

Water and food at festivals and gatherings

The above discussions of food and water supplies apply to living sites rather than large gatherings. At organised festivals, water has to be supplied in order to receive a license. For drinking, there are standpipes and huge water containers. The former can lose pressure and temporarily cease, while the latter need refilling from a tanker. These are potentially dangerous, as disease can transmit rapidly in such closely packed groups of people sharing a limited supply. So, it is crucial for an efficient organiser to ensure a regular supply.

For washing, water from a standpipe can be used, or enterprising groups set up showers, even sweat lodges. Hot showers can be fire-powered or solar, and are communal.

A sweat lodge is usually sited in a bender - creating the native American equivalent to the Scandinavian sauna. Steam from hot coals or embers fills the bender, and refreshing pails of cold water stand outside. Toilets are a combination of portable cabins; screened trenches, usually individually partitioned; and urinal troughs.

At unauthorised festivals, the facilities are not provided. Stonehenge free festival-goers could use the toilets in the public car park near the monument, but at places such as Castle Morton, there was nothing organised. Water may come from taps a great distance away, and there is great danger for those who use streams and cattle troughs. As these may be used for drinking and washing, they become polluted quickly.

As mentioned previously, whilst full-time Travellers have shovels, punters don't. So urination and defecation may happen along all hedgerows or wooded areas - anywhere providing some vague privacy. Contamination and disease spread, especially in the hot weather associated with summer parties.

Food, however, is a different matter. At both organised and illegal gatherings, there are a vast array of foodstuffs available. Commercial companies provide 24 hour outlets, recipes prepared in hygienic conditions. At Glastonbury, for example, there are the 'Gremlin Diner', 'Pennine Pizza', '24 Hour Munchies', 'Fat Vegan Heaven', 'El Fred's', the 'Real sausage company'...amongst many others. On the fringes, more basic fare is available, sometimes at lower prices. There are takeaways, cafes, and restaurants - and bars and hot drinks or all-day breakfasts.

Even at an unauthorised gathering, enterprising individuals set up food outlets. Ranging from cafe marquees, to pots of stew on a fire; from bars to cups of tea sold from the back of a van. Some mobile traders take advantage by situating hot-dogs stalls and ice-cream vans on the fringes. And there are many informal shops, and off-licences, where canned or cartoned food, cans of beer and scrumpy are sold.

Company

People have differing needs in terms of companionship. This is just as true for Travellers as the settled population. The main advantage of a mobile base is that it is relatively easy to move and change. This may be practised in several ways. Those who need time alone can park-up in isolation, joining smaller groups or big parties when needed.

Even on a site there are those who prefer a quiet corner to a central situation. Vehicles can move beside friends, or away from noisy neighbours. Some live in relatively permanent groups, moving around together; others meet up after diverse travels.

Milking goat

Pets also provide company. There are always dogs on site, not merely for company, but also for protection. Whilst being friendly on their own, they can appear threatening in a pack, barking at a visitor. Outbreaks of distemper or parvo virus occur occasionally - just as they do in any other closely populated area. As we have previously mentioned, the lurcher or long dog is a very popular breed with Travellers. They have adopted the preference of Romany Gypsies who found that the lurcher combined the speed of a coursing dog such as the greyhound, with the intelligence of working dogs such as the collie. Add to that, lurchers are protective towards children, whilst being born hunters. Lurchers are relatively easy to train.

Cats, although reputed to prefer a constant situation, seem to adapt readily to a mobile life. Their only problem seems to be on sudden eviction when the cat is away prowling. Horses are not only used for towing, but for recreation. Several children have ponies and ride well at a young age.

In all, most sites have a wide assortment of company, both human and animal. The major advantage over a house is that of choosing your company according to your needs, and extra flexibility.

♦ ♦ ♦ ♦ ♦

Having considered these practicalities, there are two other areas which seem to have become necessities amongst modern Society: **services and possessions**.

Services.

There are many services considered essential by settled communities. Yet, responsibility for these is taken by the individual Traveller, who selects according to needs and finance.

Power of some kind is needed. Obviously, networked electricity is only available on authorised sites. There are several methods, however, that Travellers can use. On a basic level, batteries power torches and radios. Car batteries can be wired up to larger appliances, especially televisions or lights. These may be charged on blat motors, at garages, or even by a solar trickle-charge.

Boat-travellers frequently have a bank of up to six batteries for domestic power as well as a battery for starting the engine. Powering up and running the engine for an hour a day usually provides enough power for the rest of the day. Some vans and caravans can do the same.

Petrol or diesel generators are increasingly common, powering tools, lights, music centres, P.A. systems etc. And those preferring alternative energy rely on wind-powered generators to re-charge batteries. Lots of us have no electricity at all, so light has to be powered alternatively. Candles are adequate; hurricane-lamps are safer. Bright light can be provided be Aladdin lamps or tilley lamps, fuelled by paraffin. They are also effective outside.

Then there is gas. Again, the national pipeline is unavailable. But calor or butane bottles can efficiently provide light, refrigeration, heat or cooking facilities. From a camping canister for emergencies, to a large bottle lasting several weeks, it is cheap and quite readily available. Again, cooking without gas is perfectly possible - on a fire or a stove.

Communication can also pose a problem for those constantly on the move. The Royal Mail provides a varied service, depending on area, but it is generally very effective. Most postmen are willing to deliver to an obvious mail-box at the site entrance, as long as there is a recognisable address. And Post Offices, if forewarned, will accept mail to hold, either 'poste restante' or 'care of'.

P.O. boxes are difficult to obtain without a permanent address; but some Travellers solve the mail problems by using the address of friends, workplace, family and calling occasionally to collect. Others receive no mail.

Recent telephone technology has spawned the use of mobiles. They have heavy power consumption, but are useful. As are the 'bleepers', some of which now print out a message rather than requiring an instant response to a central number. Obviously, the public telephone service is the main provision which is unavailable to most Travellers. The biggest problem is sometimes location - having to walk miles or cadge a lift to call at an appropriate time.

The heavy reliance on a massive network of contacts and friends throughout Britain in passing on news, results not only in efficient messages by word-of-mouth, but also in the development of rampant 'hippy rumours', which like the parlour game 'Chinese Whispers' bear little or no, relation to the original! Travelling in a small vehicle to visit friends socially is known as 'going for a blat' and is a common form of communication.

There are also networks of printed information available to those with an address. Some are aimed at house-dwellers, whilst others have Travellers as their primary audience and are circulated at gatherings or meetings. Such publications include Festival Eye, Tribal Messenger, Monolith News and the Free Information Network leaflets - published by several local areas in the U.K.. Groups like the Rainbow Circle and I.C.A.S send outlines of forthcoming events; while S.C.F and some Traveller Education Services have also provided updates on legal developments or local facilities. 'Unique Publications' have a newspaper called the 'Glastonbury Gazette' which chronicles local news of interest to Travellers in the Glastonbury area.

Settled communities rarely have to take **refuse** to the municipal tip, except on occasions when large items, or garden waste have to be disposed of. But, although a recognised site may be given skip facilities, those on unauthorised park ups have to transport rubbish themselves. Most combustible waste is burned on stoves or outside fires, but the rest has to be stored and taken away. Dustbins are impractical, so sacks are used and have to be kept on roofs or flat-beds away from dogs and children. This looks untidy, but it is safer than leaving them on the ground. Whilst some Travellers use the recycling facilities increasingly provided in settlements for glass and cans, others are less responsible, leaving such rubbish lying around dangerously.

The untidy appearance is enhanced by vehicle parts and other scrap that accumulates during maintenance. This is collected, sorted and weighed in with a local scrap merchant. Sudden forced eviction does not give people time to collect and dispose of such items. This is particularly true after large gatherings, although there are still those concerned about the environment and their reputation, who stay behind and clear everything they can.

There is lots and lots of mud.
It is very squelchy and sloppy.
You are very sticky in the End
by Bali Gill

Sustaining a lifestyle

Shopping facilities are taken for granted by everyone, but are not always available to Travellers. Those without transport rely heavily upon local general stores, where the welcome is inevitably tempered by public feeling in the area. Some larger shops may also discriminate against individuals regarded as deviant, banning them altogether, or in groups. This happened in the area around Malvern and Upton where the Castlemorton illegal festival took place. The police requested that pubs and shops should not serve Travellers.

Recreation is important and public facilities are sometimes open to Travellers. Attending sport or swimming centres is beneficial for children in particular, and they are given a source of hot showers. However, there are bans from some such places, and the use of public parks may be restricted by injunctions. The use of libraries is almost impossible unless residing in a permanent area, as membership can only be acquired with proof of identity and address.

Possessions.

The restricted space of a home on the road means that the compulsive materialism of conventional society is not viable. Possessions have to be transportable and economically stored. When a vehicle is tatted down, all free standing objects must be packed away safely. Not only does this avoid breakages, but it is safer than having items falling during travel. Possessions gain value for their sentimental or practical qualities, rather than their initial expense. There are fewer ornaments, crockery and clothes than in most houses; and these

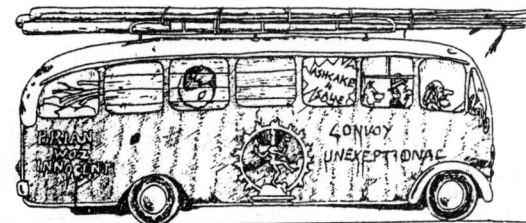

can usually be replaced. The horrific trashings of the eighties, and rapid evictions, have shown that little is sacred to the authorities.

> *"Have nothing in your homes except what you know to be useful, and believe to be beautiful." William Morris*

Insurance is rarely available, so Travellers may feel vulnerable when everything they own in the world is contained within a 18 foot by 8 foot space.

There are certain items that are crucial to everyone. Whilst settled people may expect televisions, domestic equipment and electric appliances as necessities, they are luxuries to Travellers. Basic equipment includes a shovel, an axe, a bow-saw, water containers, a kettle, some crockery and cutlery, bedding, boots, a tool kit, matches and candles. Obviously, everyone acquires tat and may accumulate attractive or precious possessions over time which replace previous objects. Thus, most mobile homes are full of aesthetically pleasing items, such as rough-hewn wood; African or Indian artefacts; scraps of items; photos and sketches or newspaper headlines on the walls; crafted or old-fashioned objects such as cast-iron frying pans...etc. Romanies collect Royal Doulton and Spode china; we have other 'treasures.'

Where do Travellers live?

Travellers are not confined to a particular geographic region and they may be drawn to areas for a multitude of reasons - explored in the following section.

It is seasonally affected, but during the winter months, Travellers tend to try and be more settled. For some, this means retreating to houses for a while; but for the majority, it means locating a site where vehicles can be overhauled, a woodpile gathered, and the need to move during adverse weather conditions is avoided. These sites, whether rural or urban, have to be carefully selected.

Although some authorities provide authorised sites, places are limited and generally available only to Gypsies. Recent legislation (see Chapter 5) has removed local responsibility for site provision, although some areas, such as Avon, have granted authorisation to illegal sites. On the whole, however, illegal sites remain so and are subject to eviction. Landownership is the vital factor. Laws of trespass and public nuisance can be more quickly enforced on land with private ownership. But equally, a landowner welcoming one or two rigs onto land is subject to prosecution anyway, unless planning permission has been obtained. And this is almost always opposed.

Particularly popular areas include the Welsh borders, Hereford and Worcester, Kent, Avon and Hampshire, all of which were traditionally associated with areas visited seasonally by Romanies. There is also the 'New Age' cultural appeal of Somerset, particularly Glastonbury and the West Country, and especially Totnes.

Common land was traditionally available to all who had owned or farmed strips under the old open field system, and was a regular spot for Travellers of all types passing through. Its use is increasingly controlled now, and several have been designated as areas of special scientific interest. Some that have been used occasionally for years are now ditched, with no vehicle access.

Greenlanes are historically used by travelling people but are also now subject to laws of obstruction, or have passed into private ownership. These ancient by-ways, rarely used by anyone other than farmers, dog walkers or horse riders; would seem ideal locations for park-ups - but new laws prohibit this. Road verges are usually council owned and as long as vehicular access is unrestricted on the metalled road itself, less easily evicted. But unless wide, and bordering quiet lanes, are unsuitable for those with animals or children.

Other council-owned areas of land are generally the best bet. Eviction could be challenged in a judicial review, although new legislation may eradicate this. These areas may range from rural recreation parks to urban derelict lands awaiting development after compulsory purchase. As the latter in particular is rarely destined for any immediate use, it seems a waste to prevent anyone else from temporary inhabitation.

Private owners who leave industrial or commercial properties empty after bankruptcy or sale, or whilst awaiting modernisation, increasingly tend to erect barriers or dig ditches. Disused airfields, quarries or M.O.D land are also popular park-ups. Although the space is rarely used by the owners, eviction may still be rapid.

Large lay-bys became the last respite for many traditional Travellers alongside authorised sites, and are increasingly fulfilling the same role for newer Travellers. Again, they are far from ideal for animals and children.

Squatted buildings with surrounding land may be viable sites, or rigs may park-up on the edges of industrial sites. Sometimes, Travellers simply head for the first seemingly suitable space; sometimes they have reconnoitred the locality for prospective sites; sometimes they return to a previous park-up, or join friends; sometimes, contrary to popular opinion, they are even invited to park-up on someone's land.

Sites to which Travellers are invited may be for specific reasons: most obviously, work or entertainment, such as fruit picking, other farm work or fairgrounds/shows. Some individuals make private arrangements with landowners who want or need them; others have access to land owned by friends or family. In the case of Talley, people bought their own land, but have fought for years for the right to live there in an ecologically sound manner.

"In 1990, when I worked on the Skool Bus, funded by the Travellers School Charity, I lived on 26 sites and visited many more. The 26 comprised:

> *6 areas of common land*
> *6 green lanes*
> *4 disused airfields*

3 areas awaiting development
1 verge area
1 commercial festival
1 council-owned recreation area
1 farmer's field with permission
1 farmer's field without permission
1 national conference
1 field under disputed ownership."   *Fiona.*

Another factor affecting sites is their purpose. Whilst obviously being a place to live temporarily, they may be utilised for along winter park-up, or a short summer party. Travellers also congregate for small gatherings, music festivals, or the raves which take place in an assortment of city warehouses, barns and disused premises. People hoping for a big event need to find a large area with plenty of access; those wanting privacy and peace need a secluded and safe site.

Basically, Travellers live wherever they can with minimum harassment. Few deliberately antagonise authorities, but we do need somewhere to go. Eviction does not solve the problem. Travellers are growing in number, especially in the summer months and are unlikely to 'go away' despite government proclamations that they will make every effort to make Travellers' lives difficult!

Paradoxically, support for permanent transit sites has come from a number of police sources, who are often frustrated by having to carry out the job of moving Travellers around the country. Mr Hadfield, the Chief Constable of West Midlands police, who is also chair of the Chief Constables' Public Order Committee, has said:

> *"The idea of permanent sites with all the facilities has to be considered.....Perhaps we should see if a piece of land near Stonehenge can be found for these people to gather on every year. If we do not consider solutions like that, we will simply go on playing pass the parcel with them."*

When do Travellers move on?

There are so many reasons for moving on, or not, that they are impossible to catalogue. A suggestion of some reasons may, however, be made. It must be remembered that those of us who live nomadically carry the ideal that we have the means to move when we need to, rather than when others enforce it. And whereas, orbitals forced into mobile accommodation may want to remain in a particular locality, other Travellers may move hundreds of miles quite regularly. This has been particularly true of Travellers who have heard that particular countries such as Eire or Spain are more receptive, and have moved temporarily, or permanently overseas.

Media and public perception seems to be that Travellers only move on after eviction. To an extent this is true. For instance, of the twenty six sites previously listed, fourteen were subject to enforced movement either when Fiona left, or imminently. Three still exist. Eviction occurs for a multitude of reasons (see chapter 5) In cases of large gatherings, it is expected that

"AS A GENERAL RULE OF BIOLOGY, MIGRATORY SPECIES ARE LESS AGGRESSIVE THAN SEDENTARY ONES. THERE IS ONE OBVIOUS REASON WHY THIS SHOULD BE SO. THE MIGRATION ITSELF, LIKE THE PILGRIMAGE, IS THE HARD JOURNEY: A 'LEVELLER' ON WHICH THE 'FIT' SURVIVE AND STRAGGLERS FALL BY THE WAYSIDE. THE JOURNEY THUS PRE-EMPTS THE NEED FOR HIERARCHIES AND SHOWS OF DOMINANCE. THE 'DICTATORS' OF THE ANIMAL KINGDOM ARE THOSE WHO LIVE IN AN AMBIENCE OF PLENTY. THE ANARCHISTS, AS ALWAYS, ARE THE 'GENTLEMEN OF THE ROAD.' "

BRUCE CHATWIN

everyone will move on fairly quickly. But it is frustrating to be constantly harassed when trying to find a suitable site for a few weeks or months. One group of people in 1990 were subjected to five evictions in six days.

When the police accompany a group of Travellers, it makes finding a temporary site/park-up a near impossibility. One of the problems with fighting eviction is that this involves legal knowledge and some individuals need to be prepared to be named on legal documents. Constant harassment by police, and the final eviction order will be a main reason for leaving a site.

A problem with some sites is that they start small, but become larger as news travels on the grapevine that eviction is being challenged. Some of the conditions are then broken, and eviction can then proceed anyway. Vigilante action or local pressure can also precipitate movement.

For instance, whilst the media reported that one site moved on after security guards surrounded it and created constant overnight noise, the Travellers themselves said that they heard nothing and left on the date dictated by legal notices. There have also been instances when locals have clubbed together in order to pay the Travellers to leave.

There are however, many positive reasons for which people may move on. One is work. Those who rely on seasonal, agricultural work may follow it across the country to join gangs and park-up on the farmer's land as part of the contract. Those with circus, fairground, musical, craft, or practical skills and equipment, participate in a multitude of commercial events and unauthorised gatherings. They set up a diary of work commitments which involve frequent movement.

Some Travellers have trade or skills of value to others on the road, or settled people, and travel

to complete required tasks. Another seasonal influence is the summer festival and rave scene. It is not only for Travellers, who gather to party; their numbers are swelled by ravers from houses and squats who have travelled for the same reasons. And people move to join friends or family, to meet new people, to holiday or see new places.

Now that there seems to be a policy of preventing transit site development, some people are less inclined to move than in the past. Abandoning a park-up before eviction no longer means that it may be available again next year, but that it will be lost for ever.

What do people do all day?

Although the actual details may be different, we do the same as people in houses:

> domestic chores
> work
> recreation.

Domestic Chores

Several of these have already been described. There are regular water and wood runs. Shopping, cleaning and cooking must be completed. Kindling needs to be gathered or chopped. Children participate at a much younger age in helping carry out these tasks. They are also given a great deal of time and attention - all adults take part in their entertainment and learning.

An enormous amount of energy is expended in vehicle maintenance and home restoration, rebuilding or redecoration. Maintenance of engines is crucial for people who need to keep moving. Almost everyone, male and female, has some competence with mechanics. The most basic jobs are learned early, as children watch adults, ask questions, and are invited to help out.

> *I love this bus*
> *That I call my home*
> *I dig this coach*
> *That allows me to roam*
> *My little space*
> *That can take me any place*
> *My sanctuary*
> *No matter where I be*
>
> *And when I know that she's ready to go*
> *And a time to travel's dawning*
> *Reaching, to start her heart*
> *She turns, she breathes, she fires, she vibrates gently*
> *We move into the morning*
> *Wondering whence we do depart*
> *Knowing that there's nothing wrong with where I am*
> *Some folk simply do not understand.*
>
> > *CG*

Aside from the more mundane mending, there are more specialist jobs requiring advice or assistance. There are many very efficient mechanics and welders on every site, who either have formal training, or have learned through practice. A major job, such as changing an engine, requires co-operation and shared tools as well as time. These tasks are made harder by the poor facilities on site - power tools need electricity, for example. Other than the engine, there is the chassis and body to maintain and the home itself to work on. There are increasing numbers of vehicles requiring restoration. It can take years to pay for materials and complete the work with hand tools only. But it is always worth it in the end, when an old vehicle has been beautifully rebuilt.

Even modern caravans and trucks can need structural work. Such development includes the skills of carpenters and joiners to strengthen or replace bodywork. Once the shell has been satisfactorily completed, the interior must be organised. Furnishings may be free standing or purpose-built, again taking time. Then there are the paint jobs, inside and out, that complete a vehicle.

All these tasks are time consuming, and are easier in good weather, on hard standing. It can take weeks or months to complete a job, but there is the satisfaction of knowing that it has been personally finished.

Hot ragging the engine

Blat-motors, small vans or cars used for short runs, or social blats around the country, also need maintenance regularly. Most are legal, but bought cheaply because the M.O.T. or tax has only a couple of months to run. Their life is extended by engine transplants, or welding or replacements of axle, brake, clutch etc.

Travellers are heavily reliant upon one another for other daily chores, as well. Those with blat motors and flat-beds can share transport in order to collect wood, water or shopping. There are regular runs, incorporating lots of people on site. The Travellers' community is close-knit by necessity, as well as by choice.

Work.

Although the media image of Travellers emphasises their reliance upon government handouts, many have skills and trades which they want to use. As discussed previously, there are a multitude of skilled tradespeople on site. As well as mechanics, welders and joiners, there are carpenters, electricians, engineers... the list is endless. These skills can be traded both internally and in the local area, either for cash or as an exchange. The rate is much more reasonable than a commercial firm, and the work is generally as good. Individuals gain recommendation for success, which is passed on by word of mouth.

> *"When my horsebox had been rebuilt by relatives, a friend*
> *travelled a couple of hundred miles to complete the welding*
> *and mechanical work - the truck, having been immobile*
> *for months, passed its M.O.T. first time."*   Fiona

There are also many people with academic qualifications, whose professions can be used either on the road; or who can take up a post because of their mobility. There seem to be a number of photographers, teachers, nurses and journalists, amongst much more diverse careers. Skills can be used for the benefit of the whole community, as well as freelanced within settled Society.

A multitude of crafts are associated with Gypsies, and the newer Travellers have followed in this tradition. Beautiful pots, jewellery and clothes can be made throughout the winter months for sale during the summer .The materials can often be stored easily and the products appeal not only to other Travellers, but also to those house dwellers who have an awareness of, and sympathy for, ethnic crafts. Some Travellers have even successfully applied for business start-up grants, Enterprise Allowance funding, or to the Prince's Trust employment funds. A spin-off is that children can learn many money making skills easily, and enjoy the chance to earn their own pocket-money.

Another predominantly fair-weather occupation is that involving the fairground or circus. There are lots of people on site practising such skills as juggling, stilt-walking or fire breathing. Hours of dedication are necessary for success, but increasingly these skills are learned by children, who become interested and involved at a young age.

More and more Travellers seem to be buying and restoring such traditional equipment as swingboats or small roundabouts. These need a great deal of maintenance to ensure safety.

All these pastimes can be used at commercial events, or for busking. Busking with musical instruments is also common, and every town with a Traveller encampment nearby is likely to sport a 'hippy' on one corner with a penny whistle. There are also beggars, especially in such cities as Bristol and Brighton, whose affluent inhabitants can provide quite a reasonable income.

In the past, Travellers of all origins have relied heavily on the scrap trade. Collecting metal, stripping and separating it, then weighing it has always been quite lucrative. However, descending prices made this less popular; then the government introduced bills limiting the transport of scrap metal to specially licensed vehicles only. This had quite an impact on those who made a lucrative living from dispensing of the waste dumped by conventional society. There are still those who rely on tatting and collecting in order to make a living, and they perform a service for us all.

Wire-stripping

Seasonal agricultural work originally employed a combination of Travellers and locals; the numbers were swelled by poor city-dwellers who took their holidays working. Now however, the gangs which often include Travellers and the local unemployed, face the challenge of immigrants imported daily to fields from such cities as Birmingham and London. All gangs roam throughout the country, providing agricultural services as diverse as fruit picking, vegetable harvesting and wild oat pulling. Whereas travellers require a place to park-up temporarily, local or urban gangs do not require accommodation. There are many people who return annually to particular farms where they are welcome, and work long hours to complete the job in time.

The summer festival scene provides an income for all Travellers, whether they are performing, trading crafts or selling skills. Large commercial events require a massive site crew for several weeks to erect fences, dig trenches, distribute bins, set up communications and so on. In turn, this spawns a need for site kitchens, mechanics and field organisers. It is often forgotten that an army of litter-pickers is required for up to a fortnight afterwards - and it is not the ticket buying punters who collect their own refuse, but usually teams of Travellers paid to complete the job well. It is filthy and potentially dangerous.

Illegal gatherings provide a chance for those with travelling stages, sound systems, marquees and cafes to make money.

There are still some drug dealers on the road, as there are anywhere - punters come to them; rather than the methods of the small urban dealer who may recruit punters in pubs, clubs or at

school gates. They supply a need rather than creating it in the first place. But they are a minority - despite media emphasis otherwise.

> *"Some of the original Travellers were dealers getting away*
> *from all the busts in town - but it was never hard drugs.*
> *There was an agreement, no hard drugs on site......because*
> *they'd watch us all day, the smackheads; sitting back, scratching,*
> *watching us work our butts off, and at the end of the day, they'd*
> *rob you. So you'd earn all your dosh at Stonehenge, then*
> *they'd nick it, on the way to Inglestone, or wherever. So that was it."*
>   *Phil.*

Everybody on the road has a means of making a living, but the current legislation limiting sites and the proposed clamp down on raves, under the 1990 Environment Protection Act, is making it increasingly difficult to do so. There are few people who want to resort to relying on state benefit and be labelled as scroungers, but there is little encouragement to do much else.

Applying for conventional jobs can be difficult when encountering prejudice; and uncertainty about the possibility of being allowed by the authorities to remain in one place does not make for a secure base.

Many people have gathered a lot of expensive equipment, such as generators and tools, in order to complete both daily tasks and commercial enterprises. These are almost impossible to insure, so are particularly valuable to their owners. Most people want to be economically independent, but are forced into accepting the benefits to which they are entitled. In reality, the level of benefits paid out are less for unemployed house-dwellers because they do not include housing benefit.

Recreation.

There is a popular misconception that those living on the road have little to do apart from relax. Quite the opposite is in fact true. Admittedly, though, once the chores and work are completed, Travellers value their recreation time. As daylight fades, and evening closes in, outdoor activities become impractical, so there is time to socialise, or pursue individual pastimes. This is also true of rainy days!

Walking is one of the few daytime pursuits that combine pleasure with work. Everybody walks, either to have a shit, collect wood, or exercise dogs. Those on isolated rural sites are particularly inclined to spend spare time exploring the locality. Children learn a great deal on expeditions with adults, especially those who know about the natural environment. There is also interest in any historic landmarks, such as ancient forts to which groups may walk or cycle.

Reading is another common form of relaxation. There are books and magazines in abundance on every site. They range from classical novels, to science fiction to underground magazines. Generally they are shared, even read aloud. Children participate in the enjoyment of reading, and also see the benefit of hours spent pouring over practical books such a vehicle manual. Most Travellers are literate and enjoy time to read. It is seen as a means of extending

knowledge and following up areas of interest, as well as escaping into fantasy.

The common contemporary pastimes of television, even videos and computer games are also popular on site. It takes relatively little energy to power a portable monochrome television set. Just as the familiar sound of 'Neighbours' theme tune echoes through settled communities and sites; so there is also a cult following of the Radio 4 series: 'The Archers'. The plot and storylines are avidly discussed and they've even had their own invasion of Travellers in the past!

Children enjoy the gameboy and similar hand-held graphic games, as do those adults who get their hands on them! Video recorders allow communities to share films or favourite programmes. With the limited energy supplies discussed previously, Travellers tend to be more discriminatory about how they use their electrically-powered resources. Children in particular, learn to select thoughtfully.

Music has been quite comprehensively outlined in another section. It must be emphasised that the radio and cassette or CD players provide entertainment in almost all rigs. Acoustic musicians play for themselves, or with others, practising whenever they have a chance. There is also heavy emphasise on games, using cards, boards or characters. These are really sociable activities and have been abandoned by much of conventional society. As well as card games, there may be tricks performed, or the tarot read. Popular boardgames include Trivial Pursuit, Monopoly and Backgammon - all of which benefit children. There were cult followings of the Dungeons and Dragons style adventure games played on a complex series of levels. These are still very commonly enjoyed, especially amongst Travellers embracing the whole 'New Age' philosophy.

Conversation and discussion on site is usually very stimulating. The diversity of individuals, experiences and outlooks provides a range of viewpoints to talk about. Mundane, practical debates about the relative worth of different vehicles are balanced by knowledgeable ecological and ethical discussions. Travellers are great raconteurs, presenting anecdotes with vigour and vision. There are often common concerns to talk about, like plans for moving on, or facing legal action. Then there are media articles to read and debate; gossip about friends and fellow-Travellers to enjoy. During 1990, the 'gobslip board' was a central exchange of graffiti gossip on a blackboard, which entertained everyone. The art of speech, and sharing both problems and solutions is very powerful on site.

Just as the settled community associates alcohol with relaxation, so do Travellers. Pubs and clubs often ban them on the basis of clothes and reputation, so drinking usually takes place on site. The 'Brew Crew' image of crusty individuals clutching cans of Special Brew is cultivated by the media, but the fact remains that precise mechanics cannot be achieved by a bunch of drunks. Individuals have preferences of all kinds, often based on economy. Champagne tequilla slammers were sold at Treworgey, for example, but a lot of people make their own home brew. It is also quite easy to make wines from the hedgerow, orchard and vegetable products so readily available.

On a less toxic level, fresh ground coffee and herb teas are as available as instant coffee or the common tea-bag!

"The use of drugs by Travellers such as myself, (Gubby, Ludden Foot), in particular cannabis, is almost universal. Most will have experimented with the available range of psychoactive substances - including those who no longer use drugs at all; some have been recruited on to the road through local drug scenes or in order to escape heavy drug scenes.

To the average Traveller, though drugs are an integral part of the lifestyle, they are seldom the dominant factor; it is quite difficult to maintain a full-scale habit in the countryside and heroin in particular is usually actively discouraged. As regards the softer drugs, cannabis is a drug particularly well-suited to the life of the Traveller. It is a great reliever of tensions between people and - since most Travellers by necessity live in very close confines - it is useful in making petty arguments and irritations seem irrelevant.

Cannabis may not instil one with great ambition, assertiveness, or desire for hard physical labour, but - speaking as an artist of sorts - its enhancement of the creative and imaginative elements is almost essential. One can work regardless of the time the job is taking, regardless of the opinions of others, or of comparisons with other work; it can rid the brain of peripheral thought processes that are such a distraction to the artist, and concentrate the mind purely on the doing and the enjoyment of creative activity for its own sake.

Alcohol has become increasingly evident on many sites in the last few years - to the detriment of the atmospheres on the site and its reputation in the locality. Chronic alcoholism seems to be on the increase. I enjoy heavy drinking myself and reckon site parties to be wilder and better than any others I have been to, but I cannot regard this as the main part of my life and it makes me sad to see how essential it has become to the lives of many. It seems to cause more trouble than any other drug.

LSD, mushrooms and other hallucinogens are fairly popular drugs. They cause few problems among Travellers and those that do occur can usually be dealt with on site as long as the authorities do not get involved. Their presence usually exacerbates the problem, not to mention the ham-fisted and obtuse methods they have for dealing with anyone suffering detrimental effects. I know of people who have suffered long term mental damage through the actions of the police and hospitals and believe they should be criminally liable for their actions.

I have lived on some site where amphetamines have been freely available. Though I personally dislike this drug, it seldom seems to harm the atmosphere on site; sometimes it is quite advantageous, particularly for mechanics and general physical labour. Some people do get in a mess with amphetamines and they, like other Travellers who abuse drugs - end up living in cities where it is easier to maintain the habit.

Cocaine is not as actively discouraged as heroin, but its price and availability confine its use mainly to cities. I expect most of my friends would accept a free line, but it is not a common drug amongst Travellers.

I think most Travellers have a fairly healthy attitude towards drugs; a person may be ostracised for his actions while under the influence but seldom for the taking of a particular drug. Travellers' opinions and preferences are open; there is little of the hysterical prejudice so common in mainstream society. Children learn early and honestly about their effects and drawbacks and, without the taboos in currency elsewhere, I believe are far less likely to get into trouble for their use."

Gubby

Travellers are great party people. The big summer gatherings are but a part of the constant series of small celebrations. The solstices and equinoxes are such a focus. Although Stonehenge has now been subjected to comprehensive injunctions, people still gather at other points to enjoy the sunrise or sunset.

Similarly, the full moon is important to people living close to the elements. It is powerful in history, and, more practically, gives enough light for an evening sitting around an outside fire.

Birthdays are celebrated by the whole site, parties spilling from caravans. And children in particular tend to have a great day, incorporating adults and animals as well as their friends. People may travel a substantial distance in order to catch up on news whilst having fun. They are a powerful contrast to the sheer drudgery of much day-to-day existence.

◆　◆　◆　◆　◆

This chapter has attempted to provide some insight into a culture which defies definition and generalisation. Travelling is not any easy option in life, but the hardships are outweighed by the advantages. We have not even touched on the weather - the most unstable factor much of the daily life of a Traveller necessarily happens outside. Not only the obvious chores outlined earlier, but also fetching equipment or meeting up with people. Relentless rain is depressing, as a site without hardstanding quickly becomes deeply rutted with mud. Wet clothes, boots and dogs steam by the fire, and some important tasks, such as vehicle maintenance, are awkward.

Alternatively, every aspect of life moves outside on hot summer days ... cooking, eating, washing up... everything. This proximity to the elements is lost to a certain extent in a house. It inevitably affects behaviour, but also makes for a resilient community.

Another aspect that needs a mention is the fact that a high proportion of Travellers have family in settled communities. There may be little, or no contact. Conversely, there may be plenty of communication. Even third generation Travellers may have great-aunts or cousins who are part of straight society. There are close family groups on the road but the extended network is

reliant upon established friendships. Children grow up with a mass of contemporaries, and adults work together to survive.

Who? Why? How? Where? When? What? This enigmatic group of people cannot be categorised despite all attempts to do so. We have merely offered a few insights, but living on the road is a constant voyage of discovery. It is worth following, as long as you remember to...

Bury your shit!

Snowy site

ANCIENT SITES

Avebury, Wilts: A 28 acre henge with 27 of the original 100 stones remaining; the village has developed within the monument.

Cantlin Stones: Sussex.

Chalice Wall, Somerset: A covered spring at the foot of Glastonbury Tor, whose water is tainted red with iron, giving rise to the legend that the Holy Grail is hidden within.

Cissbury Ring, West Sussex: Iron Age hill fort constructed on the site of Neolithic flint mines.

Clun: Forest in Wales used for gatherings.

Glastonbury Tor, Somerset: A conical hill with ridged slopes and traces of a spiral path winding to the summit; linked in legend with Avalon, and King Arthur, giving access to ancient lands. Also the Holy Grail mystery.

Old Sarum, Wilts: Site of an Iron Age fort, then Roman, Saxon and Norman settlements; part of a ley-line aligning Stonehenge, Salisbury Cathedral and Clearbury Ring.

Rollright Stones, Oxon: The stone circle is known as The King's Men; a single 8-foot standing stone, as The king Stone; a burial chamber of 5 large stones, as the Whispering Knights.

Stonehenge, Wilts: Monument of massive stones in concentric circles, constructed from approx. 2800 BC onwards.

Uffington White Horse, Oxon: 365 foot long figure cut into chalk centuries ago above the Vale of the White Horse; Dragon Hill - a mound - and The Manger - a steep combe - are nearby.

Westbury White Horse, Wilts: Of ancient origin, the present horse was cut into the chalk in 1778 and lies on a slope of Salisbury Plain below Bratton Castle, an Iron Age earthworks; Cherhill and Alton Barnes White Horses can be seen from the earthworks.

Chapter Four: Education and Welfare

We do not inherit the earth from our forefathers, We borrow it from our children.

Chief Seattle.

Children are an integral part of the Traveller community. The origins of the movement have ensured that there are new adults, raised on the road, who are bringing up their children the same way. The high proportion of young adults on the road has also led to many babies being born and raised nomadically. The legislative difficulties faced by parents in daily life provide a challenge in bringing up children responsibly. These are compounded by limited education and health facilities; and constant negative media attention. Children, are on the whole, brought up in a caring environment, with an alternative experience of life.

Bender life

Social and Moral Welfare

This is a very broad area to discuss, including the individuals immediately caring for a child, and the more general living environment of all Travellers.

Family

The traditional nuclear family has gradually been eroded in Britain, and single-parent families are as common on site as elsewhere. A fairly high proportion, however, are headed by men.

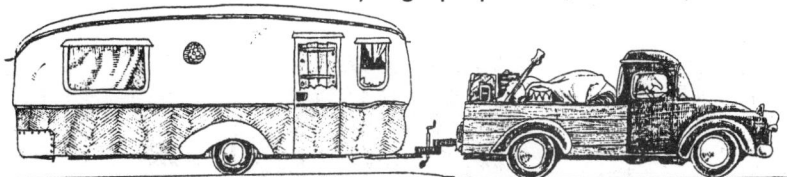

Although there are some married couples, most tend to have a commitment to be together, rather than an official agreement. Due to the high level of young adults, there is a degree of changing partners frequently, which may leave some women pregnant and alone. There is no stigma attached to single parenthood, and new partners are rarely deterred by the presence of children. Indeed most adults become involved in the communal care of children. There is a strong sense of responsibility for the next generation. Adults encourage children to participate in daily chores, such as collecting kindling. Those involved in work are also receptive to young people showing an interest. Most site children are confident mechanics, for example, and are treated as such.

Whilst conventional society tends to regard children as too young to join in many activities, site communities willingly involve them in everything. Most of the children are given a lot of responsibility - and also have the scope for lots of fun. They can play outside for hours with little fear of abduction, as strangers rarely hang around sites. Supervision is a communal concern, not really delegated, but undertaken by anybody who's outside, including older siblings. Single children benefit from the environment, because their friends become an extended family, and lots of homes are available for play, meals, or overnight stays.

It is inevitable that some people are more natural carers than others, and children gravitate towards them, reaping the rewards of sharing time to play and learn. Obviously a mobile home cannot store as many toys as a playroom in a house, but because their is so much invitation to communicate and share, there is usually a good range throughout a site. Outdoor equipment is especially popular - bikes, pedal cars and rocking horses, for example; but children also get the chance to play imaginatively, building dens or bases. An agile adult will usually sling a rope swing from a suitable tree, and see-saws are equally easily constructed. Due to mud in winter, and sudden evictions, toys may be abandoned, but others are soon collected or made to replace them. Inside, children generally have an area regarded as their own, where favourite toys and special objects may be stored.

The summer months are often spent almost entirely outside by children, and even in winter, they can soon warm themselves up by a cosy stove if they've been active outside for a while. The diverse talents of adults can also provide challenges for children, and many learn basic music and juggling skills quite young. Whilst it may appear that:

> *"Filthy toddlers in tattered clothes play*
> *outside in the dirt....children faced a*
> *terrible risk of illness as they were left to*
> *fend for themselves....no children's toys*
> *in sight...."*   *News of the World 6/9/93*

This is a generalisation based on inaccurate first impressions, rather than informed observation. A site can provide a loving, generous community in which to develop. Yes, children may become dirty - but they can soon be cleaned up. They are usually articulate and confident because they communicate freely with adults, and learn their talents or limitations very young. The varied geographical environments create learning through casual study, and provide a variety of local attractions, such as parks, wildlife areas and historic buildings.

Play reflects experience

Many Traveller children have extended family within settled Society. The reactions of parents to their adult children living on the road are varied, but include fear and anxiety, further fuelled by media myth. Some disown their offspring; others speak out in their defence:

"The love remains as strong as ever,
perhaps strengthened by the need to protect
them from....criticism."
D.Wingett, Independent, 3/5/93

On the whole, there seems to be a balance between the two; a combination of tolerance and perplexity. Young children form a focal point for these feelings.

Those who benefit most are those whose relatives, such as grandparents, uncles and aunts, invite them into their own homes at times, to experience the house-based life of the majority of British Society. Others are distanced for ever from such experiences, especially when concerned relatives resort to legal action, attempting to enforce Travellers and their children to resettle. This may result in a complete severance of trust and contact, so depriving everyone.

Custody battles between separated parents are uncommon, but are most likely to occur when one has decided to return to a house, while the other continues to travel. This can be resolved by giving the child an option, especially for those wanting a specific education. On the whole, those Travellers who have made a conscious decision to live on the road, recognise that their children have the right to experience all kinds of lifestyles, so that they can choose for themselves, and re-integrate later on, if they want to. Those who have been forced to live

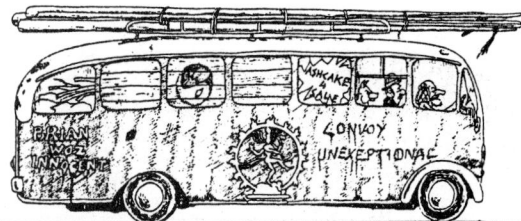

nomadically may have less inclination to expose their children to the negative influences they feel they have escaped. Just as settled parents may escape for a few weeks a year on a caravan or tenting holiday, so it is equally pleasant for a Traveller to be able to relish in the luxuries of a house occasionally.

Modern civilisation includes a multitude of influences on children beyond that of their parents Traveller children spend a great deal of time with family and friends, and are more protected from these distractions. Young babies are never alone, left to sleep in a separate room, but are always in a space shared by other people. Adults tend to work on site, and children become involved; and they are usually taken on off-site expeditions too. Surely such constant contact and communication is beneficial, especially in an age when it is all too easy to allocate daily care elsewhere.

Social Welfare

There is much concern about the dangers of the late twentieth-century. There are public debates about the vulnerability of children in the face of an increasingly technological array of pastimes. Media and individuals alike discern the influences affecting children and their development. These are comprehensively outlined by David Parker in *'Children at Risk,'* and are worth a brief consideration here, in the context of Traveller children.

Some of the major influences he cites are:
> ***Television, computers, advertising and fantasy role playing games.***

There are televisions on site, but, as their power is on limited supply, watching tends to be selective. A car battery has to be recharged, and a generator refuelled, so nobody leaves the set on all day. Children still have favourite programmes - which they usually watch in adult company; either because they are working in the vicinity, or they fancy a chance to relax for a while. Such shared viewing stimulates discussion. Some children may help with the earning of money for fuel, and value their viewing.

> *"Tom(aged 13) sold his portable mono set to a couple in the*
> *caravan next door, and can now watch it for free with them, while*
> *they worry about the power supply." Herring.*

Whilst some Travellers may have video recorders, their use is, again, limited. Children rarely have access to them whilst alone - if there's something showing, everyone on site wants to see it. Those selected are usually popular comedies or classic favourites. There was a good birthday party which concluded with the children sitting down to watch a 'Magic Roundabout' video - soon to be accompanied by adults !

A home computer is not very practical in a place without constant electricity, so those Travellers using them tend to have access to a house on an occasional or permanent basis. As an educational tool, they can be very useful, though children should have mastered the mechanical skills first. Even with something as basic as a calculator, for example, the number relationships should be understood beforehand.

Like children everywhere, those on site are fascinated by hand-held games, and play them enthusiastically if they're around. However, such solitary contests take place within the context of a physical and varied lifestyle.

The twentieth century bombards everyone with advertising on television and radio, on billboards and in shops. Slogans and jingles echo around us all the time. To a certain extent, sites are protected from such incessant sales techniques. Children seem very aware of what can be afforded, and soon learn that practicality is more important than currant trend. Most are happy to browse in jumble sales, tat shops, or at a car boot sale, and to choose their own favourites from such selections.

Fantasy role-playing games have evolved rapidly in recent years, and computer software makes complex challenges readily available. The game 'Dungeons and Dragons' has been a cult pastime on some sites, though play is usually without the expensive figures now sold in specialist shops. Games may last hours or even days, and provide communal entertainment and competition amongst all age groups.

Making their entertainment

Moral Welfare

There seem to be three principal concerns today about the moral development of children and, most particularly, teenagers:

sex, drugs and crime.

Sex

We have witnessed no child abuse on site. It would be untrue to say that none are neglected by their parents, but in those uncommon situations, the communal care considered earlier comes into force. Parents with temporary difficulties are not isolated, and other adults will

ensure love, clean clothes and hot food for their children until they sort themselves out. This care comes without the condemnation that may occur in housed populations, and is therefore more valuable. It is agreed that authority care is a poor alternative, so the whole group will make sure that no child is left alone. Sexual and physical abuse is also uncommon. The sheer proximity of homes, the thin walls, and the constant personal interaction between those on site means that everything is seen and heard. In one case, years ago, when a single man interfered with some children, they joined forces between themselves to burn him out, destroying his possessions.

One problem for sexually active parents may be the closeness of children's beds to their own, but this can easily be overcome by having time alone in the datime, or asking someone else to let the children stay overnight. As children grow older, they need their own space. There is little privacy, so children are familiar with bodies, but may become embarrassed through puberty. Several families with teenage children tow a small caravan as their bedroom; help build a bender for privacy; or construct a room at one end of the bus.

The high incidence of teenage pregnancy throughout Society, reinforced in polls revealing an ever-younger age of sexual experience, is probably reflected on site. But in a way, our children are more mature, having been part of the community all along, participating in the responsibility for survival.

Drugs

Recreational drug use has also expanded in recent decades. Popular music trends have promoted the designer drug culture, subsidised by common social use of soft drugs. Restless youth has turned towards harder drugs, not only in the urban areas. The difference with teenagers experimenting with drugs on site is that it is within a more tolerant adult community. Hidden use is not necessary, so the danger of misuse is less common. Children may have seen the effects on others, so understand more about the substances.

> *"I taught one teenager, for example, who occasionally smoked hash.*
> *But she always waited until after the daily lesson, because she knew that its use*
> *impairs short- term memory and concentration."* Fiona.

There are older adults who have come through hard drug addiction, and whose advice to abstain is more readily accepted than the conventional parental attitude of repulsion based on written, rather than real, experiences. Those who live on city sites, such as Bristol, may see the ravages wrought on those in squats or on site, who rely on a daily fix, be it illegal or prescribed. This builds an awareness of effects, and the potential of a more responsible attitude. Whilst drug abuse remains a danger for young people everywhere, its use in specific places, at particular times, may be more understood better by those on site.

Crime

Teenage criminal activity is attributed to a multitude of causes - family breakdown, boredom, poor job prospects, to name but a few. Family relationships on site rarely breakdown completely. They may go through transition, but there is not often a complete lack of contact between parents. There is also the development of adult bonds outside the family unit, so that close friends travel together for a while, one leaving an immediate family unit to join another. Children on site rarely have time to be bored either, the older they become, the more

involvement they may have in general activities. Some may focus on domestic chores, or sibling care; others use and develop skills and trades. Most particularly, engines can be tinkered with and tuned; or trials bikes can be built, rebuilt, and used away from the roads. Because children are accepted as 'people', they are viewed on their merits; there is less need to prove their independence through crime.

Chopping wood

The prospect of life on the dole, with no obvious role within Society, is less apparent on site. Whilst young people may not be able to make much money, they soon learn to barter their skills in exchange for others - or even cash. Most adults share tools and equipment, and demonstrate techniques. So while the immediate future may seem reliant on state handouts, teenagers can practise towards some means of ultimate financial independence.

One reason for teenage crime which is commonly unmentioned, is the consumer age in which we live. Material possessions, especially cars, clothes, or jewellery, gain an unreal value, and may only be acquired illegally. With the less materialistic view of objects on site, teenagers may be less inclined towards criminal activities. They will still blag items they find useful, or even nick them from somewhere if the opportunity arises; but they will rarely set out deliberately to challenge the law - they have all seen too much of that anyway, at each eviction.

It would be wrong to say that childhood on site is ideal, but in many ways it is a good compromise. The influence of parents and other significant adults is less challenged than in settled Society. The life is hard but rewarding; involving everyone equally. Even on the most

squalid of sites, children have advantages over those trapped in inner-city, high-rise flats, surrounded by strangers. And on the best they have enormous chances to develop. On all of them they are integrated into every aspect of life - chores, parties, evictions, fairs........a whole vista of experiences to learn from, and become adults in their own way.

> "In fact, there are few places in the world more beautiful than the English countryside. To be a child among woods and fields gives you an understanding of changing seasons, growth and decay, life and death."
>
> John Mortimer. Mail on Sunday. 13/3/94

Education

It is a common misconception, reinforced in most State schools, that attendance is compulsory. It is not.

> *"Parents are obliged to ensure that their child receives efficient full-time education suitable to the child's age, aptitude, or any special educational needs that he or she may have, while of compulsory school age."*
> *Section 36 Education. Act 1944*

Education is very important, but the blind acceptance of State provision is not only often opposed by parents on the road, but is also, in practice, often hard to obtain. At one stage in the development of the current Traveller sub-culture, it seemed that parents were offering their children a broad knowledge of life and skills, but little in the way of conventional schooling. However, the danger of regression, of successive generations being decreasingly literate, seems to have been recognised; and most parents are actively seeking some form of acceptable education system.

Traveller children often have exceptional skills in oracy and numeracy, gleaned from general site life; but reading and writing usually have to be specifically learned. Once mastered, however, the child then has the potential to learn as and when appropriate. It would seem that there are three broad options available to parents for consideration:

Learning through life; State provision; alternative education.

In fact, most Travellers opt for a combination of all three, dependent upon a mass of individual circumstances. On the whole, the trend seems to be towards the child's point of view being taken into consideration, and discussed in the light of parental opinion and practical possibilities.

Learning through life

The nomadic lifestyle previously outlined provides a great deal of stimulation for most children. By children being in close proximity to adults at work and leisure, they are exposed to a

multitude of experiences. Imitation in play amongst pre-school children reflects this - toy vehicles, for example, may be hitched up, customised, or even 'scrapped', as well as being dismantled and rebuilt. They also observe and learn daily tasks.

> *"My daughter talked my mum through lighting the hurricane lamp*
> *one evening, even though she'd never done it herself."*
> *Fiona.*

They participate in cleaning, maintenance, cooking, collecting kindling, gathering berries etc., and often have specific tasks they adopt as their responsibility. As they grow older this becomes more developed, and they find particular areas of interest.

> *"Young girls already have motherhood skills and a seven year*
> *old boy would be able to change the oil on a huge lorry."*
> *Barbara Perez NW report*

Mending the taxi

We would also add that this gender stereotyping is rare, girls and boys choosing whichever role they find best. Teenagers gain independence young, always having been part of the adult community. In addition, geographic and historic knowledge is learned through movement around this, or other, countries. Simply observing changing landscapes leads to deduction and development.

> *"Beren has seen the Alps, and understands how they are an international border."*
> *Roddy.*

Many 'school' subjects, such as science, home economics, arts, languages, metalwork, woodwork, maths; are encompassed in daily life.

> *"To them, (Travellers' children) the tests are just everyday common-sense.*
> *They know that pieces of wood float. They've probably tried to get across*
> *a river on a piece of wood that floats!"*
>   *Barbara Perez NW report*

Less easily categorised lessons, such as sociology, cultural differences, moral debate, are also freely available.

> *"Barry went to Europe with the 'Tofu Love Frogs' as their guest star bodhran player*
> *for about three months visiting Belgium, Switzerland, Austria, Slovenia, Croatia and*
> *France. They played some refugee camps in Slovenia and Croatia and at a blind school.*
> *They delivered some stuff there too. Fossil did an aid run to Bosnia in his truck didn't*
> *he?" Es.*

J.M.Forrest notes in a discussion of sociology of education, May 1990, that reliance on this form of learning as total provision; "seems to be the position of many of the older children, particularly those of the more anarchic groups." This must be tempered by the fact that parents of older children sometimes settle temporarily in order to allow them State education facilities.

And we would also wish to repeat the fact that many Travellers fear a regression in standards, removing the option of children re-integrating into Society as an adult, if literacy is lost.

State provision

The State education system has fine principles; that a basic curriculum be available to all children, regardless of background. This is not always as straightforward as it may seem, however, and there are usually three sections of the education service encountered by Travellers.

Schools

Mainstream schools vary enormously from area to area. Just as settled parents consider aspects like results, culture, truancy rates, so do Travellers. They cannot always move into, or remain in, areas where the schools meet the needs of their children.

But reservations aside, the availability of mainstream education to Traveller children is variable. The attitude of a particular school is one of the principal factors. Legally, a school can only refuse a place to a child if the roll is full. However, delaying tactics, or enrolment forms demanding a permanent local address, can effectively exclude a Traveller.

Those schools which welcome Traveller children are often pleasantly surprised:

> *".....they often cope better with the community of the school than some of our more*
> *protected children.........they are very good with our handicapped pupils........the*
> *children are clean and come appropriately dressed."*
>   *Mrs. Segger Times Education Supplement 18/12/92*

Basic reservations include:

• Religious indoctrination, where pupils take part in a predominantly Christian day, while   parents may have rejected these beliefs.

"The worst bit is having to sit through all those God-songs every morning."

Steve (7)

• The limited value of short term inclusion, after which children are wrenched away from a new set of friends and teachers.

• The National Curriculum, which represents a reinforcement of principles rejected by parents. Political history, for example, may be considered less relevant than social history to those currently part of a new sociological trend.

• The narrow categorisation of children by age rather than ability. It is neither normal, nor natural, for children to be surrounded entirely by peers of an identical age group. They are used to interacting with younger and older children as well, thus developing other learning skills.

One of the main advantages is that they usually want to learn and be in school, instead of having been forced to attend from the age of five. The attitude of the school authorities may not be reflected by local parents and their children .

"You can have the best school......excellent staff.....but if the parents are difficult, the kids are difficult, and they can make our kids' lives an absolute misery."

Lin Lorien, Traveller parent, Times Education Supplement 18/12/92.

Prejudice within the classroom is an enormous burden to a young child, and becomes an even greater problem if it extends to playground bullying. Although Traveller children are pretty resilient, such negative approaches are hindrance to learning.

"In Cound I found the school very friendly, very helpful. Very countryfied; the teachers quite keen in having the children, the problem being after two days we were forced to move somewhere else, which was rather annoying, having got them used to the school. We thought we might send them to Dothill, where we were parked outside the local school. When first we got there, we all sat down to watch the news to see what they had to say about us, and saw one of the parents picking up her children from the school saying that they thought they should get a machine gun and shoot us all. After that I thought it might not be a good idea to send the children to that school.

I think they see us as something completely alien to their way of life. Also as a bit of a threat. I think a lot of people are frightened of us, as they don't understand us, and it needs to be pointed out that we are people just the same as anyone else. We have families, children, we have pets, we have the same everyday problems that other people do. The only thing we don't have is houses."   Es

---

It is difficult to remedy biased opinions, and a high percentage of children in all schools have experienced some form of verbal or physical bullying. Traveller children are not unique in being obvious victims - so are the fat, the thin, the intellectual, the slow learner, the spotty, the tall, the short, the racial or ethnic minority, the religious, the rich, the poor, the dirty,....and so on.

The close relationship between Traveller children and their parents means that the children may quickly learn to recognise discrimination, and the choice facing Travellers is that of withdrawing, or integrating sufficiently to appreciate both the 'static' and Traveller culture.

> *"They're all right in the classroom, but outside, they call me names like gyppo or crusty....and I'm not!"*
> *Frances (13)*

There are also the uniform requirements to consider. Parents quite simply cannot afford to buy a complete change of clothes for a series of different schools. When this includes games kit, aprons, or even coats, the cost of kit is totally prohibitive. Thus the child stands out as differently clothed; or second-hand garments have to be adapted; or a sympathetic Educational Welfare Officer/L.E.A/school will offer funds from a welfare fund. Washing and drying clothes nightly is often impossible in winter, so they must be worn carefully.

Once actually in school, accepted by parents, children, staff and governors, and adequately attired, there are other considerations which come into force:

Teachers must be ready to adopt a new range of teaching strategies, as the adult-child relationship is perceived differently by Traveller children. They have often been encouraged to explore and discover, to question and deduce, rather than accepting the dictates of an adult as totally correct. Such experiential learning has often been acknowledged in educational circles as a much stronger foundation than simply learning theories.

The **children** are often unaccustomed to an organised daily routine based on time rather than opportunity. They may feel restricted by desks, or by the limitations on personal choice. This is true of all children entering a State school, but is increasingly awkward for those children adapting to a different routine in each new place.

> *"He didn't want to be sitting there with a book, he wanted to finish his painting. Nobody explained why he had to move, they just told him he had to."*
> *about Ro, aged 5.*

Parents encouraging their children to go to school may have emphasised the need for minimum skills in reading, writing, and basic maths. The children may then resent time spent in other activities. It can easily become a confusion over priorities and cultures.

> *"The teacher said that she (my daughter) seemed to think that school was for learning to read, write and learn numbers, and that she was reluctant to complete tasks in the sandpit. Quite frankly, I'm happy with that. It seems a pretty sound attitude to me."*
> *about Freija, aged 4.*

As children become older, the lack of continuity in their education becomes more obvious, and considerable gaps in the knowledge required by school may be noticeable. This may complete the self-fulfilling prophecy of failure of Travellers, as they cannot hope to compete equally in public examinations or tests, unless parents have made a considerable effort to back up sporadic conventional schooling.

Most of all **resources** within schools rarely incorporate any form of traveller culture. Whilst there has been a great pressure educationally to include racially and culturally divergent

resources, these do not often include alternative nomadic cultures. Emphasis is placed on awareness of gender, mental or physical disability, class divisions etc., but there is little constructive debate about Travellers.

Young Traveller children instinctively draw vehicles rather than houses; or address parents by the first names they hear repeated by the whole community; but there is little in most State schools which reconciles these images in books or pictures.

> *"I gave them a list of our names, and where we lived, but she still came home calling us mummy and daddy, clutching a painting of a house." about Freija, 4.*

The school system is rarely used by Travellers as an exclusive form of education. Those whose travel causes them to return regularly to one area, especially to a house, may adopt a distance-learning scheme. The school sets up a programme of workpacks which are completed, returned by post, and marked. Thus the children maintain a standard, and quickly assimilate themselves back into the system. Similarly, those children on secure winter park-ups may go into school. The current legislation is making it almost impossible for Travellers to return annually to an area, so children are having to adapt each year to a new system, and different experiences. Some parents choose to join their children in the classroom, working towards integration and understanding, and providing specific knowledge on occasions.

> *"I went in three days a week in Norfolk, with about half a dozen kids who went every day. They gave me my own little drama group of straight kids, as well as ours, and it was really good." Liz.*

Some children opt into the system during their teens in order to gain recognised qualifications. This may necessitate temporary settlement, or the child may choose to live with another relative currently in a house. On the whole, the mainstream school is regarded with a healthy degree of scepticism.

> *"Personally, I can think of few places as detrimental to the development of a child between the ages of 8 and 13, as a school - and I say that as a teacher, as well as a parent." Fiona.*

The fact remains that many Traveller children would probably benefit from more access to schools, if only it were less hassle, and they were able to negotiate a balance of terms.

> *"I like living on the road because it's more free, easier to do things and there's more space to do 'em in. I goes to school sometimes. I wanted to go to the school my brother goes to (a primary), but they wouldn't let me 'cos I'm eleven. I didn't want to go to the big school on my own 'cos I'd have to wear uniform; my mum can't afford it*

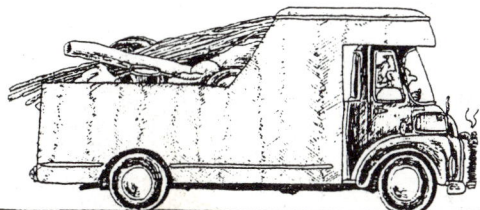

and none of the other kids go there off site, so I'd have no-one to play with. I'd be the smallest kid there and have to be in the small class and I'd get picked on."   John, _aged 11 years, after four and a half years on the road._

Education Welfare Service (E.W.S)

The second State sector affecting Travellers is the Education Welfare Service. Their work with schools concerns following up cases of extended absence, and to ensure the equal opportunities for all children to be educated. Individual Education Welfare Officers, (E.W.O.'s) are as different as the regions in which they operate.

Some believe in forcing the children of Travellers to attend school. Others point out to parents that a school attendance order may be enforced by the county if parents cannot prove that the child is _"receiving efficient full-time education......"_   And others turn a blind eye, encouraging and helping provide an adequate home education. Some Traveller parents do not realise that once a child has been registered at a particular school, regular attendance must be maintained. Sudden eviction, or even planned moving-on, may not mean that a child has been de-registered. Whilst prosecution does not usually follow, the E.W.O. may have responsibility for checking up.

This gives a degree of flexibility in interpretation of 'unauthorised absence,', which should help Travellers. Some E.W.O.'s actively encourage school attendance by arranging a taxi service, or obtaining bus-passes for those Travellers on a low income. Unfortunately a few antagonistic individuals have made their profession unwelcome to some parents, who dislike their authoritarian links. This diversity was reflected at a conference where one EWO wanted ideas on seeking a voluntary teacher of reading for an 18 year old, whilst a colleague's suggestion was: "send him to the Adult Literacy classes." Similarly, he gave out leaflets on DSS benefits, while she took Travellers to the office and helped out with making claims.

At present there is a move towards unifying the E.W.S nationally, and a body has recently been established to promote training and sharing. A few Travellers have been invited to advise on some issues, or to present workshops and discussions about our lifestyle.

"Usually, schools and E.W.O.'s are quite helpful. Well they have been so far. I mainly winter-up in Shropshire and a good relationship with the E.W.O." Es.

```
The DFE Draft document on 'School Attendances Policy and Practise on categorisation of Absence'
includes the following recommendations:

TRAVELLER CHILDREN
44) The special position of Traveller families is recognised by section 199 of the Education Act
1993 which protects Traveller parents from conviction if the parent can demonstrate that:
     - he is engaged in a trade of such a nature as requires him to travel from place to place;
     - the child has attended at a school as a registered pupil as regularly as the nature of
     that trade or business permits;
```

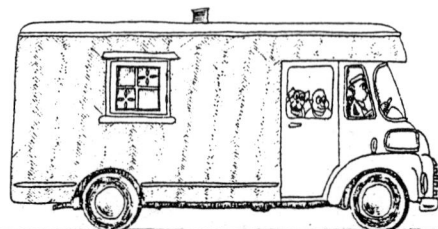

- where the child has attained the age of six years, he has made at least 200 attendances (i.e. 200 sessions or half days) during the preceding twelve months.

45) The purpose of this section is to protect Traveller parents from unreasonable prosecution for the non-attendance of their children at school. It does <u>not</u> mean that part- time education for Traveller children is legally acceptable, nor does it relieve parents of their duties under section 36 of the Education Act 1944 to ensure that children are receiving suitable education when not at school.

46) In general, the aim should always be to ensure that Traveller Children, in common with other children, attend school as regularly and as frequently as possible - 200 attendances should not be regarded as a norm. A difficult balance has to be struck between, on the one hand, the need for action in individual cases in the interests of the child and, on the other, adopting a sensible and sympathetic approach which recognises the lifestyle and cultural traditions of the family concerned.

47) Schools may authorise absence of Traveller children where they are satisfied that a family migrates, but gives reasonable indications that it has every intention of returning. This includes Gypsy and other Travellers, Circus and Fairground families leaving sites and winter quarters, with every expectation that they will return. Some schools in these circumstances are able to maintain contact with the children by outreach work or the provision of distance learning packs, although such activities should not be viewed as a preferable alternative to attendance at school. Some reasonable latitude on absence might also be offered in respect of families who have moved from, or been evicted from, unauthorised sites while the family finds another site. However in the latter circumstances, all efforts should be made to encourage the maintenance of attendance at school.

48) Where Traveller children are registered pupils at a school and are known to be present either at a site (official or otherwise) or in a house and not attending school, the absence should be investigated in the same way as that for any pupil.

Traveller Education Service(T.E.S.)

Section 76 of the Education Act states that Local Education Authorities must:

> *"have regard for the general principle that so far as it is compatible with the provision of efficient instruction and training and the avoidance of unreasonable public expenditure, pupils are to be educated in accordance with the wishes of their parents."*

Neither the State school system, nor the E.W.S provide this, and the third facet of State-funded facilities is the Traveller Education Service. Many T.E.S employees are members of the National Association for the Teachers of Travellers, and are dedicated to making education accessible to all children. Traditionally work has been with fairground, circus, Romany or bargee families, so adaptation is needed to the very different needs of newer Travellers. These include the fact that most of the Traveller parents are literate, and can support children with schoolwork; and also the fact that some have deliberately rejected the present school system.

The role and scope of T.E.S units vary immensely. Some counties established mobile schools which visit sites regularly. Those from Oxford and Sussex worked with the Skool Bus in 1990 (see Fiona's Diary of the Skool Bus later in this Chapter.) About 16' long, these modern vans had light and heat generated by batteries. There were play, reading and activity areas, with lots of culturally friendly resources available. These were stocked daily from a school base, so could be changed over according to the ages and abilities of pupils. The teachers were patient, concerned and helpful, welcoming adults to learn or chat, as well as children. Even then, however, counties began to issue limitations; and some mobile classrooms became restricted to authorised site visits only, with no acknowledgement of children on unauthorised sites.

Other T.E.S employees have a much wider role to play:

> *"I see my job as multi-faceted. I am not here to offer in-class support*
> *to Traveller children all the time - that is a form of discrimination.*
> *I am here to help them integrate into school. I can also support schools*
> *who request help, especially with resources and approaches.*
> *I see myself as being able to show non-travelling children some positive*
> *aspects of a culture about which they have pre-conceptions.*
> *And we want to produce culture-friendly resources that everyone can use."*
> *Rowena, Hants T.E.S*

Government funding has altered as more counties have bid for a proportion of the allocated total amount. They all have varying degrees of continued commitment to Travellers, and different approaches. Whilst some continue to build up, others, which had a large proportion of finances in the past, have been forced to cut back. Pat Holmes of the West Midlands T.E.S made a pertinent statement in *'World Fair'* magazine:

> *"It should be a nationally organised business so that the level of service*
> *across the country is uniform, so that contact is continued and not just*
> *as long as the family is in 'my patch'."*
> *15/01/93*

The most important contribution of a T.E.S advisor, is to encourage schools to recognise their legal obligation to offer an education to all children within their area, if a place exists. The developing Grant Maintained School status of State education discourages such offers, and is already affecting some areas. The most worrying development of all, however, is the tendency for counties to adopt a policy of integration. This is not an educational policy objective, but seems to be a preferred option for many local authorities. Whilst it is not directly linked to the proposed implementation of the Criminal Justice Bill, the current government's obsession with national conformity has threatened the work of caring T.E.S workers wanting to help children learn on the road.

Integration is not always practical, even within families:
> *"Elouise happily went to school, but Rohan did not want to attend.*
> *I made up a package of resources and dropped them off unofficially one day."*
> *T.E.S advisor 1993*

Nor is it in accordance with the conditions of the Education Act, 1944. No child should be forced into education, whatever the background, and this can be particularly harmful to nomadic children needing continuity.......not conflict. It would be a tragedy if T.E.S units begin to adopt a sole policy of integration, as they would lose much of the goodwill built up with Travellers.

◆ ◆ ◆ ◆ ◆

Through State schools, the E.W.S, and T.E.S units, the Government provides something for Traveller children, but its value is debatable.

> *"In its present state, school provision for Gypsy and Traveller children is characterised on the whole by a need for adaptation and innovation."*
> *C.E.C. orientation document 'School Provision for Gypsy and Traveller children.'*
> *Jean-Pierre Liegeois.*

The Government funds local education authorities, who cannot give funds to schools. Money can only be spent on approved projects: e.g. teachers who can support a school. The reality is that the scope to develop flexible 'education' is curtailed; Travellers' children usually have to conform to schools who are almost inevitably restricted in what they can offer them, and generation gaps are introduced. It is a system which many settled parents accept unquestioningly.

> *"I was recently asked by a student whether the State education system made adequate provision for Traveller children. My reply was that, in its present form, it does not make adequate provision for the majority of children, whatever their backgrounds."*
> *Fiona.*

Alternative Education.

An important statement in the Education Act 1944, is that the child must be:

> **"receiving efficient full-time education.... either by regular attendance at school or otherwise."**

For many Travellers, attendance at school most emphatically does not represent an efficient full-time education. In the widest sense, education is achieved through life experience; in its narrowest it is taught at school.

For those parents who are forced by circumstance, or who choose it, providing an alternative education is better challenging and satisfying. Again, there are three obvious choices:

Home education is an option which seems to hit the media only when a prodigy, like maths scholar Ruth Lawrence, or teenage author Caitlin Moran, prove the value of a personal timetable with close adult contact. Teaching at home is the ideal of many Travellers, but the reality is much harder than it originally appears. Making time is difficult. A child in school should have a minimum of 25 hours teaching contact time. Although this is conditioned by the fact that at least a dozen, possibly as many as thirty other pupils will be sharing the teacher's time; it is still necessary for a home educator to make some time each day for specific one-to-one learning. When the weekly existence includes wood and water runs, shopping, signing on, tatting, vehicle maintenance etc.; this is often easier said than done.

In addition, the child must be willing to learn from its parents.

> *"There was no point even trying to carry on with my two. They just didn't want to know unless a 'real' teacher was telling them. But I've taught other kids on site perfectly okay....... just not mine."*
>
> 　　　　　　　　　　　　　　　　　　　　　　　*Chloe.*

Then there is the curriculum to consider. Whilst the value of the current National Schools' Curriculum is under debate, it is true that children need varied stimuli in order to develop broadly. Generally, however, site life provides a whole range of adults willing to pass on skills and knowledge, so this concern is mostly overcome.

> *"My mum teaches me more than any kid would have really, 'cos I've got loads of other people to teach me things too like. Things that grown-ups do like fixing things and making things. I'm learning to ride a horse; I can make candles. I've been to school, but I left when I was 7. It was boring; they don't teach you anything really. It takes about three years before you learn anything. You learn more on site really. I want to make lots of bits and bobs and sell them at festivals. I've been making a newspaper - I've done issues 1 & 2 and I'm working on 3. I imagine I'll do lots more when I'm older." John*

An organisation which helps all home educators to share experience and skills is 'Education Otherwise.' Whilst principally aimed at advising and assisting settled people, it welcomes enquiries from Travellers. Education Otherwise has a number of publications which clearly lay out legal requirements of educational standards, as well as regular updates via newsletters. To house-dwellers, the main advantage is being able to contact other home-educators in the locality, to share time and resources. To Travellers, the legal advice is useful, especially if threatened by E.W.O.s and L.E.A.s. The emphasis from Education Otherwise is that children's skills can be fully extended without a conventional school education, and they have offered many of us invaluable support over the years.

There are two major implications of home education. First, it is better for the child to have contact with some children, other than siblings, for both work and play. Whilst this is usually no problem on site, there are people who park up alone, and whose children have no youthful contacts. It is crucial for social development that they learn to play; but it is also valuable for them to have companions with whom to share more formal learning.

Secondly, resources are not automatically available for children taught at home. The Government allocates an annual sum to schools, based on roll, but there is no amount available for those seeking to offer an alternative education. Stationery aside, a range of reference books and specialist equipment are not only expensive, but also difficult to store. Complex scientific apparatus, different artistic mediums, modern atlases, are but a few examples of high cost items

Home education is rewarding and fulfilling, and many Travellers regard State schooling as an easy option for parents who want to pass on the responsibility of child care. Those who are dedicated to the advancement of their children try combine the provision of basic educational skills with alternative skills such as circus practise; thus offering a potential career.

The constant mobility allows Traveller parents to escape constant supervision and county

council surveillance to which settled home-educators may be subjected. But there are many who have successfully taught their children to examination standard.

Private schools provide another option for parents wanting to bypass the State system. Whilst the image of public school is hardly in keeping with that of an alternative lifestyle; Montessori and Steiner schools have policies and approaches which appeal to liberal parents. The educational theory is based on giving children the freedom to learn when they are ready, rather than dictating a standard. In fact, there is active discouragement of subjectively assessed learning in the early years. Children are encouraged to learn experimentally, and to be creative. Their presentation shows a care and pride often lacking in conventional exercise books.

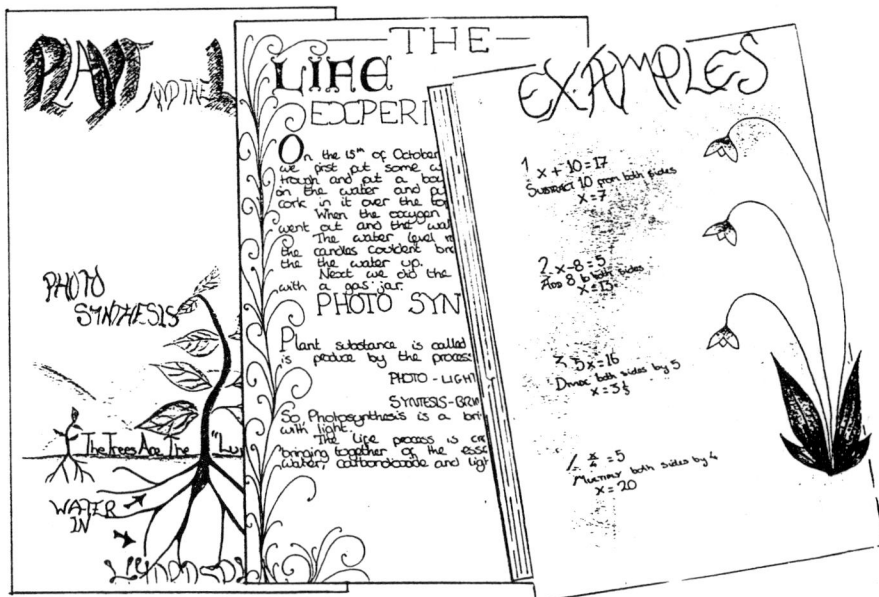

Ria and Polly

The cost of Steiner school education varies across the country. One or two offer the chance to negotiate fees in exchange for some teaching time from a parent. Some are linked to alternative communities, who offer schooling for their own children and also to children living in the area. For those believing in this active learning environment, Steiner schools are of increasing interest.

Some groups of people establish their own form of schools, or areas of learning. The Rainbow Circle, for example, holds ten day camps in which skills are shared and learned. Some sites establish a school area in an unused caravan or bus. Some counties have small parent -run schools where teaching is shared, and numbers are low. In the mid-eighties, the Orpington site in Kent established a school bus for its children.

The Travellers School Charity (T.S.C.) exists to offer advice for home education, and directly provide mobile classrooms. It was established in the late '80s when a group of young parents envisaged a permanent mobile school travelling with them, helping them provide a positive alternative education. It was realised that charitable status would help fund-raising, so trustees were gathered, and the venture developed. Soon, enough cash had been raised to buy and

convert a unique vehicle. Previously used by the Welsh Tourist Board as a display base at shows, it was soon known as the 'Skool Bus.'

Skool Bus '90

A couple of small events at Clyro Court in the Welsh borders established the Skool Bus's place amongst the Traveller community, and it set off on the road. The T.S.C swiftly realised that the original idea was unsustainable; that no group of people really did live and travel together the whole time, and that this classroom resource should be nationally available. By 1989, a couple had volunteered to take it on, driving to various sites where there were children, and teaching there. A geodesic dome (bender-type structure of precisely measured metal poles) was bought as a play area for younger children, and the Skool Bus seemed to be doing well on many sites. It spent a couple of weeks at Glastonbury Festival, as part of the Green Field children's area; and was later a focus for children at Treworgey Tree Fayre in Cornwall.

However, divisions between trustees, voluntary workers on the road, and parents themselves, resulted in a major rift; and the Skool Bus left Cornwall with new caretakers. By Christmas, however, the outlook seemed grim; few funds were left, and the initial enthusiasm had given way to the hardships of gritty reality. Meanwhile, the T.S.C. had helped a qualified science teacher to convert and equip a Bella Vega bus as a mobile science workshop.

> "It was at this point that I negotiated a post as paid teacher on the Skool Bus, agreeing to £70 p.w. on a self-employed basis, calculating hours as I went along. I was lucky to have a brilliant year, just before the police crackdown on gatherings, and left to set up my own caravan classroom in 1991, as did another parent. A couple of other mobile classrooms had also been set up, and we established a small-grants fund for Traveller parents needing resources. The T.S.C. produced culture-friendly books, such as Creative Play Handbook, and ABC book."   Fiona

Further rifts grew between Charity administrators and people on the road. Nobody would take responsibility for the Skool Bus; and different people accepted set-up grants for new teaching initiatives, only to lunch them out. By the summer of 1993, it seemed that there was no motivation for a T.S.C. based education opportunity, and the Skool Bus was weighed in at a great loss. T.S.C. morale was low, the focal point of its energy gone. But a new Science

Workshop; the flying teacher; and Fiona's purchase of a horsebox for specific conversion as resources truck; combined with the continued needs of children, has brought about a shift in focus. As Government-funded T.E.S. units increasingly encourage integration policies, so the T.S.C. needs to use its charitable status to generate monies to help those who cannot, or will not, accept the State education system.

It is envisaged that the T.S.C. will concentrate on creating, collecting and collating resources relevant to children on the road, and distribute them nationally. A network of support and advice should be available to parents, as well as children. The T.S.C. will move forward to meet the needs of Travellers abandoned by the State system. In order to do so, it is reliant upon charitable trusts; private benefactors; subscriptions from friends; fundraising events; Traveller goodwill; donations from companies; etc.

At the time of going to print, nothing is certain. But we do have hope.

BRIEF DIARY OF THE SKOOL BUS, 1990.

By Fiona

First, let it be said that the spelling in the mural on the side of 'Skool Bus' had nothing to do with me; and I got more stick for that than for anything else. As an English teacher, it offended me greatly, and nobody ever really gave an adequate explanation; other than it representing an' alternative' school with no conventions.

Second, this was the most rewarding year of teaching that I have ever completed; and is the basis for my continued commitment to making a positive contribution to Traveller children's education.
Thirdly, I don't really know how I got involved, other than having been sent Richie's address for the T.S.C. by both Kenneth Clarke, then Education Minister, and Gwen, founder trustee, whose son I'd been teaching on site after my straight school job each day.

1. WINTER SITE.
Skool Bus arrived mid-Jan, filthy and neglected. Richie very disheartened. I was full of energy and visions! Friends and trustees help strip contents into dome for sorting. Body rebuilt, engine overhauled, M.O.T. passed. Interior scrubbed and repaired, roof mended. Inside repainted, rainbow colours for chairs, shelves etc. Resources bought new, and from private school closing down, tat shops and jumbles, donated. All stored.

2. WINTER SITE
Arrived at dusk. Moved on properly in morning. As I wasn't willing to drive, nearly every move necessitated a return trip in my car for the drivers. This was often sometimes a couple of hundred miles.
About two dozen children, from babies to 11 years. Three at local school, but attended afterwards. Lots of interest and support. Open everyday, including most weekends.

Rough timetable:

9.00-9.30	open up, games	
9.30-11.00	English, Maths, Science	School-age children
11.00-11.30	dog walk together	
11.30-1.00	all other subjects	School age children
1.00-2.00	lunch-usually prepared together	
2.00-3.00	activities, painting, music etc.	All ages
3.00-5.00	playtime	All ages

Attended local playgroup a few times. Health clinic on board one day. Lunch food donated. Site tombola for party funds. Parents joined in, other adults gave specific workshops. The Skool Bus range was slow to warm up, but was very effective once hot. It was used for cooking in the evenings by some people, and for drying washing once the kids had gone. My evenings were spent preparing worksheets relevant to each child, and chatting to parents.

3. STONEHENGE

Spring Equinox. Used by some children, though more a chance to show it was in use again. A base for music and entertainment. Site bucketed. Walked to the stones in the morning to celebrate and leave flowers - which the authorities cleared.

"How can they put beautiful flowers in bin bags - they'll kill them" Elouise.

4. WINTER SITE

Half a dozen children. Very short stay.

5. TEMPORARY PARK UP

Rejoined a group from site 2, with about a dozen children.
Filmed by students, including Herring from Newcastle Poly. producing a T.S.C. promo video. Loads of art workshops in dome, run by students. Shadow puppet show by firelight. Adult party on board.

6. WINTER PARK UP

7 Children, and Science bus on site. Filmed again, and visited by T.S.C., T.E.S. teacher, and fundraisers. Birthday party - 8 cakes from the skip, all iced individually.

7. NEW PARK UP

Some people moved on in my absence. Met up, and found bus completely spring cleaned. It was really good to return from a fortnight's break to find the whole bus had been thoroughly cleaned. I'd kept it tidy, insisting that kids cleared up one activity before starting another, but a complete clear out was great. There was also a leaking roof, so some tat had to be stored in bin bags.

Dome erected by parent for young children to play when 3 others moved on. Watched cat produce kittens. Zoe gave science lesson in dissection, when one of the dogs caught a mole. Cured the skin. Liz moved on - keen to teach. Also Jeff, a natural playleader. And another child.

8. FESTIVAL

Hectic journey. Set up as part of central area, with Wango Riley's stage. Dozens of children. Good weather, so had doors open all day. Bucketed successfully. Presented 'Dinosaurs: all that rubbish' on Wango's stage - directed by Liz, Jeff and Zoe, because I was chronically ill. Dome used as home base by friends of bus.

9. SMALL SITE

Few children. Recovery period. Jeff mended Bus bikes. There were two lots of chaos to sort out. 1st, every time we moved, I had to tat down my trailer, and the Bus. But there was always something which fell down - 2 gallons of glue being the worst. We ended up sticking a rug onto the carpet that time. 2nd, a mass of children playing, reading, making props and costumes had left a real mess.

10. FESTIVAL

Small gathering. A couple of dozen children. Quite laid-back. Lots of outdoor stuff. Joined by Tom, P.G.C.E. student on alternative teaching experience, and his girlfriend, Emily. Whenever we could, we spread a couple of carpets outside and put paints, toys and games out there. We also had a number of mobile toys, and a sand-pit in a tin bath.

11. SUMMER PARK UP

Most children from site 5, so caught up with learning. Activities organised by Liz, Jeff, Tom, Emily, and a new volunteer, Graham. Trip to local wildlife park. Engine mended. And I had a driving lesson in the Bus. That once was enough. I found the vehicle cumbersome, with awkward gears, and resolved not to go on the road with it.

12. FESTIVAL

Summer weekend. Further from the stage. Dozens of kids. Liz evolved new game 'Pin the brew can on the drongo.' Bucketed successfully.

13. PARK UP

Back with site 7 again. Time not teaching spent sorting out plans for forthcoming commercial festival, and collecting resources.

14. FESTIVAL

This was local, and quite small. As we were getting set up for Pilton, we took all the outdoor stuff for a day. Science bus went there.

15. GLASTONBURY FESTIVAL

Horrific journey. Struggled onto Skool Bus field, enclosed space between paying festival and permitted Traveller gathering. Set up dome, and tarped area. Borrowed bouncy castle. Joined by a couple to supervise that, and Lavina, to help out. Total crew: me, Liz, Jeff, Graham, Zoe, Tom, Emily, Lavina, Spread and Jenny.

Chris also gave hours to bucketing. Volunteers gave hours to main festival.

The week became increasingly hectic, and by the time of the main event, plans had been abandoned and we all did everything we could. The bouncy castle was rationed, but was still chaotic to supervise. We ended up hardly using it. Time off was spent bucketing, and we raised an enormous amount for the Skool Bus and Science Bus. Money raised on the road went into a P.O. account to be used for fuel, maintenance, resources, etc., while the T.S.C covered insurance, M.O.T, etc. We arrived at Pilton with about £30, so it was vital that we raised enough to keep going another 6 months.

After the festival masses of materials donated by other children's areas - all to be sorted and stored.

10. LITTER PICKERS

Moved to lower field as school for children of litter-pickers. Tom and Emily back home. Organised as school again rather than play area. About twenty children. Liz, Jeff and Graham moved on. (The success of the school prompted me to return with my caravan classroom in 1992, as a school for site crew children who are on site for several weeks.)

17. N.A.T.T. CONFERENCE

Parked up in car park with Richie and Celia. 3 workshops held on board. Met S.C.F. mobile classroom. Attended seminars. Small collection made. Resources donated by Arthur Ivatts, H.M.I. Traveller Education.

18. FESTIVAL

Small weekend gathering. Quite a lot of children. Joined by Zoe and Tom. Met Ben and Kay - volunteered to drive for the rest of the year. Previously, a volunteer would drive Bus and I'd follow in car and caravan, then drive them back to the original site.

19. PARK UP

Half a dozen children . All new to me. 2 days only. The arrival of the two volunteer drivers was a huge relief, It widened the scope of travelling, and meant that I could move independently at last.

20. FESTIVAL

500 mile journey. Left my rig half-way and had my first trip in the Bus. Thunderstorm 10 miles from destination drenched everything inside. Pulled onto last piece of hard standing. Quite a lot of children. Brilliant atmosphere. Herring helped out . Bucketed. The T.S.C had always maintained that no-one should sleep on board. But at gatherings it was actually better that someone did - if only to prevent squatters who didn't take kindly to an invasion of children at 8 o'clock in the morning. So I stayed on board this time - and got even wetter.

21. SITE

Took it to new site with a couple of dozen children. Left it there with Liz, Graham and Jeff while I had a break.

22. SITE

Met up with the Bus again. Same children as 21. Mainly activities. Liz taught them how to build an outdoor fire. Bouncy castle at other end of site. Engine repaired.

23. SITE

Joined various people met previously and some new. Lots of pre-school - responsibility of Jeff and Graham. These two were brilliant with children, having endless patience, a similar intellectual level and sense of humour. T.E.S mobile classroom visited twice.

Feeding the ducks

Kala and Nissa '90

24. STONEHENGE

Autumn equinox. Skool Bus was nearest the stones. Little child-based activity. A good focus for meeting to chat.

25. SITE

Back to 23; Bus left care of Liz, Jeff and Graham while I travelled abroad.

26. WINTER SITE

A couple of months. Couple of dozen children mainly from site 2. Back into routine. T.E.S mobile classroom called once a week. Drivers left. Liz setting up caravan classroom elsewhere with Jeff and Graham. Midnight feasts on board twice, with older kids sleeping there with me. Heavy snow.

I woke one morning to drifts a few feet deep outside the caravan. Staggering through the blizzard to the Bus, I found it with internal drifts of its own, several inches deep. I despaired. Gwen and Diane saved it, sweeping it out and drying it as the thaw set in. Alex taught breadmaking. All kids made a family meal to take home on Thursdays. Winter solstice, Jeff arrived to collect the play dome. Others took over the Bus.

◆　◆　◆　◆　◆

By this time I was burned out. I'd had a really good year but had no energy left. The Bus, looking fine in theory, was very impractical on a day- to-day basis. Its height made it slow to heat up; and the lack of opening windows made it stifling on hot days. The side doors had fallen open twice on journeys, and needed repair. The roof leaked constantly. the steps were broken. As the others who had helped out had gone off to personal projects, so I too, went away, and set up my own, smaller scale, Caravan Classroom.

If nothing else, 1990 proved that the children wanted a mobile school. Now that the T.E.S units are likely to lose theirs, or have severely restricted use, it is more important than ever that Travellers establish their own school bases. There are quite a number of individuals trying to do so, but funding remains the main hurdle.

There are an increasing number of culture-friendly resources now available to parents and teacher and they can also create their own. The following 'panto' is an example:

THE SKOOL BUS PANTOMIME

The Three Dirty Hippies: A Modern Fairy Tale

Adapted from a well known classic by Liz

A Christmas Pantomime performed by: -

Rowan -	1st Dirty Hippy
Antony -	2nd Dirty Hippy
Vicky -	3rd Dirty Hippy
Charlotte -	Dodgy looking character
Amber -	Policeman
Willow and Maria -	Dogs

With a special appearance by "Fat Boy" Steve - as the mother.

First performed on Christmas Day 1991 on the Skool Bus

ONCE upon a time, there were three dirty hippies who lived with their mother, 3 dogs an a 12 foot Sprite Alpine (Caravan).

One day just before Christmas, their mother said to them; "You can no longer live with me, 3 dogs and a goat in this 12 foot Sprite Alpine. You do no wooding, no washing up, you never sweep the floor and you treat this place like a bloody hotel. Now get out all of you."

The poor dirty hippies pleaded to be allowed to stay. Their mother was a hard woman and would not be persuaded, but as it was Christmas she did make some compensation and gave to each of them a clapped - out illegal Box Truck and £100 in cash. With these gifts the dirty hippies set off to make their own ways in the world.

The first dirty hippy was driving along the road in his clapped out illegal box truck when he saw a dodgy looking character and pulled over to speak with him. "Oi! Geezer, wanna buy some cheap brew?" (1) asked the dodgy looking character. The first dirty hippy spent all his money on a stock pile of brew for Christmas and then went into the back of his truck for a quick swig.

Shortly there was a knock at the door and a gruff policeman's voice said: "Dirty hippy, dirty hippy, let me come in."

"Not by the hair on my chinny chin chin, I will not let you in." Replied the terrified first dirty hippy.

"Then I'll huff and I'll puff and I'll take your vehicle in". With these words the policeman impounded the first dirty hippy's truck. The poor dirty hippy only just managed to escape with his brew.

The second dirty hippy was driving along the road when he saw a dodgy looking character. "Hey man, want to buy some cheap hash?" (2) asked the dodgy looking character. The dirty hippy spent all his £100 on hash for Christmas, then went in the back of his truck for a smoke.

Cont'd.........

(1) Brew = poisonous alcoholic drink made by a Danish Brewery
(2) Hash = a mild recreational psychedelic drug made from cannabis resin

Shortly there was a knock at the door and a gruff policeman's voice said:-
"Dirty hippy, dirty hippy, let me come in."

"Not by the hairs on my chinny chin chin, I will not let you in." Replied the second terrified dirty hippy.

"Then I'll huff and I'll puff and I'll take your vehicle in." With these words the policeman impounded the second dirty hippy's truck. The poor dirty hippy only just managed to escape with his hash.

The third dirty hippy was driving along the road when she saw a dodgy looking character and pulled over to speak with him.

"Wanna buy a cheap cover note and M.O.T?" (3) asked the dodgy looking character.

The third hippy spent £45 of her £100 on the documents and then carried on her journey to the post office where she purchased a six month tax disc. She then proudly displayed the Tax disc in the windscreen of her truck and went into the back for a rest.

Shortly there was a knock at the door and a gruff policeman's voice said:-
"Dirty hippy, dirty hippy, let me come in."

"Not by the hair on my chinny chin chin, I will not let you in." Replied the third dirty hippy.

"Then I'll huff and I'll puff and I'll take your vehicle in."

When the third dirty hippy heard these words, she leapt out of the back of the truck brandishing her documents. The policeman had such a shock on finding that the dirty hippy was legal, that he had a heart attack and died. The policeman never bothered another dirty hippy again.

After a little while there came another knock at the door. It was the first and second dirty hippies with lots of brew and hash but nowhere to live. The third dirty hippy immediately invited them to live with her. They all had a wonderful Christmas and lived happily ever after.

The End

Education is an important consideration for all parents, but Travellers have a great many variables to take into account. Few opt for one scheme only, and combine a balance of all methods, according to the needs of the child and the practical means. By giving children choice, they usually respond positively.

Sharon's report:

Elouise was soon to experience State school education; I had taught her to read and write by this stage. She attended her first school for 8 weeks, her teachers were impressed with her academic skills. From that point, she attended various schools around the country through the winter months.

I'd always given Elouise the choice....she only went if we were parked-up on our own; she went more for social experience than for learning, which she would receive from us anyway. Some schools were extremely biased, in which case she didn't stay long, it being pointless her going if there were no friends. On the other hand, there were some good schools.

Ro, is very different; he prefers to stay on site, kids or no kids. He spends a lot of time with his dad. His first experience of school was when Fiona pulled on site with her Caravan Classroom. Elouise hadn't attended any State schools for quite a while; and kids from other sites quite close to us were in the same position. Fiona brought them all together and taught them, each having individual attention - on site, and all together as Travellers' 'learning.' I'm sure this gave them extra confidence in themselves. It also showed we parents how to run our own caravan classrooms. I was always amazed by Fiona's unstoppable energy as a mother and teacher.

HEALTH CARE

This is not only a concern for children, but for the whole of the nomadic community. Generally deprived of basic sanitary provision, and with limited water supplies, hygiene has to be considered constantly. Traditional Travellers have separate utensils for tasks like washing themselves, washing clothes and washing crockery, for example. The need to bury excrement and dispose of rubbish is recognised as a fact of life.

However, children raised in a totally sterile situation seem to be prone to infection. Travellers lead a predominantly healthy lifestyle - they are outdoors a lot of the time, exercise adequately performing daily tasks, eat quite balanced diets; and have different stresses in their lives from housedwellers.

But everyone, everywhere has a need for medical attention at one time or another, and Travellers are no different. As with education, though, it is increasingly difficult to use State facilities; and there are many who hold alternative beliefs, anyway.

Alternative Medicine

Throughout society, there has been an increased modern belief in the benefits of alternative forms of healing. This has long been recognised and practised by nomadic peoples of all kinds.

> *"Herbal medicine is the oldest form of medicine known to mankind,*
> *using plants and plant extracts as remedies, it was the mainstay of many*
> *early civilisations......."*
> *Home Health Fact File.*

Simple herbal remedies are used regularly on site, especially rescue remedy. Infusions and tinctures are taken internally, while ointments and poultices are applied externally. There are individuals who are effective herbalists, and, whilst most modern chemical drugs are based on herbal origins, the latter are less likely to cause side effects. In addition the qualities of various herb teas are often known and used - raspberry leaf tea in the last stages of pregnancy seems to help a swift and safe birth, for example. Although homeopathic treatment is available on the N.H.S, most people who use it on site do so on the advice of respected Travellers.

> *"I don't really go to the doctors unless I've got some physical problem I know he*
> *can sort out. I've got basic homeopathic knowledge, herbs and stuff - same as*
> *most people. There's a lot of stress involved in simply going to the doctors, so*
> *I've developed a sort of holistic philosophy, treating the whole person." Es.*

Aromatherapy is a practise in which massage with natural essential oils is seen as an aid to health and relaxation. Blends of oils are made to suit the individual, and through massage are absorbed through the skin whilst the body is manipulated. Again, conventional medicine now makes this available, but there are many competent aromatherapists on the road.

Yoga and meditation are used, particularly by some of the original Travellers, to promote general health and well-being. Some ancient martial arts are also practised for similar body control and purity.

Maybe the most common approach to cure on site, is that of holistic healing. This uses a whole range of orthodox, alternative and unconventional therapies to treat the body as a whole, rather than one isolated part.

> *"The application of holistic methods avoids the supremacy of the doctor or healer*
> *and the passive acquiescence of the patient, instead promoting an interaction*
> *between them that takes account of the total experiences and circumstances of*
> *the patient."*
> *Tony Thorne, 'Fads, Fashions & Cults.'*

There are usually a number of alternative healing practices available, especially at large gatherings and events where a peaceful 'healing circle' may be established. It is not only those who believe strongly in such methods who use them, but also those who will not, or cannot, easily use the State provision.

National Health Service

The changes in the N.H.S. have been widely discussed nationally, and have inevitably affected Travellers. Apart from problems with the availability of health service, Travellers also have to face quite considerable prejudice in some quarters.

> *"They told me I had to wait outside, and they'd call. When I asked why, it was 'cause of my boots....so I offered to take them off, but then they said other patients may not want me there."* Ben.

General practitioner funding has undergone radical changes. The media has focussed attention on the fears of elderly people, or those needing regular medication; as doctors may find them too expensive to keep on their register. Doctors seem to need a balance of patients to ensure that expenditure does not exceed their financial allocation.

> *"I wanted to register with the doctor here, but they would only let me be a 'temporary resident'; they said it wasn't worth sending off for my records. That has pissed me off a bit because I've been using the Post Office for nearly two years, so I could easily have a local doctor, but they won't have it. They were doing these sort of human 'MOT's' - checkups. So I arranged for me and my son, John, to have one. When we turned up for the checkup they told me it was only available for patients on the books, not for temporary residents."* Es.

Travellers often need to register as a temporary patient in order to receive treatment, but this means naming the doctor with whom they are registered. Whilst orbitals may still be near their original practitioner, others may not even recall the name of their last doctor. Those, such as diabetics, who have a regular prescription have to ensure a registered base for reference.

> *"I'm okay at the moment, as I'm still in the area. But I'll have to make sure they don't know when I move about, 'cause they could take me off the list. I'm expensive, you see, high risk."* Mush.

The procedure can be time-consuming and complicated. As with schools, subtle discrimination like demanding a permanent local address, or deferring appointments, are potential deterrents. Combined with indecision about whether to use traditional or holistic medicine, some Travellers are easily put off. The need to be a local resident for acceptance at breast clinics or for smear tests makes them very inaccessible. Travellers also experience problems with records being lost, or not passed on, and vital information being unavailable.

Hospital treatment is a last resort for most people on the road, but in some ways, it is more accessible than GP care. Some ailments that could have been adequately treated by a GP, if one be found, are taken instead for treatment at a local Accident and Emergency unit. These are less common than before and may involve long journeys. In emergencies, the A&E units are as crucial to Travellers as to any other members of the public. Those who need continued care may try to find a local site as a base, or even move temporarily into a house.

Hospital births are less common amongst Travellers than in the settled community. There are a multitude of moral, practical and social reasons, and the attitude of the midwife is important. Those whose babies are born in hospital rarely stay long.

> *"I left the next day, for example. I had a good hospital experience, but many do not, and this puts new mothers off. Personally, the benefits of a bath and a bidet for 24hrs outweighed the disadvantages of stifling heat, patronising attitudes, starvation and boredom."* Fiona.

> *"I parked up outside the hospital when Peach was born. Jill had to stay in a few days, and nobody seemed to mind me in the car park."* Phil.

Midwives have a wide range of attitudes when it comes to home births, especially when they are confronted with a proposal that a home birth should occur in the middle of a muddy field, half a mile away from a phone or running water.

Tracey's report:

"I arrived in Scotland 2 weeks before I was due to have Harry. I went to the hospital in Glasgow to inform the midwives that I was going to have a home birth in the bus. The doctor came to see me and said:

> 'Look at your hair, look at your clothes, look at your hands, look at your way of life. I bet you inject heroin! You don't deserve to have a child. I refuse to have anything to do with you.'

I went into labour a week and a half later, and two midwives came out to the bus. The bus was full of people drinking and singing and the midwives couldn't handle it at all, especially after Maggot fell in the burner and knocked it over twice! They kept telling me to go in to hospital, although there was nothing wrong. They wouldn't let me smoke or even drink water.

In the middle of the night they called the pigs, so that they had radio contact with the hospital, but that just caused more drunken chaos. Maggot drew a line on the drag and wouldn't let them past, and then dropped his trousers and showed them the scars on his arse that he got at the Beanfield.

Two younger midwives arrived and the old ones fucked of. the first thing these midwives said was:

> 'I've got a packet of fags, a tin of iron brew and a packet of crisps if you want them. Where can I go for a piss?'

They were ace.

They delivered my baby left-handed so everyone could see. As I was having him, everyone was singing: 'Hurry up Harry, we're going to the pub'. So I called him Harry. I had no choice really. After I'd had him, the head midwife for Glasgow came round with a pan of vegi slop, 2 loaves of bread and a carrot cake, because she thought that everyone had forgotten to eat because of the excitement.

Soon after, I took him to be registered, but none of the doctors in the area would register him. I had to get the midwife to report it to the Area Health Authority to force a doctor to register him."

Sympathetic and efficient midwives become well known within a locality, so that mothers-to-be return there deliberately.

Imminent birth can, but not always, temporarily postpone the threat of eviction. Once common misconceptions about warmth and cleanliness have been overcome, some midwives are very positive about births on site.

> *"She was born five minutes after the midwife arrived.....it was ace.....really easy. Garry was just washing his hands, thinking he'd have to do it, when she got here. It was ace." Cheryl.*

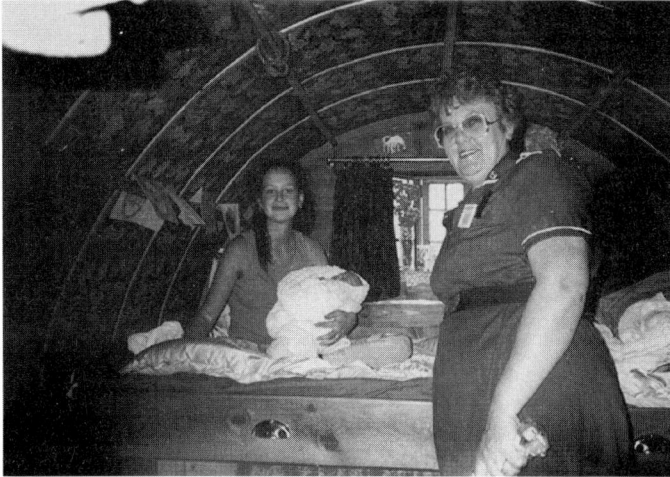

Ruby, aged five minutes, with Cheryl and midwife Molly

There are also births without the attendance of an N.H.S midwife. Just as women of other cultures efficiently deliver one another's children, so do women on site. This particularly applies to women who choose to deliver somewhere special to them - there are always babies born at Glastonbury Festival for example.

Health visitors have a variety of roles. They offer care for babies as part of the service after the midwives. Again, some are quite positive about site life, others very negative. Although a new mother has usually a great deal of community support, a tolerant health visitor can help out. Babies are rarely separated from their mothers at all, usually sleeping in the same space so bonding is rarely a problem.

However, once children grow older, the persistence of a health visitor may appear threatening to Travellers. Unlike social workers they are not linked to the judiciary, but can still seem very authoritarian. Immunisation is usually considered by parents, and an awareness of growth progress may be useful, but attendance at clinics is not always easy and may just be avoided.

There are campaigns to make condoms widely available to Travellers, and to promote safe sex. Admittedly, as amongst any young community there is a degree of promiscuity' but at least everyone knows where everyone else has been before, and knows about the exploits of potential partners. It is difficult to have sex in a caravan without everyone knowing about it!

Similarly, some urban sites with heavy heroin dependency have had sterilised needles made available. Nationally, heroin use has increased dramatically this decade, and some addicts who

could not hold squats together have moved onto the travelling scene. Whilst such initiatives are beneficial to some, there could be some much more helpful health facilities available to the majority. Mobile clinics dispensing nit lotion for example - because if one person needs it, everyone needs it, and you can't usually get a prescription for thirty bottles; or with family planning advice (rather than 100 condoms appearing in a box) ; or distributing first aid equipment; would be much more useful.

Dental Care

Few dentists now take on new N.H.S patients, and private care is very expensive. For people constantly on the move, regular check-ups are almost impossible, unless they were lucky enough to be registered somewhere before the changes. Even then, a permanent address is needed for reminders and appointments. As a result, teeth may be neglected of professional care until an emergency - excruciating toothache occurs; then the A&E department of hospital will usually cope.

> *"I really need a dentist; have done for a while, but I haven't met with much*
> *success round here - they're not into taking on any more NHS patients. "* *Es*

♦ ♦ ♦ ♦ ♦

Overall, the State responsibility for healthcare and education seems to be available only to those who do not deviate. Government funding for both is based on registration in one place. For those unable or unwilling to do this, the funds are unavailable, and alternatives have to be found. Fighting for children's rights to appropriate education, and everyone's rights to healthcare, is balanced, however, by generally more positive social and moral environments on the road.

> In some ways the Government campaign of 'back to basics' epitomises
> this lifestyle........... So why do they try so hard to force conformity?

ABBREVIATIONS

A & E: Accident and Emergency Ward
BRU: British Romani Union
CJA: Criminal Justice Act
CJB: Criminal Justice Bill
CSA: Caravan Sites Act
DoE: Department of the Environment
DSS: Department of Social Security
EWS: Education Welfare Service
FFT: Friends and families of Travellers
LA: Local Authority
LCTR: Labour Campaign for Travellers' Rights
LEA: Local Education Authority
NATT: National Association of Teachers of Travellers
NCCL: National Council of Civil Liberties, now Liberty.
NGCE: National Gypsy Council for Education, Culture, Welfare and Civil Rights
POA: Public Order Act
SCF: Save the Children
TAT: Travellers Aid Trust
TES: Traveller Education Service and Times Education Supplement
TSC: Travellers' School Charity

Chapter Five:
Living on the Edge

Anyone who makes life difficult for these people, has my blessing.

Margaret Thatcher

If alternative values means a selfish and lawless disregard for others, then I won't understand.

John Major

There are no accurate figures for how many people are living on the edge of legality on someone else's property, but the Council of Europe estimates that there are over 100,000 Travellers in the U.K., (this includes the media named, 'New Travellers,' Showmen, Gypsies, Tarmac and Labouring gangs and itinerants squatting on empty land or derelict buildings). There is a wide spread attitude that only a very small proportion of these people are 'true Gypsies,' and most, extraneous to this definition, should qualify for no status other than that of 'no fixed abode.'

Historical records on the origins of Travellers are few and far between, as most travelling cultures rely on an oral tradition, rather than literacy; the information that does exist relies heavily upon external, romantic interpretations of their ways of life. The contemporary travelling community is a product of hundreds of years of people turning to a nomadic way of life as part of a changing Society.

Many people believe that the only 'True Gypsies' are those with Romani connections who can trace their ancestry back through the nomadic tribes, (such as the Kalderash and the Romungri), that originated in the 18th and 19th centuries, and hailed from North West India and the Middle East. (The word ' Gypsy' itself is a derivative of 'Egyptian.') Any narrow racial or ethnic definition excludes indigenous nomads, the English, Scots, Irish, New Travellers, Circus, Showmen, and many others of non-Romani heritage. While most Romani families are brought up as Travellers, many other groups have chosen a nomadic lifestyle. There is a long history of nomadism originating from changes in economy, government, wars and famine; from the break up of the Feudal system through to the major recessions of the both century. In Scotland the Highland clearances forced people from their land; in Ireland whole tribes of people were dispossessed by English settlers under William of Orange, and the Potato Famine of 1845-8 forced many people to travel in search of food. Although denied recognition, Travellers are part of a long established history of native people adopting a travelling life as part of a changing society.

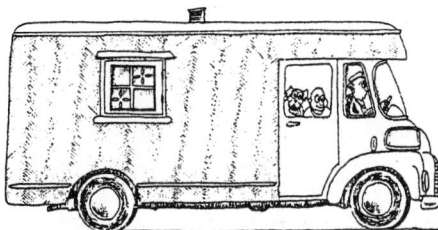

Face-to-face

In the next section we look at how legislation has always been used against Travellers and is now enforced by local authorities and the police. However, 'life on the edge' is also made difficult by media hype generating moral outrage; the problems of obtaining benefit payments; the complexities of legalising a vehicle, and the limited funding for welfare groups who try to support Travellers.

Legislation

Currently the question of defining Gypsy status is central to much of the proposed legislation which will effectively criminalise nomadism as a way of life in the UK. More than half of all land in Britain is owned by one per cent of the population, and three quarters by about five percent. So called 'Public land' is owned by various Councils, Highways Authorities, the Forestry Commission, Ministries of Defence, Transport and the Environment, Water and Coal Boards and the various associated private companies, likewise, British Rail and its offshoots, and finally, the Crown, all of whom can take legal action as owners against trespassers. The traditional recognition of certain places used by generations of Travellers as stopping places was denied by the 1965 Commons Registration Act. Since everyone has to live somewhere, but 'everywhere' and almost 'anywhere' is now somebody's property, thousands of people have nowhere to go.

With an already overwhelming amount of legislation penalising travelling and nomadism on the statutes and more in the pipeline, the Government's new proposals for reform of certain notorious parts of the 1986 Public Order Act, and a comprehensive repeal of the Caravan Sites Act 1968, are currently enjoying parliamentary debate under the auspices of the Criminal Justice Bill.

In general, Travellers have enjoyed a relatively tolerant, if haphazard, pattern of relations with Local Authorities and Police under the Caravan Sites Act 1968, (C.S.A. 1968). This Act makes

it the duty of the Local Authority (L.A.) to provide sufficient caravan sites for those Gypsies
"resorting to or residing in"
their area. These provisions are based on the Department of Environment (DoE) figures taken
from six-monthly 'caravan-counts' of Gypsies conducted by councils. Official counts fail to
include newer Travellers, but of the 12,000 to 16,000 other Travellers that they did count,
nearly 40 percent were on unauthorised, illegal sites.

The law obliging local authorities to provide sites can currently be used against them, and
Possession Orders stopped if the authority has failed to provide adequate sites. However, once
an authority is deemed to have provided sufficient sites for those 'Gypsies' it counts that
"reside or resort" in its area, the council can apply to the Secretary of State for 'Designation.'
Once designated, councils can evict any Travellers not included in their local count, even if
parked on unoccupied land they have permission to use. The problem is that councils often do
not count all the Gypsies in their area, and use creative interpretations of the words ' Gypsy'
and "reside or resort to". Courts have never yet made an order against councils or the
Secretary of State to make them do their duty, even when they have found against them.

In theory, when Travellers arrive in a different local authority they should make themselves
known to the council's Gypsy Liaison Officer, who should then liaise between them and the
council, finding a suitable site for them to stay on, with minimum impact on the local
community. In practice, this is rarely the case; most Travellers are suspicious of authority
representatives, often with good reason:

> *"We were parked at Fewston near Harrogate in 1988, and some
> council officials, accompanied by police, attempted an illegal eviction.
> When I asked one of them who he was and what was he trying to do to us he
> said; 'I am employed by the council to harass people like you.' "* Sue

> *"A big problem for us Gypsies is the councils. They seem to keep Gaujas and
> Gypsies apart. Then when they want someone to blame they can blame us!"*
> Charlie Smith, Gypsy poet and Chair of Gypsy Council for
> Culture, Education, Welfare and Civil Rights.

Many Gypsy Liaison Officers see their jobs in different ways, as described recently by one
district liaison officer:
> *"I am employed by the council to locate unauthorised Traveller sites and evict
> them."*

If Travellers make no representation of their needs to the council, they can be evicted without
delay. Councils act like any other landowner in this respect; they do not advertise their
statutory obligations and as many Travellers are unaware of their rights, most do not challenge
councils for provision. At present, landowners (including councils) can apply for a Possession
Order through the courts to remove trespassers from their land. This can be achieved within a

week of people pulling on the land and although the plaintiff (landowner) is required by law to inform the defendants (occupiers) of their intention to recover possession of the land in court, notice is rarely served in person, usually being addressed to "persons unknown," and haphazardly pinned to the nearest gatepost or entrance. Thus the majority of Travellers have experienced being awoken by bailiffs and police enforcing a 'forthwith' eviction.

The length of time which can elapse before an eviction is enforced is seldom at the discretion of the judge granting the Possession Order. Although most judges are unsympathetic to non-landowners, if the defendants can discover when and where the Possession Order is being sought, they can make their representations to the court. In extenuating circumstances, such as a baby being due, severe illness, or livestock needs and depending upon the proposed use of the land, the judge can persuade the plaintiff to agree to a period of grace on the site. However many landowners push for immediate evictions, sometimes using unrealistic plans for land use as leverage.

Case: A group of Travellers who were parked on Press Heath Common in Shropshire, were served with an application for an immediate Possession Order in June '92. They had all travelled in Shropshire for a number of years, often using the Common as a traditional park-up, so were suspicious when this eviction was rushed in. They attended the court hearing, and noticed that the application for possession was made by a company calling itself Press Heath Holdings, registered in the Channel Islands, which none of the Travellers had ever heard of before. They questioned the accuracy of the land ownership, asking for it to be proven, and the case was adjourned until the afternoon. A second document was produced at the afternoon hearing, registering the owner of the land not as Press Heath Holdings, but as Pressheath Ltd. of a different address in the Channel Islands.

The Travellers asked the judge if it was acceptable legal procedure for the name and address of the applicant to be changed halfway through a case, and whether it cast doubt on the sworn affidavits of the solicitors and land agents for the applicant, both of whom appeared to be working for a company whose correct name and address was not known to them until after the initial hearing. The police had also supplied incorrect information as to the number of vehicles and people on the site. Luckily, the judge threw the case out of court, admonishing the applicants and ordering them to pay the costs, but it was only due to the local knowledge and perseverance of the Travellers that the true facts of the case came to light. Most Travellers do not scrutinise land ownership or 'official' documents so carefully, and so it is fairly easy for bogus companies to secure illegal evictions and Possession Orders for land to which they have no legal right. Police later evicted the site using the Public Order Act.

---

*"The erection of any building or fence whereby access to land to which
this section applies is prevented or impeded, shall not be lawful."
(Law and Property Act 1925, Restrictions on Inclosure of Commons)*

*"The tenant farmer was enraged when Travellers broke through a padlocked
gate. Today, Whitchurch Police assured him that steps were being taken to
evict the Travellers under the 1986 Public Order Act."
(Shropshire Star, Oct 1987)*

If unpressurised by landowners or police, bailiffs can sometimes prove sympathetic to families being pushed from 'pillar to post,' and grant a 'stay of eviction' of sometimes up to a month, though this is happening less as bailiffs act on police recommendations. Even when Travellers are given permission to use land as a park-up they can be evicted by a 'stop notice' under the Town and Country Planning Act 1990. Seasonal workers on farms are permitted to reside on land for short stay periods only, and landowners allowing Travellers to remain on land with permission can be fined several thousands of pounds per day per caravan. Those landowners turning a friendly 'blind eye' to Travellers on their land can be directed by local councils to instruct occupiers to leave and in some, cases be forced to start eviction proceedings.

The Visit

Case: Police tried to 'Public Order' a site near Stratford in 1993, after the council failed to secure a civil eviction through the land owner. The police forced a number of Travellers off the site and bulldozed and trenched the land to prevent re-occupation. This outraged the landowner, as it destroyed over two years complicated irrigation and drainage work. He slapped an injunction on the police excluding them from his land and invited the Travellers back on. His attitude was that the police did far more damage than the Travellers, who were harming no-one, and should be allowed to live their lives in peace. The council could not prosecute him for running an illegal campsite as he lived in the Channel Islands.

Even Travellers who have bought their own land to park-up on are usually evicted as the planning permission required is refused in 90 percent of applications.

Case: A family of Travellers who own land at Dinder in Somerset have applied repeatedly over the last five years for planning permission to station their caravans there. Permission is always refused and the council has prosecuted them for having an illegal campsite, fined them for every caravan stationed on the land, and threatened to impose a compulsory purchase order, yet no alternative site has been offered. They are left in a catch 22 situation, being unable to live on their own land.

Despite the possible penalties under the Planning Acts, it is becoming fairly common practice for landowners who have been denied planning permission to manipulate councils using Travellers as leverage:

> Case: "We were about to be evicted from Ashford Hill and this bloke turns up in a Beemer, saying he's got some land we can park up on. Everyone was sceptical: What's the crack with this then? But me and Luke went off with him and his missis to take a look. It was a good flat well-drained field, screened from the road and away from houses, with a standpipe! Luxury running water! Turns out this guy's been refused planning permission, but knows that if he reapplies for it as a reason to evict Gypsies the council will rush it through. So we get a cushty site for a while, and he gets his planning permission sorted. Funny thing was, his wife was terrified of us when we set off to look at the site, admitting that she would avoid all contact with Travellers, having believed what she'd read in the papers. But after an hours conversation (and being charmed by Luke), she was astonished how her sympathies had changed, and was quite looking forward to her next visit."
>
> Herring

A favourite form of eviction is the use of the infamous section 39 of the Public Order Act 1986. Despite constant government assurances to the contrary, in effect it enables police to evict sites at any time of the day or night; with the powers to arrest people who fail to leave, and to impound any homes, vehicles or possessions remaining.

Serving eviction notices

Councils and landowners prefer 'Public Ordering' sites, rather than incurring to the costs, time and hassle involved in obtaining a Possession Order. Supposedly, to be 'Public Ordered' a site has to have met certain criteria:

1) Two or more persons must have entered land as trespassers and are present there with the common purpose of residing there for any period, and have been asked to leave verbally by the owner of the land.

i) There must be (currently) 12 or more vehicles on the land.

ii) There is damage to property

iii) One or more of the trespassers has been abusive or threatened the land owner, his family or employees.

The senior police officer present (who can be a constable) must reasonably suspect that the criteria in (1) plus one of the tests in (i, ii, iii) have been met before a direction to leave can be given.

Interpretations of the above criteria bear varying relations to reality: caravans, bicycles, tat-trailers and motorbikes have all been interpreted as 'Vehicles' and counted in the 'Over-12 - vehicle test.' Also counted may be visitors to the site. For instance, the police counted the midwife's car at the Binegar site near Norton Radstock. This brought the site total to over 12, and police evicted despite a woman going into labour. On another occasion, a woman miscarried and lost her baby after suffering 5 public order evictions in 6 days.

In a survey by Maternity Alliance (Traveller Mothers and Babies - who cares for their health?), it was found that one third of local authorities would evict a pregnant woman from an unauthorised site; 30% would evict a woman close to birth, and just over a third would evict a mother with a new born baby. In fact, the high proportion of Traveller mothers and babies suffering through ad-hoc and inhumane evictions led to the of the _**SAFE CHILDBIRTH FOR TRAVELLERS CAMPAIGN**_ which petitioned the Government to issue guidelines on the use of section 39 of the Public Order Act. A Home Office circular (37/1991) was published as a result, which listed guidance on serving section 39 notices, suggesting points to be taken into consideration:

i) The consequences of giving a direction to leave: if eviction would lead to further trespass in the locality.

ii) The consequences of not giving a direction to leave: disorder is likely to ensue if the site is not evicted.

iii) Whether all or some of the trespassers should be directed to leave, depending on circumstances, available sites etc.

iv) The personal circumstances of the trespassers: whether well being would be jeopardised by a move.

v) The duration of the trespass: section 39 may not be an appropriate remedy where an occupation has lasted many months or years.

However, it also states that this guidance is not prescriptive, and that the decision whether to issue a direction to leave remains with the police in charge. In practice, police who are Public Ordering a site take little notice of pieces of paper, even if they are from the Home Office.

Case: "We were down in Sussex for the fruit picking and had been evicted 3 times in a month. I applied to the council for a legal site where we could settle down to do some work, but they couldn't offer us anything. Sue was away in hospital, so I was staying on her bus looking after the kids. The next day we were moved again, to another site. At 8pm that night there was a knock at the door, and it was the police again. I was cooking the kids' tea so I turned round to them and said: "What do you want now?" And they told me we were being Public Ordered again, so I tried explaining that it wasn't my vehicle; that I was only babysitting the kids while their mum was in hospital, but no - "MOVE". So we tatted down and moved again the next morning." 'H'.

Tyre marks have been interpreted by police as: 'Damage to property.' 'Abusive or threatening behaviour' does not have to be proved; only reasonably suspected by police. If people do not move their vehicles 'within reasonable time,' which may amount to only a few minutes, they can be arrested and often vehicles are impounded or trashed.

Case: "There were a few of us parked-up in a lay-by. The pigs turned up one morning; tooled up to Public Order. They told us to "Move Now!" So we tatted down as quick as we could and sorted tows out. A few vehicles couldn't tow, so we thought we'd have to do some to-ing and fro-ing. The next problem was where to move to? But that wasn't the top of the list at the moment. We needed to get out of the lay-by and away from the pigs.

One of the lads was away and we were looking after his trailer for him, but we hadn't got a tow for it. We organised all the vehicles, tatted down and hitched up as quick as we could, just chucking everything into cupboards, the bed, the floor, the police shouting all the time, walking up and down the lay-by, poking in our tat,:
            "Five minutes, and we'll tow you off!"
Everybody's panicking, lining up and getting jumps. I tried to explain to the officer in charge that we'd have to take the first lot of trailers up the road a couple of miles and then come back for the rest, including Jim's, as he was away. The only reply I got, was:
            "You've got two minutes to go and keep going. Anything left
            here will be towed off."
But they just lost their patience and started the tow truck up. It was chaos after that; people started to pull off, and those that couldn't were panicking. I was desperate:
            "Please can't we come back for Jim's trailer. We won't be
            more than half an hour?"
            "You'll go and keep going!"
They smashed into Jim's trailer with the tow truck and then escorted us out of the county, leaving Jim's home and tat spread in a heap over the lay-by."   Tracey

It is clearly the case that, despite the specific intentions of parliament in passing section 39, it is routinely abused to secure swift evictions (especially by local authorities where a civil action would raise issues of duty under the CSA 1968) even where no actual threat to public order exists. Police forces have marshalled newly evicted convoys and forced them out; sometimes across several counties and directed them onto long term residential sites in unlawful occupation, and then used section 39 to evict the entire site, as happened in Shropshire in February 1993;

Case: A small convoy of vehicles that had been evicted constantly throughout the winter months, were escorted from a site near Wakefield by police. They were taken down through South Yorks, Derbyshire, Leicestershire, up into Cheshire and finally into North Shropshire in a non-stop, forced push, where drivers were told to get in and drive or be arrested. It was a marathon journey stopping only for fuel and a bare minimum of a couple or hours rest for drivers, having no consideration for their exhaustion, lack of funds for long haul amounts of fuel, or the well-being and safety of their families and children, and that of other road users. They were finally escorted onto Goldstone Common; a site on common land which had been peacefully occupied for years. Ownership was in dispute and the council could not use a civil eviction.

The new convoy swelled the numbers on the site to 'Public Order' potential and the 'significant' increase in numbers as a 'threat,' was used even though they were forced there against their will by police, and were so physically exhausted and stony broke from the journey that the only threat to public order comprised of the loud snores emanating from their vehicles. The whole of the Goldstone site was 'public-ordered' by a local, notorious, Police Inspector.

Families were uprooted after 2 years, children removed from school with no notice, and the site was split up into several different convoys, with no regard for family ties. The convoys were then escorted out of the county in different directions.

Evictions such as this have taken place in Gloucestershire, Avon and Somerset and probably elsewhere. Increasing numbers of Travellers find themselves in confrontational situations with police, so travel in larger groups (safety in numbers) between the fewer sites that are left, and are more likely to suffer hardships such as family stress, losing access to medical services, education and employment opportunities.

Which way forward?

The new proposals under the **Criminal Justice Bill** include a clause, number 45, which gives police powers to evict when there are only 6 vehicles on the land; thus extending powers to small family groups (as one family can easily extend to 2 caravans, a lorry and a car). This will amend section 39 of the existing legislation, and will have the effect of splintering communities still further. The definition of land has been further extended to include the highway verge and public rights of way of all kinds. This removes the option of using lay-bys and other remaining traditional stopping places, as temporary camps; even in emergencies such as breakdown or illness. Also people can be 'Public Ordered' off land they were originally legitimately occupying. In theory, you can now be public ordered off your own land!

Clauses 54 and 55 extend the Public Order Act 1986 prohibiting 'trespassory assemblies,' and increase police powers to arrest members of the public visiting sites. They also enable police to set up 32 mile exclusion zones and roadblocks which will effectively stop free festival culture, thereby destroying much of the self-supporting Traveller economy. These proposals combined with the proposed denial of social security benefits for 'non-householders,' mean that many families already living on the breadline will be reduced to begging and scavenging.

In reality, the threats of possible arrest and impounding of homes means that police threats to 'Public Order' a site are rarely challenged, especially in light of such police trashings as the infamous 'Beanfield'. Only the bravest; some would say naive, people most sure of their legal back-up and witnesses; would challenge a mob of tooled up riot police, risking their home and liberty to a Judicial System where Travellers' accounts of events stand no chance against the word of 'the Law.'

Usually, people park-up on disused or derelict land, ideal sites being deserted farms, disused railways, industrial wasteland or any land not in use, preferably where ownership is in doubt or in contention. There is approximately one and a half million acres of common land in the U.K., and the fact that these traditional stopping places are no longer available is due in part to the Commons Registration Act 1965. This is effectively a modern Domesday book, chronicling the ownership, commoners' rights and access to the public. Some commons now have no commoners, and no public access, but there are reputed to be nine commons in England where the Lord of the manor put into the deeds the right for Travellers to stop off on the land. However, Travellers are now denied access to most traditional stopping places, if not legally then by obstruction; trenches and mounds of gravel or manure are often found blocking droves and the entrances to commons.

Blocked in

There are long waiting lists for Local Authority Gypsy site provision, and it is rarely available to 1st or 2nd generation 'New' Travellers. In fact, the definition of who Gypsy-site provision should be available to is the central question hotly debated in the many current Judicial Review cases that Travellers have brought against their local authorities, alleging breaches of the Caravan Sites Act. 1968, through non-provision of sufficient sites.

> Case: "We have been living on the unauthorised site in Granville Country Park for over a year now. We have sent over 50 applications for authorised pitches and numerous letters to the council but they still refuse to make any provision for us. They tried to evict us 7 months ago so we took our case to the High Court in London for Judicial Review, as there is nowhere else for us to go. We asked the council if we could use temporary facilities while the case was heard, but we have been refused access to water and sanitation as:
>
> > "it would have cost too much to provide."
>
> Yet the council think nothing of spending on average £30,000 a year on evictions, whereas it would cost a paltry £2,750 to provide basic transit site amenities (a standpipe and chemical toilet), thus saving them £27,250 of public money; the police, the courts, and the bailiffs, a lot of wasted time and effort. It would also enable families in the area to secure a safe place to live, whilst settling their business and get their children into school, without disrupting the local community."
>
> > Herring.

The question what is a 'Gypsy' has always been a central issue in the implementation of the Caravan Sites Act 1968. The Act defines a 'Gypsy' as:

"a person of nomadic habit of life , whatever their race or origin."

Despite this clarity, there have been many court cases contesting the definitions and duties. One of the most recent was a tri-fold Judicial Review involving three 3 sites in Gloucestershire, Warwickshire and Devon. Mr. Justice Harrison, presiding, held that:

> *The definition of 'Gypsy' for the purpose of the C.S.A. 1968, was capable of embracing persons other than traditional Gypsies, so long as they could be said to have a nomadic habit of life, which imported more than just the habit of wandering or travelling, but moving from place to place with a purpose in mind as a necessary characteristic part of their lives."*

Mr Kerswell, vice chairman of the National Gypsy Council supported the Travellers' application saying,

> *"It is my conclusion, from my observations, that the style of life of the persons I saw and spoke to was more or less indistinguishable from that of traditional Gypsies. Indeed in some ways they appear to be continuing traditions which are dying out among traditional Gypsies on authorised sites."*

Two of the cases are now going to appeal on the correct definition of the word 'Gypsy. One case will deal with whether or not the local authority alone is responsible for making a judgement on Gypsy status.

Almost twenty years after implementation, most councils have not fulfilled their statutory obligations under the 1968 Caravan Sites Act. There is a significant shortfall between the number of pitches available on authorised sites, and the number of Travellers needing legal stopping places. This shortfall is due, in part, to unreliable methods of ascertaining need for provision. Local authorities conduct their own caravan counts, which cannot guarantee accuracy, as nil caravans counted, equals nil provisions required.

For example, over 80 caravans stationed on illegal sites in Shropshire, July '93, were not included in the D.o.E. count. The D.o.E. count conducted on 21/7/93 returned a total of 12,810 caravans for the whole of England; an absurd estimation when compared to the National Gypsy Council and Council for Europe estimates of over 100,000 Gypsies in the U.K.. In any case the number of available sites currently stands at 4,556 caravans, so even judging by the grossly underestimated Government figures, legal sites are available to only one third of the 'official' Gypsy population. Of the 401 district councils in England and Wales, only 108 have been designated by the Secretary of State as having fulfilled their statutory obligations for provision of Gypsy sites under the '68 Act; and therefore have powers to evict, and are not under obligation to provide any more Gypsy sites. In fact 62 percent of local authorities cannot use their powers under the '68 Act for the very reason that they have failed to comply with their statutory duty to provide sites.

Even as long ago as 1976, it was clear that the Caravan Sites Act 1968 was not working. The Government commissioned Sir John Cripps to prepare a report on ways to improve conditions for Gypsies. The Cripps' Report urged toleration by councils and Government departments. (DoE Circular 57/78):

> "If the local authorities cannot provide sufficient temporary stopping places, a policy of non-harassment (should) be followed and/or temporary stopping places be provided on Government owned land, supervised and serviced by the local authority wherever possible......"

In a similar vein, DoE Circular 28/77 states:
> "Successive governments have repeatedly emphasised that until enough sites have been provided, Gypsies should not be needlessly moved from place to place."

It's all over

It's all over
For this sanctuary
I have no answers
And long run out of questions
Desperation keeps me lingering on
'Til the silly season warms my flesh
And I need no shelter
And there are no convictions
Except where's the party?
When's the eviction?

CG

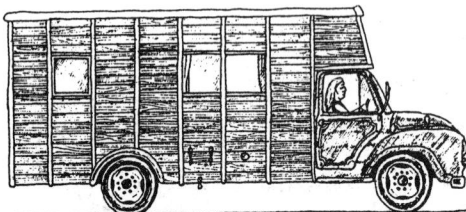

However the Government is currently attempting to implement a comprehensive repeal of the 1968 C.S.A. under the Criminal Justice Bill. It is proposed to increase the powers for local authorities and police wanting to evict Travellers from land in their district;

> *"making it a criminal offence to park a caravan on any land without the landowner's consent;*
>
> *new powers for local authorities to tow away illegally parked caravans, if they obtain a warrant from magistrates;*
>
> *new powers to prevent offenders from returning to the same site within 2 years, once evicted;*
>
> *and local authorities to be given powers by magistrates to seize caravans, as an alternative to fines at the last resort. "*

This means that to live in a caravan or vehicle on any land,(be it private or public, rented, squatted or even your own land!) without site planning permission, will become a criminal offence. Homes and vehicles can be impounded if not removed to a legal site and further trespass will be punishable by fines of up to £5,000 and up to 3 months imprisonment.
The new law will not provide anywhere for Travellers to go. As a result of a very limited consultation exercise, even the Association of Metropolitan Authorities called for a national strategy on Travellers:

> *"This may include increased powers to move them off inappropriate sites, but only in the context of adequate alternative provision being available. The Government's plans will lead to Travellers being shunted around the country and instead of solving existing problems will cause them to escalate. "*

Indeed the proposals did not address what many Travellers define as the problem: a shortage of campsites, partly because local authorities' refusal to carry out the '68 Act, and partly because of the difficulty in obtaining planning permission for private sites.

The effect of part five of the Criminal Justice Bill will be to make an extra 180,000 plus people and their children into homeless criminals. Three main groups of people who will be criminalised are:

• The otherwise-homeless:(clauses 45, 46, 51, 56, 57, 58-60);

• Travellers who simply lack anywhere 'legal' to put their homes,(clause 61 cancels any hope of this remedy);

• Approximately 60,000 squatters, who more conventionally, and less conspicuously, occupy otherwise empty property.

• Protesters and demonstrators are criminalised in clauses 52-54.

• Young people ('ravers') in clauses 47-50.

Unless compensatory legislation is introduced to:
a) Provide alternative legal accommodation for the newly homeless.
b) Recognise the legitimacy of objectors in a democracy.
c) Allow for self-organised, inexpensive cultural gatherings for the young,
it is likely that thousands of people will be forced into breaking the law simply to survive.

THE DARING BUDS OF MAY?

STOP THE CRIMINAL *IN* JUSTICE BILL.

NO CULTURAL CLEANSING! - BIN THE BILL!

PRESSURE ON - MOMENTUM GROWING

More events related to Stage 5 Criminal InJustice Bill? Info & donations to **Freedom Network**, The Old Dolehouse, 372 Coldharbour Lane, London SW9 8PP. **Groups** please rip this off, put your name here & p'copy lots.

NETWORK please photocopy ten times and display in your area **NETWORK**

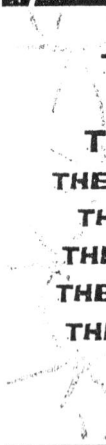

THERE IS A NEED TO DANCE
THERE IS A NEED TO TRAVEL
THERE IS A NEED TO SQUAT
THERE IS A NEED FOR PROTEST
THERE IS A NEED FOR OPEN SPACES
THERE IS A NEED TO CELEBRATE
THERE IS A NEED FOR COMMUNITY
THERE IS A NEED TO COMMUNICATE
THERE IS A NEED FOR TOLERANCE
THERE IS A NEED

TO BE HEARD

THE CRIMINAL JUSTICE AND PUBLIC ORDER BILL

will make a criminal offence out of
- peaceful protest
- attending an unlicensed celebration
- a travelling lifestyle
- occupying empty buildings

It contains laws that contravene international human rights laws.
It wil result in your friends, and other innocent people being locked away in the newly privatised prisons.
It must be opposed. By you. Bring a picnic.

If all the world was as
    gentle as the breeze
    within my hands;
If all the days weren't
    numbered for those who
    walk aimless down
    the high road;
If the space between us was as
    solid as I feel it,
    there'd be no sad song.

CRASS

Much of the remainder of the Bill provides the machinery for dealing with the newly dispossessed 'criminals,' including extending prison accommodation. (e.g. Clause 76 which *"enables the Secretary of State to declare to be a prison any floating structure..........and any structure provided by a contractor to be a prison."*)

The escalation of police, local authority and courts' time and manpower (needed to enforce evictions, man 32-mile exclusion zones, roadblocks, operate permanent vehicle pounds, deal with arrested persons, collect fines, pick up the social consequences of a massive increase in homelessness and human distress) will create major expense and conspicuous wastage of resources. Such evictions are purely repetitive; the same families being moved on **again and again**. These consequences are not acknowledged in the proposed legislation, which states that:

> *"No other provisions of the Bill are expected to have significant public service manpower effects."*

There is no logical reason why 'preventative operations' should be smaller or cheaper than 'full-scale' ones; on the contrary, they are more likely to create complex ongoing 'guerrilla' situations which may stretch police resources beyond reasonable or affordable bounds. It is hard to envisage how, if 'full-scale' operation costs, are, as quoted £400,000, a further 60 additional special operations might take place a year with combined police costs of £0.3 million, which assumes that each operation costs only £5,000.

Roadblocks '92

A further example of this flagrantly misleading data are the costings given for vehicle pounds: five vehicle pounds may cost £500,000 to provide, but what about administration? Leaving aside the fact that the same land and money would provide basic transit sites for a high proportion of those whom these vehicle pounds will render homeless, this counter-productive extravagance is excused thus:

"It is envisaged that the current costs will be recovered through the fees charged for the release of the vehicles".

How are the homeless Travellers going to raise the money, especially in the knowledge that their homes may be re-impounded at any time?

Clause 51 governs the imposition of such charges. No indication is given as to likely sums. These will be at the Secretary of State's discretion, via statutory instruments. Charges for removal (towing to pound) retention, (storage), and also disposal and destruction of vehicles/caravans after 6 months:

"shall be recoverable as a simple contract debt".

To expect homeless families to pay police/council costs for the confiscation and destruction of their homes is both stupid and cruel. Recovery of such debts from people who have no property will be virtually impossible. Such vehicle pounds have already been in operation for some years, and this clause retrospectively legalises the ad-hoc practices of many local authorities.

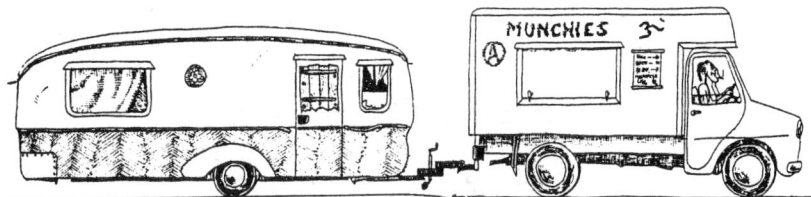

Around Bristol, for example, charges for the return of impounded caravans have been £20 the first day, £40 the second, £80 the third and so on. Families unable to raise the cash instantly (and vehicle pound operatives habitually refuse to release vehicles until evidence of a 'legal' pitch is provided), have generally had to abandon their homes and possessions, acquire a 'scrapper' caravan, and start afresh in acute poverty. This is the reality that pounds will impose on siteless traveller families. 'Illegal' encampments won't shrink; they'll just get unhealthier, scruffier, and angrier. Huge social costs will be the result. The British section of the International Commission of Jurists wrote in their response to the 1992 consultation paper:

> *"We believe that if the duty to provide accommodation is removed and new criminal laws are introduced for unlawful camping, there is a danger that it would be impossible for Gypsies and others to pursue a nomadic existence within the law. This raises important considerations under international agreements as to the rights of nomadic persons - a matter which is not addressed in the consultation paper. In the case of G and E v Norway (99278/81) concerning Lapps, the European Commission expressed the opinion that:*
> *'Under Article 8 (of the European Convention of Human Rights), a minority group is entitled to claim the right to respect for the particular lifestyle it may lead as being private life, family life or home.'*
> *Article 8 must be read in conjunction with Article 10, which forbids discrimination in the enjoyment of the Convention rights and freedoms by, interalia, minorities."*

The failure of the '68 Act could have prompted various courses of action: the Government could have taken powers to ensure local authorities carried out their obligations under the '68 Act. The planning system could be changed to facilitate the establishment of private Gypsy sites. But, the Government's new policy, which follows the 'Thatcher principle' of legislation without consultation, goes directly against these suggestions; abolishing the duty to provide sites and it will make it harder to provide them privately within the planning system.

Vehicle Legality

It is difficult enough for Travellers to find safe sites on which to service and repair their vehicles in order to keep them 'legal', i.e. M.O.T.'ed, taxed and insured, or to remain in one area long enough to receive log books and licences in the post. (For example, you can be fined up to £400 for having inaccurate details on licences and registration documents.) Keeping a vehicle fully legal and insured is already a complete nightmare, and yet instead of making provisions for these problems, the Government is introducing further laws which will force people out onto the roads in illegal vehicles, where police can arrest them, impounding and destroying their family homes.

Where an eviction occurs, bailiffs must ensure that they do not break the Road Traffic Act 1988 or the Highways Act 1980. It is an offence, in certain circumstances, to tow vehicles without a fixed bar, an independent braking system and proper lights on the towed vehicle. Caravans should, by law, be removed to a legal site. Bailiffs should not evict vehicles onto a roadside, as highways' authorities argue that this constitutes an obstruction. Mostly there are no legal places in a particular county, and police and bailiffs may employ threats in the hope that Travellers move themselves, turning a blind eye to illegality just to get them off land. Thus 'passing the buck' occurs; hoping that some other authority will have to deal with the Travellers' next illegal parkup.

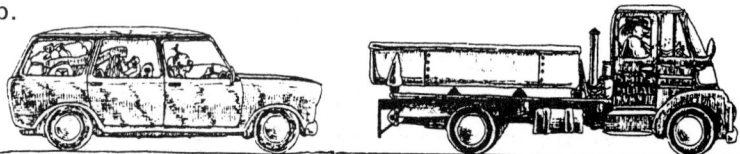

**Escorted to the county line.
Dorset/Somerset '92**

Recently, a Gypsy family, who were parked up between two mounds of gravel dumped in a lay-by, turned an 'obstruction' charge on its head. The local authority tried to win eviction by charging them with obstructing the passage of traffic into the lay-by, but as the Gypsies proved, the mounds of gravel occupied twice the space their caravans did, so the council were charged to remove the gravel instead!

> _"I was stopped at 3 o'clock in the morning on the A34 'cos one rear light was blown, which I didn't know about. I hadn't got my licence and was told that I would be arrested, despite the presence of my baby daughter. Eventually, I argued my way out of it - the licence was 200 miles away in my trailer, and nobody could have fetched it for me." Fiona_

The licence itself should have the current address; a physical impossibility for many Travellers. Most leave it at the last permanent address they had, which is usually OK, as long as vehicle documents are also registered at that address. M.O.T. requirements for cars are quite straightforward, but a larger vehicle is subject to a plating test unless registered as a mobile home. New laws have made it difficult to convert a vehicle individually - commercial refitting is generally required before it can be re-registered as a caravanette. To qualify for a class 4 M.O.T., a living vehicle must have a bed, sink and cooker as permanent fixtures. Then, the test is still very rigorous, and has to be conducted by a D.O.T. station, not just an M.O.T. garage. Some are known to be more tolerant of Travellers than others, but all are extremely thorough.

> _"I got through, even the emissions test, except for the fact that I haven't got a padlock to secure the fuel tank cap. So I grabbed one off a tat- box, and I was OK - I got my MOT Class 4!" Fiona._

Insurance is the next obstacle. Travellers find it almost impossible to find cheap third party cover for living vehicles, as companies are obviously cautious about high risks.

For those who move little during the winter, the road tax is a real waste of money. Paying £70 for using roads on three occasions, for example, is rather irritating. There is also the argument that, as we have no freedom of road use during Summer months, we should have this reflected in the cost of a tax disc. So, legalising a vehicle is not always straightforward. It is

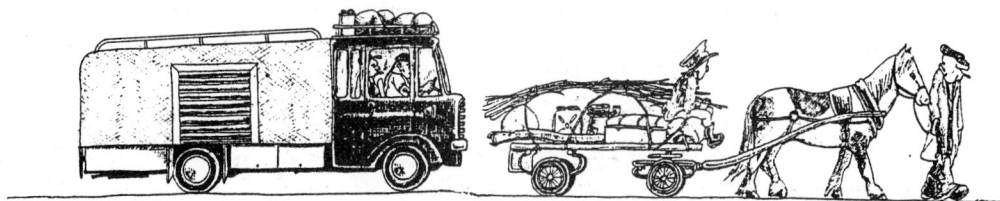

also practically impossible to adequately insure contents without vast expenditure. The attitude of individual police is also an important factor.

> *"I got stopped on the A303 near Stonehenge the day after I'd bought my truck - no M.O.T. or tax, though I had three day insurance. I proved it was on the way for M.O.T. work, & showed the fail certificate from 2 days previously & the bill of sale, and they let me off. Yet on the way to the pre-booked M.O.T., I was pulled by different cops - and got an £80 fine!" Fiona.*

Case: We had set off to join friends on a well established site at Stratford, but it had been 'Public Ordered'. After a few days of total chaos I finally found out where my kids were (we'd been split up by police in the confusion of roadblocks and cordons). We pulled up outside the site; I walked on and found the kids in a bus with Penfold, they're fine. We get some helpers to lift the trailer out of the ditch and push it onto the site. At the last moment the police landrover at the gate reverses so that we can't get past. When I tried to explain the situation, the driver tells me I'm a liar, gets on his radio and confirms it:

> "No more vehicles allowed on the site."

The kids will have to get their stuff together and we must leave. The trailer must be removed from the road now! We are trying to move it off the road and onto the site. 12 riot vans turn up, fresh from the Cleeve Hill eviction; 6 blocking the road in each direction. All traffic is made to turn round and sent back the way it came. We don't want to block the road, we want to get in, have tea and go to bed. But we're not allowed to. Finally, I discover which officer is in charge. People are milling around, arguing, questioning, all the riot police are out of the vans, standing in the road. I try to talk to him calmly. We cannot get onto the site, or leave it in the road, so I offer to move it onto the grass verge, where it was to start with. Another officer says that is no good either. As I talk to the first officer, the second orders his men to pick up the trailer and move it to the side of the road.

By now almost all the people from the site are out in the road, and over 100 police officers. One is shouting at me to get in the taxi and start it up. I explain that the driver, my kids, their trailer, dogs and tat are still on the site and I can't leave without them, not again. Also I cannot move the rig anywhere, as the road is blocked both ways by people and police. The officer in charge tells me to disappear! I tell him I can't. I can only move forwards or backwards, and when I do , if they still follow me, we will still be causing a roadblock/disturbance. He must get his officers back in the vans, off the road and out of the way. He can't see that.

> *"Just tell me where to go, don't tell me to disappear!"*.   Es.

Vehicles are not safe, even if temporarily parked up of the road. A newly evicted convoy of Travellers had been escorted by police onto a lay-by near Bath. They had been told by police that their vehicles would be safe there for a couple of days, so some had gone on site reconnaissance, leaving only a couple of people with the vehicles. While the site was small and empty, police seized the opportunity to break the convoy up still further. They raided the lead vehicles, arresting the only occupant, who was asleep, and impounded the vehicles on the grounds that they were causing an obstruction. They later released the man without charge. (This often happens to people who are classified N.F.A., of no fixed abode, and cannot prove an address.)

The vehicles were now in the pound. The Travellers tried to retrieve their homes and were told that first they had to pay a towing fee for removal to the pound and charges for storage. So they set about raising the money, whilst staying with friends. Two weeks later they returned to the pound with £200 to cover the towing and pound fees, only to be told that they couldn't have their homes back as an environmental health notice was now in force. They had not been allowed to collect any of their possessions, and the vehicles had been rifled through, not properly tatted down before they were taken to the pound. In consequence, some of the food in cupboards which had remained untouched in the pound, and had gone off thereby attracting vermin. The police maintained that it was a health hazard and refused to release the vehicles. One man was denied access to even his family's clean washing. This stalemate situation continued for several weeks, with pound fees mounting and the Travellers still without their homes. Finally, the police saw fit to destroy one of the vehicles, a double decker bus with a Gardner engine worth over £1,000 scrap value, selling it to scrap yard for £200. This £200 was used to pay overdue pound fees. The Travellers lost their home and all their possessions and were informed that they still owed pound fees and removal charges.

"I grew up in the 1930's with an unemployed father. He didn't riot he got on his bike and looked for work." Norman Tebbit, Tory Party Conference 1983.

"The open road? My dad, he lost a leg in the war. Afterwards he'd pull onto a common and the police would come and move him on. What did he fight for? Freedom?" Bill.

"We're the people who got on our bikes and got on with our lives. We do for ourselves; we've got our own homes; we fetch our own fuel and water. But now that's not good enough. We got on our bikes and looked for work and now the Government keeps trying to push us off them. No matter what, we'll get up and walk if we have to. We're not the sort of people that will just lie down and take it." Herring.

Double take

There has also been the recent, sinister, 'Operation Nomad,' in which many Travellers have been photographed inside and outside of their vehicles, with number plates clearly visible for identification purposes by the police. These are then transferred on to a national file recording 'Travellers.''

Media

There are many reasons why people take to the road and the number of Travellers in the U.K. is rising at a phenomenal rate. This increase in the nomadic population has lead to an 'overflow', whereby Travellers of all denominations have been forced into the glare of publicity, no longer a local problem that can be conveniently swept under the local authorities' carpets.

As a visible problem, Travellers and the homeless are now embarrassing to a Government that prefers to champion it's privatisation campaigns, whilst neglecting the problems inherent in cutting public services. The only answer the Government has so far offered has been to initiate, through a largely slavish media, a campaign of moral panic and vilification, attempting to incite hysteria about cultural deviance by hi-lighting instances of offending behaviour:

> *"A SWARMING TRIBE OF HUMAN LOCUSTS" Daily Telegraph (7.6.93)*

> *"RAVAGING MARAUDING DRIFTERS AND ECSTASY DOPED YOBS"*
> *Daily Express(7.6.93)*

> *"TRAVELLERS ARE A GRISLY REMINDER OF HOW LOW HUMAN DEGRADATION CAN GET"   Daily Mail (30.7.92)*

> *"LOCK UP YOUR KIDS - RAVE. PARTY FEARS" Derby Telegraph (11.5.92)*

The press has unfailingly produced a maledictory catalogue of often fictitious crimes committed by the infamously anonymous 'New Age Travellers,' with their circuit of culturally deviant 'Free Festivals,' causing panic among parents whose offspring attend such events. This moral outrage now encompasses most local press coverage on the mere existence of temporary roadside camps. Most Travellers have had first hand experience of hostility from settled communities; if not actual vigilante action. Those on the receiving end of petrol bombs and paving slabs through windows usually have little legal recourse and can do nothing save tat down and move on.

Case: **Durley School:**
We were there for a couple of weeks. The landowners noticed that some of the building materials were missing and hired a private security firm to search the vehicles leaving site. They were positioned about half a mile from us at the end of a long private drive. We only saw them when we came on or left site. The pigs 'Public Ordered' us (16 vehicles). 2 days later the local paper reported that we'd been driven away by constant drumming at 4 a.m.. But we had heard nothing, and this report was all bullshit. The only reason we left was because of the Section 39.

Glen.

Local newspapers tend to emphasise problems and ignite opinions. Media coverage was favourably disposed towards the farmer, who in 1993, attacked a group Travellers by attempting to overturn their caravans with his JCB. He had all charges against him dropped. A small convoy of vehicles had pulled onto the land on the A525 at Marchwiel, after being escorted through Wales by the police. The Travellers were exhausted from non-stop eviction and needed a day's rest. The farmer attacked the camp with his JCB damaging five vehicles, overturning one which had people and children inside it. He showed no regard for the lives or safety of any of the people. The charges were dropped because; only 10 of the 18 Travellers were able to attend the hearing to give evidence; there was some evidence that the throttle of the JCB was stuck (this was never proven) and the court decided that the farmer had the right to defend his property against trespassers.

> Case: "We were parked in Yorkshire in 1988, and were driving to a scrapyard when we passed a bus parked by the roadside. We stopped to chat; it was Phil who we hadn't seen for ages as he liked to park quiet by himself. A new baby and a new family, We said we'd visit next week. A week later there's no sign of their bus, but another visitor to our site informs us that a paving stone had gone through their window into the baby's cot one night. Fortunately, the baby wasn't in it at the time. You wonder why we board our windows, we sure as hell don't park on our own anymore."   Sue

The press campaign that had built up to a climax by the summer of '92 effectively halted the free festival economy which had been thriving since the 1960's; in '93 the highlights of the circuit included;

♦ **TOUR GUIDE** ♦
Summer Season 1993
Festivals

● ● ● ● ● ● ● ●

♦ A fortnight's tour from picturesque Stratford on Avon, through the beautiful Cotswolds, accompanied by officers from Thames Valley, West Mercia, Gloucestershire and Avon Constabularies in full riot regalia, (and full overtime pay).

♦ A bank holiday break on the M5, again with a full complement of her Majesty's finest for company.

♦ Numerous battles to leave lay-bys in the West Country, with a ***Special Solstice Riot*** at Ford Street site, kindly advertised by 'Spiral Bribe' (or Tripe) as cover for a big-bucks and bullshit party they conducted elsewhere.

♦ A traditional torrential weekend in the Elan Valley.

♦ Culminating in a 'fait accompli' in Norfolk where everyone finally partied.

All in all it wasn't an economically successful summer season, except for purveyors of DERV and police officers, who made a tidy packet out of the run-around. Of course, the scheduled commercial festivals were also included on many peoples itineraries; Forest Fayre, Phoenix, Pilton, Strawberry Fayre. Travellers provide music and circus acts, stalls, cafe's and site crew which are the backbone of commercial festivals.

> *"But there is growing disenchantment with 'closed shop' mentality, such as that exhibited by Michael Eavis's 'NO TRAVELLERS' policy, (he was so grateful for the 2 decades of free festival culture that forged the current commercial success enjoyed by his Glastonbury Festival, that he now pays a private police force £500,000 to keep Travellers out)." .....and ..... "The sheer terror at the 'security' tactics employed at the Phoenix Festival at Long Marston Airfield, (which included harassing potential 'Traveller types' by dousing with petrol and interrogating cultural and ticketed status with a lighted match!)"   Herring. *

Whilst the majority of the tabloids continue their biased, hysterical reporting, a few publications are more balanced in their approaches. A few broadsheet Sunday Supplement magazines, women's interest magazines, educational and health publications, as well as most of the music and biker press; have included articles which show Travellers in a more favourable, if patronising, light. There is also a fringe press which is associated either with Gypsies or the New Age and Festival scene. Romanestan Publications, Unique Publications, Traveller Education, Monolith news, Zine, Fevered Imaginings and Tribal Messenger are amongst the outlets for the voice of Travellers of all kinds. Certain writers contributing to the 'quality' press, such as Polly Toynbee and Jeremy Sandford, have also offered an 'alternative' perspective on Travellers, which is less stereotyping and describes the daily lives of Travellers without resorting to 'hype.''

Our place in Society is reflected in many commercial situations. Jeremy Beadle, for example, included in his programme, the take-over of a holiday caravan by Travellers; 'Dirtysomething,' a TV play, fictionalised a meeting between two Travellers at Glastonbury (highly likely!) and moving to squats in London; a cartoon poster of a lurcher includes a comment:

> *"General expression: gentle and friendly, sometimes looks hurt, especially after receiving bad publicity due to living with hippy convoy." Dick Twinney.*

We are part of 1990's British Life, like it or not.........

Benefit Payments

Anybody out of work is entitled to a minimum payment of social security or dole on which to survive. Travellers do have problems maintaining claims as they move around, and obstructions are often placed in their way. Sometimes people of no fixed abode are ordered to walk miles to sign on daily, thus 'proving' local residence.

* Michael Eavis says: *"I'd never even seen a 'hippy' in 1970 when the festival started. It was organised by locals, for locals, and it was only in the 1980's, when Stonehenge was banned, that Travellers attended in any numbers."* See also Michael's comments in Chapter 2.

The general reluctance to provide benefits is revealed in a document circulated around DSS offices, and sub-titled 'Not for Public Domain.' It catalogues greater restrictions on Travellers claiming anything other than a very basic survival limit, possibly less than £10 per week.

The media also constantly repeats the myth that Travellers own dogs because they can claim £8 per week for their feed and keep - this is untrue. It is important to remember that any Traveller claiming benefit is receiving half the amount available to housedwellers in the same circumstances.

"DOLE STAFF'S FIELD TRIP TO PAY HIPPY HANDOUTS"
Daily Mail (29.7.92)

Case: "We'd all pulled onto this scrap of land on top of a hill in Kerry, Wales. We'd had a good festival there the week before, no trouble and were getting ready to leave at the end of the week. Some people had to sign on for their stamp and had been down to Newtown to make enquiries at the social. Next thing we know there's a horde of DSS people setting up shop on site with a mob of journalists having a field day, total media circus. Hardly anyone signed on, maybe about 60 people form a site of hundreds. Everyone was scared of repercussions, it was generally a quiet site until the DSS set up, then we were mobbed by the media, TV cameras everywhere   and the pigs got their helicopter out to show off, they didn't do anything before except play football at the gate 'til the media turned up.

The next day 'HIPPY SCROUNGERS' was plastered all over the papers with photos of some dumb punter who didn't even live on site flashing his Giro about and mouthing off to the press. We're not scroungers, we mainly support ourselves; we've got our own homes, get our own fuel and water. Why should we be scapegoats?

The people that owned the hotel down the road that the Old Bill were all staying in, came up to site for an evening and told us that they'd rather we'd stayed in the hotel as we were far more polite and considerate than the police."   Sarah.

With media stunts such as in the above case, the public opinion of Travellers has been so defiled and manipulated by the media that it is now simple for the Government to pass sweeping new laws which amount to serious infringements of basic Human Rights, with minimum resistance from the settled population.

The law, support groups and travelling

To sustain an 'economic purpose of travel,' in other words, some kind of work or business which can survive sometimes daily evictions and continual harassment, much of on-site economy is necessarily self-perpetuating. It has for decades relied upon the summer circuit of festivals not only for entertainment, but essential trading and economic opportunities; where Modern Travellers and conventional society meet and mix to mutual advantage. The Criminal Justice Bill contains proposals that will seriously curtail festival culture and economy, depriving more people of their livelihoods.

"Any extension of the criminal law is likely to prove impractical, expensive and result in a further rise in homeless." Jon Fitzmaurice, Director of CHAR.
(Housing Campaign for the Single Homeless)

It's not alright Jack

First they came for the miners,
        and I did not speak out,
Because I was not a miner.
Then they came for he gays,
        and I did not speak out,
Because I was not gay.
Then they came for the Gypsies
        and the New Age Travellers,
        and I did not speak out,
Because I was not a Gypsy or a Traveller.
Now I've lost my job,
        the house is being repossessed,
        and my wife has left.
Then they came for me,
        and there was no-one left
        to speak out for me.
                                Jack

Conspicuous only by their absence are reports in the national press on the Government clampdowns and withdrawal of funding to agencies actively involved in helping Travellers. Only 4 national organisations have set up units to campaign for the rights of travelling people. These are Liberty (formerly the National Council for Civil Liberties), Save the Children, Bristol Shelter, and the Labour Campaign for Travellers Rights. Jenny Smith of Bristol Shelter was a particularly vociferous and well connected campaigner, running the Travelling Peoples Unit and commissioned by the EEC to write a book: 'A Right to Travel and A Right to Stop' on legal and welfare rights of Travellers in the U.K.. after the M5 blockade by police in May 93, where Jenny was acting as an independent witness, the police made complaints to Shelter head office along the lines of:

> *"Why is she helping Travellers when official efforts are being made to discourage them?"*

A number of contributors halted their donations to Shelter, and the Department of Environment, who are major contributors to Shelter funds, have expressed annoyance with her work. Thus the Travelling Peoples Unit has been closed down, although Jenny continues work on the executive of the Labour Campaign for Travellers Rights (LCTR). The Gypsy Unit of Save The Children is also the subject of insidious objections. One of the main organisers, Ann Bagehot, may be retired early and the unit is being closed down in October. There have been attempts to discredit the Unit's work by implying that it is of a political nature and therefore inconsistent with it's charity status. The Labour Campaign group is doing a great deal of good

work liaising between traveller groups and producing alternative proposals to lobby parliament.

But the harsh reality of the constantly hyped association between travelling and criminality and the continuous moral outrage stimulated by media manipulation means that Travellers are not a popular cause to support. When John Battle, Shadow Housing Minister, spoke up for Travellers at a recent housing conference, a Shelter delegate was overheard saying to a colleague:
> *"Why does John concern himself with non-issues?"*

Although the charities themselves state that the increase in the Traveller population bears direct correlation with the dire housing shortage, housing charities are not keen to bear the brunt of adverse publicity, as they rely heavily on public sympathy and sentiment for their funding. The Commission for Racial Equality consider that:
> *"The Government's proposals are both contradictory and unworkable, and are a direct attack on the Gypsy way of life."*

Traveller support groups like Save the Children and Bristol Shelter were small, energetic groups, accomplishing much. But, because they are small they're easy to get rid of. Campaign groups cannot match the media resources of the Government; the lobbyists behind part five of the Criminal Justice Bill are the County Landowners Association and the National Farmers' Union, also Tory voters and party fund contributors, including some of the richest people in the U.K., and have a combined lobbying budget exceeding £8 million per annum.

Small support groups like Friends and Families of Travellers, LCTR and even the Gypsy Council for Culture, Education, Welfare and Civil Rights just cannot compete with the might of superior resources and the manipulative control of information. So, the rights of minority groups in this so-called democracy can be eroded in ways hidden from public attention. In the light of such draconian laws as the Criminal Justice Bill and the denial of basic human rights, it will entail,

many Travellers are seriously considering forfeiting their birthright in the U.K. to seek asylum abroad rather than be hounded into homelessness and extreme poverty.

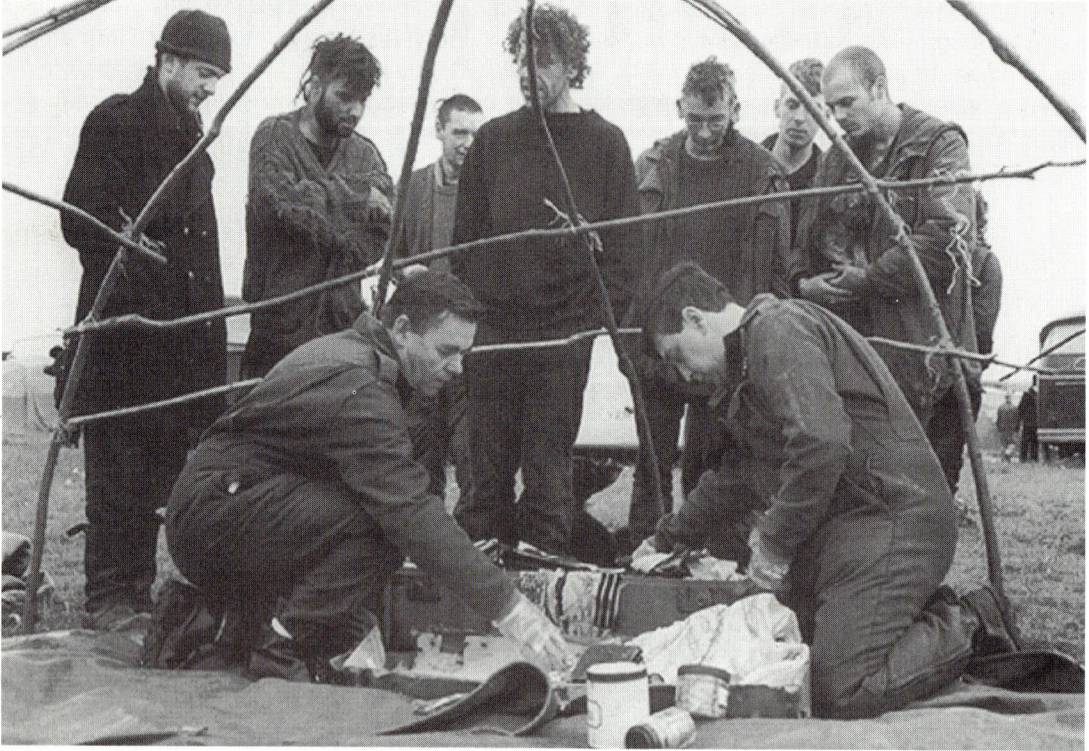

Search. Stockbridge Common '91

This bears a chilling resemblance to many of the reasons given in justification of the Criminal Justice Bill.

It was a capital offence to be a Gypsy in many parts of Europe between 1550 and 1750. In 1822 the English Vagrancy Act declared that all persons pretending to be Gypsies, telling fortunes, wandering abroad or lodging in tents or wagons were to be deemed rogues and vagabonds with a penalty of up to six months imprisonment. The Nazis sent people to Death Camps if they had one eighth Gypsy blood; more extreme than in the case of Jews. These crimes were denied prosecution at the Nuremberg Trials, as Germany argued that the persecution was not racial but because Gypsies were:
"Asocial and criminal".

"The time has come for Gypsies to be banished into the wilderness. What is needed is more harassment and more discouragement." John Carlisle (Conservative M.P. Luton)

"Society needs to condemn a little more and understand a little less."
"New Age Travellers? Not in this age! Not in any age!"   John Major

"I am only too delighted to do anything we can to make life as difficult for such things as hippy convoys."
"We are declaring war on squatters"   Margaret Thatcher.

"New Age Vermin"   Paul Marland. M.P.

"I believe that 'scum' is an appropriate term for Travellers who live in an appalling way and inflict their filth on innocent people."   Derek Conway Conservative M.P. Shrewsbury.

> There is an old Jewish custom where all the sins of the people are ceremoniously placed on the back of a goat, which is then turned into the desert to die of thirst. It is the origin of the word 'scapegoat'.

Otterbourne

Department of the Environment

OFFICIAL NOTICE

SET-ASIDE
FOR
TRAVELLERS

THIS SITE IS SET-ASIDE FOR TRAVELLERS USE ONLY

Under Section 5, Clause 23c of the Land Use Act, 1991, the land encompassed by this site has been officially designated for use by New Age travellers, fellow travellers, ravers, hippies, and any persons of no fixed abode. The site may be used for consciousness-raising gatherings, parties, musical performance, dance, and short-term accommodation. The act expressly forbids payment of poll-tax, the setting up of long-term business, or the presence of anyone in uniform on the site.

Fake DoE notice produced by Travellers which caused a little confusion!

Chapter Six: Relations with other Travellers

I like living in a caravan,
Am I such a terrible thing.
I dare to be different.
Now that is a terrible thing.

charlie Smith.

The diversity of the definition of a Traveller has been discussed in previous chapters, but this is even more relevant when discussions of traditional Travellers are concerned. Obviously, the reactions of those who travel as an inherited way of life affect those who have chosen, or been forced, to adopt a nomadic lifestyle.

We have divided traditional Travellers into four broad bands (Gypsies; Showmen; Circus and Water Travellers) in order to show the similarities and differences in outlook; but have also attempted a brief explanation of the types of people included in such broad categorising.

Gypsies

The National Gypsy Council has outlined **five categories of Traveller:**

Tinkers - from Roman descent, skilled metalworkers with particular specialisation in tools such as knives. The Industrial Revolution limited this trade, and many tinkers moved on to scrap dealing.

Pedlars - travelling salespeople providing any commodity required by outlying communities. Wares were also sold at fairs and markets, especially as the pottery industry expanded, so diversifying the range of goods.

Romanies - probably descended from Indian nomadic tribes travelling across Europe in the fifteenth century. Although the language and nationality of a host country may have been superficially adopted, their culture remained separate. The Romani language, rooted in Sanskrit, is their own.

Irish tinkers - people whose families travelled for centuries throughout Ireland, many of whom have been driven from the country by eviction, famine and poverty. Their language is Gaelic based and called Shelta or Gammon. They have been joined recently by migrant Irishmen seeking construction work.

Scottish tinkers - probably descended from Celtic metalworkers, and originally called tinklers. Their numbers were swelled by the massive Highland clearance campaigns of the nineteenth and early twentieth centuries. They are still more likely than other Travellers to use bender tents as homes.

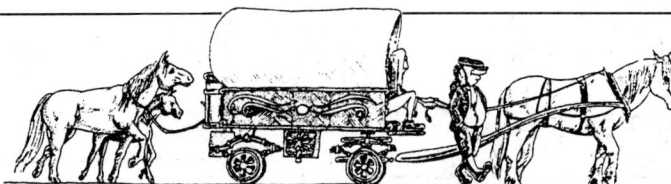

The term 'Gypsy' referred to the supposed origin of Romanies (or Roms as they often call themselves) their dark complexions mistakenly suggesting that they came from Egypt. Many other terms exist, such as didikoi or pikey, which refer to the degree of traditional Traveller blood in an individual and his family. However, many view these terms as derogatory.

It is estimated that there are 80,000-100,000 Gypsies in Britain, but generalisations about ways of life and making a living are limited by the definite divisions between the types of Travellers listed previously. It is believed that approximately half live in caravans, while the rest are now housedwellers. Small groups of Welsh Romanies known as the Kale, from North Wales and Roms and Coppersmiths from Hungary are also part of the overall Romany population.

> *".....the Irishmen.....came over in the summer and...for so many shillings an acre and so many gallons of beer would cut the meadow green."*
> *'The Hard Way up'. Edited by Geoff Mitchell.*

In looking at links between Travellers and Gypsies, we have focused more heavily on the traditions of Romanies and their culture. Gypsies have faced persecution throughout Europe, including Britain, for centuries:

   17th Century: death penalty for nomads in England;
   18th Century: persecuted for vagrancy; could be sent to workhouses in England;
   19th Century: treated with a more romantic, but unrealistic, attitude through art, music and literature - especially the writing of George Borrow;
   20th Century: massive European persecution, with over 25,000 killed in the Nazi extermination camps; later, some civil rights awareness.
   In the 1960s, the persecution by bulldozers and hired thugs and planning regulations was a forerunner to the current legislation and action against all Travellers.

Whatever the divisions, one old tinker who had survived attacks in the past said:
> *"I can understand what you're doing. Now that we're older, you're going to have to fight instead."*

Gypsies, together with all other Travellers, are fighting for a common right embodied in the European Convention of Human Rights:
> *Everyone lawfully within a territory of a State shall, within " that territory, have the right to liberty of movement and freedom to choose his residence."   Protocol 4*

◆ ◆ ◆ ◆ ◆

Gypsy culture is very different from the lifestyle of newer Travellers in many ways. During the post-war period, there was an overall change from horse-drawn wagons to motor-drawn caravans, as cars and lorries became increasingly available. The homes themselves tend to be kept spotlessly clean by the women and girls, while the men and boys are occupied outside. The caravans indicate status, especially the new chrome trailers, which are usually custom-built, and extremely expensive.

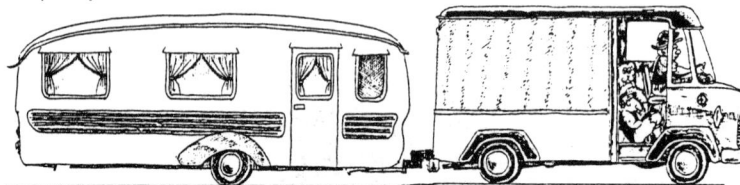

"I've always wanted a Vickers; The trailer of my dreams,
One real big and chromy, with coloured piping seams."
                                        Charlie Smith.

Gypsies treasure possessions, such as Crown Derby china, which are collected down generations, and are kept exquisitely presented and preserved. Travellers, in contrast, have a much more diverse assortment of homes, which are usually scruffier inside and out. The definitions between the sexes for domestic chores, menial tasks, money making or vehicle maintenance are far less clear. Few possessions are gathered, other than for personal preference or memories.

"At Norton Barracks, you could stand in the gatehouse and look out over
both sites. The Gypsies had clean, white and chrome trailers
with electric lights and buzzing generators; T.V.'s flickering
behind curtains, and flatbeds loaded with scrap were parked up.
On our side, there were benders, trucks, old trailers, buses
and horse-drawns scattered through the dusk. Faint candles or
hurricane-lamps glared within- and the odd T.V. was powered by a battery."
                                        Fiona.

Many Gypsies are strongly religious, traditionally Roman Catholic, but more accurately based on Romany lore and Catholicism. Some are born-again Christian. This affects their whole attitude to life, particularly to sex and marriage. In many Gypsy family units sex is rarely discussed with children, and certainly not with boys and girls together; whilst marriage partners may be comparatively young. But the success-rate of marriage is high, and the family bond extremely strong-whilst immediate family tend to live together on sites, it is increasingly being left to younger members to keep the travelling tradition alive. Gypsies were mostly oriented towards rural travelling, but lack of work has made them more attracted towards towns and cities. Extended family groups still meet up for fairs or rites of passage:

"More than a thousand Gypsies from all over Britain and Ireland
came yesterday for a funeral......" *Daily Telegraph 4/3/88.*

Travellers, however, have few shared beliefs or religions. There are a high numbers of illegitimate births, and very few marriages - though many couples are committed to their partnerships. Strong friendships are forged and maintained, as relatively few have several generations of family on the road. Also, a permanent site is not an option for most Travellers, who have to adapt to new friends and communities constantly.

◆ ◆ ◆ ◆ ◆

Education is regarded as increasingly important for Romany children. Groups such as NATT and ACERT have made schools more accessible to Gypsy children. Parents tend to recognise a need for literacy and numeracy in today's society, but are rarely in a position to teach it themselves. It is not unusual, however, for children to leave in their early teenage years to adopt the gender roles quite clearly expected by the Gypsy community. There are also sensitive areas in education, most particularly health and sex education. High moral standards are practised and expected, and it is often regarded as wrong for children to be taught the facts of life in a co-educational environment.

Alternatively, many Travellers are strongly opposed to the State education system. Those who have a high standard of education may feel confident in home-teaching, while others seek practical alternatives. It is the materialism of peers, and social conditioning by the imposition of national curriculum learning that most of them fear. In contrast to Gypsies, who are increasingly literate, new Travellers may create a decreasingly literate and numerate generation unless adequate alternatives are established. (see Chapter 4 for a fuller discussion of the issues.)

◆ ◆ ◆ ◆ ◆

It is only in the post-war years that men have become the main breadwinners. Until then, traditional Traveller means of earning income have included seasonal agricultural work, pedling crafts or charms - known as 'calling' - or fortune-telling; all of which were done by women. Scrap-dealing developed in the last forty years; and there are also some very skilled horsemen and lurchermen capable of breeding and dealing advantageously.

> "*They are contemptuous of the fact that most non-Gypsies work for*
> *someone else, and also that we draw social security.* "
> *Jeremy Sandford.*

As some Gypsies have become increasingly settled, Travellers have taken over some of these skills - most particularly the scrap and agricultural work. Some horse-drawn Travellers make traditional pegs and baskets, while others make ethnic clothes and jewellery. Whilst tarot-card reading is not uncommon on site, the selling of such skills remains linked to the ancient Romany families; as do the legendary dealers of dogs and horses.

◆ ◆ ◆ ◆ ◆

Gypsies have a circuit of fairs and gatherings at which they traditionally meet, such as Stow and Appleby horse fairs. Smaller events are held all over the country, such as Wickham, Thirsk and Horsmanden. A Kent newspaper wrote about the latter:

> *"There is even some dispute about how the fair began. Some say the Gypsies had a Royal Charter, while others argue that it began during the peak hop-picking time."* 9/7/93

Stow and Appleby, the biggest of the annual events, have increasingly attracted Travellers. Whilst this did not use to be a problem, the numbers, swelled by punters and ravers, have been reported by the press as having caused animosity. However, those Travellers who have attended recent horse fairs have thoroughly enjoyed themselves, and have been made welcome by the traditional Travellers.

Gypsies also have family gatherings and celebrations, especially for weddings. In contrast, Travellers tend to be associated with spiritual celebrations, free music festivals, or raves. Whilst these also tend to attract many non-Travellers as participants, there are also some young traditional Travellers who have been drawn to the scene.

With about half the Gypsy population now housed, many still practise their traditional culture, and

> *"might return to the road if conditions got better. Some have intermarried with non-Gypsies and they still continue to do so."*
>
> Jeremy Sandford.

Travellers may also move back into houses if the circumstances are right, though they have usually deliberately left such ties behind them.

◆ ◆ ◆ ◆ ◆

The Gypsy Council was established in 1966, and campaigned successfully for some of the points included in the 1968 Caravan Sites Act. However, whilst this acknowledged the need for sites, there was little discussion about their location or landscaping. The 'designation' clause also allowed some councils to evict the remaining Gypsies from their area, by designating it with the Department of the Environment as unsuitable for sites. There was also a growth of local private sites, often when families had made enough money to buy the land, and obtain permission for limited numbers to live there.

In 1988, David Lovegrove estimated that 5,500 caravans in the U.K. were on authority sites, with 2,500 on legal private sites.... and 4,500 totally uncatered for. Some sites are seen as little better than 'reservations,' and the Caravan Sites Act has contributed to the ending of the traditional lifestyle 'on the move'. The highest congregation of Gypsies is in East Anglia and Kent, which were originally areas where agricultural work was plentiful.

> *"It's the sites that are killing them. They shouldn't have put them here, it's destroying our way of life."*
>
> 'Colonel' Joe Harris.

The influx of new Travellers further challenged the counties in their provision of sites. Those individuals conducting judicial reviews were occasionally offered places on authority sites, though Gypsy prejudice and limits on vehicle size etc. usually made these impractical. Again, such offers ignored the needs of other Travellers in each area.

The 1986 Public Order Act (see Chapter 5) also affected Gypsies adversely, as well as the Travellers, whose pilgrimages to Stonehenge it was meant to halt. The Act was designed to prevent twelve or more vehicles travelling together and any 'damage' to unoccupied land used for park-ups. As Donald Kennrick and Sian Bakewell stated in 'On the Verge. 1990:

"Gypsy families were encouraged by this law to stop on the edge of roads,
with all the inherent dangers, rather than pull into a piece of unoccupied land."

This has been a source of conflict between Gypsies and Travellers in the past, though it seems that they are finally united in fighting the proposed legislation of 1994:

"Gypsies and Travellers lobbied the House of Commons yesterday
in protest at Government laws to criminalise illegal camping" Telegraph 11/3/93

Which the Gypsy, which the Traveller?

It is very uncommon to find Gypsies and Travellers parked up together, though not totally unknown. As previously noted, it is often the young Gypsies who may join Travellers; while horse-drawn Travellers may live comfortably with Gypsies in wagons. Jeremy Sandford's introduction   to his book 'Gypsies' says:

> *"Many people are thinking of how an alternative society could be created,*
> *and it is worth noting that the Gypsies have had an alternative culture*
> *of their own for centuries, a society which intermeshes with ours, but which is*
> *different in almost every way. Those of us who are discontented with*
> *existing available life-styles may find things to ponder in this book."*

Travellers have adopted that nomadic lifestyle, and brought to it their own origins and cultures. It is to be hoped that all Travellers will ultimately unite to fight the current appalling proposals to curtail civil liberties. Since 1989, the Department of the Environment has started to instigate a policy of divide and rule, actively encouraging county councils such as Hertfordshire, Avon, Hereford and Worcester, to provide more sites for Gypsy caravans. However, the DoE. has decreed that Travellers (called by Hereford "100 plus Hippy vehicles") are *not Travellers* and are a public order problem - covered by the Home Office.

However, this summer should show the strength of unity in all nomads.

> *"You don't own nothing really, you just borrow it."*
> *"You can't own the ground, it sort of owns you, don't it..."*
> ***Bubbles Brazil.***

SHOWMEN.

The history of the showmen goes back centuries to the rural celebrations combining holiday and religion in medieval church festivals; and also to the hiring fairs at which itinerant workers were 'bought' or hired for the season. Although Fairs initially provided mystery and miracle plays, they soon diversified to include competent original entertainers and performers who would attract a crowd.

By 1750, fairs were seen as a working class domain, and shows were for the middle classes. There was a surge of people who joined the fairs after the Napoleonic wars, partly because the

> *"Nomadic life(provided) a convenient retreat from the problems which they had left*
> *behind." Duncan Dallas;*

and partly because they had little else to do. It was only from about the 1830's onwards, as a second generation grew up on the road, that living vans were really adopted. In 1871, the Fairs Act stated that Fairs:

> *"are unnecessary, are the cause of grievous immorality and are very injurious to the*
> *inhabitants of towns where the fairs are held."*
> *Duncan Dallas.*

The showmen resisted the Victorian urge to suppress their shows, and replace them with static displays in museums, theatres etc. But the development of steam-driven rides in the last

decades of the 19th century established the Golden Age of Showmen. They set up the U.K. showmen and Van Dwellers Association to maintain their rights, and later, the Showman's Guild

The traditional showman's life has changed dramatically this century, and Travellers are increasingly adopting the skills and facilities to provide shows.

♦ ♦ ♦ ♦ ♦

"Many fairground families today....can trace their connection with the trade back to the hard times of the 1820's and 1830's." Duncan Dallas.
This sense of family has always been strong:
"Wealth is measured by families not by individuals....
The family is a source of cheap and reliable labour...
A large family is a distinct advantage to the successful showman."
Duncan Dallas."

Travellers tend to work and travel in friendship units, though they will pass on skills and equipment to their children. The whole scale of the cost and ownership of modern fairground equipment involves few Travellers. Most are concerned with presenting a traditional show, such as puppets, or operating basic rides, such as swingboats. Modern fairground rides incorporate expensive equipment which must be maintained constantly in order to reach insurance standards. It is expensive to buy, maintain, and run - but the more dramatic the ride, the more likely it is to draw punters.

"Dodgems probably need most maintenance since much of their appeal lies in being deliberately maltreated by the public." Duncan Dallas.
In contrast, those Travellers who own rides have tended to purchase and restore the old Victorian rides, abandoned after the steam revolution. These are several sets of swingboats on the circuit, erected for use at commercial fairs and events, such as Sidmouth Folk Festival.

Sharon's chair swings
at Whole Earth Fair

The 'traditional' showmen's wagons were palatially decorated, and as large as could be horse-drawn. They have been replaced by huge modern plastic and aluminium wagons which are equipped with domestic appliances, and can be moved quickly and efficiently by the fleets of vehicles.

> *"The lines of Mercedes and HGVs are mostly H registration; serious funds will soon be required to keep up the flash trappings."*   Scotsman on Sunday 13/6/93

In contrast, Travellers either adopt a ride to carry on their own trucks, or buy one of the discarded wagons to renovate and inhabit.

◆ ◆ ◆ ◆ ◆

Gender divisions in the fairground are less emphatic than on Gypsy sites. Women are still expected to maintain a reasonable domestic standard while men erect the rides, but once the fair is under way, they are also involved as:

> *"secretary, accountant, worker and business partner."*   Duncan Dallas.

Similarly, there is little difference between men and women in the Traveller culture who become involved in presenting shows - everyone unloads, constructs and takes money.

◆ ◆ ◆ ◆ ◆

Educationally, fairground children tend to be included in schools during the winter months when the fair is parked up. This gives continuity, and can be sustained by learning packs taken on the road through summer months. Some fairgrounds even employ a teacher to work with the children throughout all the moves in summer - sometimes two or three a week. Traveller children still face the limitations discussed in chapter 4.

◆ ◆ ◆ ◆ ◆

The most important benefit to showmen is the Showman's Guild, a modern trade union run with selective entry to preserve high standards.

> *"It has to fight on many fronts, against Government legislation,....*
> *property developers, killjoys and prejudice."* Duncan Dallas.

The Guild controls the letting of pitches on fairgrounds, and these are subjected to a 'Two-Year Rule' by which previous occupants have right of first refusal. The Guild also limits rentals, and protects the interests of full-time stallholders. There is almost no expansion, only 1% of new members being accepted annually, and these are usually already linked through their families to the Guild. The Guild also successfully campaigned for lower road tax for the HGVs-used seasonally - and since 1926, special rates have been available. Showmen are also excluded from permanent caravan-site legislation; as winter-quarters are only occupied for a proportion of the year. Many Travellers would like the benefits of protection and legislation that membership of the Guild provides. But, as previously said, few can be admitted. It is a close, closed group, and other societies, such as the Roundabout Operators provide an alternative.

The biggest difference, apart from the show itself of course, is that some show people:

"have become flatties, setting up snooker halls, cafes and pubs,
buying chalets and hotels, sometimes owning a ride as a subsidised hobby."

Scotsman on Sunday.

Whilst Travellers are adopting the skills of performance and presentation, they operate as individuals at gatherings or busking. Showmen operate a whole fair.

◆ ◆ ◆ ◆ ◆

A fairground winter-quarters was visited so that implications of Travellers on the lives of showmen could be discussed. Generally they said that Travellers had had little impact. All fairground bookings tend to be on council land, often in town centres and therefore not used by Travellers. The only problems are when a short term stopping place, the 'Atchin Tan' of the Gypsies, has been ditched-off due to Travellers having been evicted from the site.

CIRCUS

The history of the circus lies parallel with the development of fairgrounds until the 1950's, when they became divergent affairs. The most obvious change to the circus came in the last decade, when animal rights activists spoke out against acts involving wild animals, especially elephants, bears and the big cats. Recent years have seen the emergence of jugglers, clowns and fire-eaters etc. on Traveller sites and festivals, as well as in the commercial big top.

Uni-cyclist

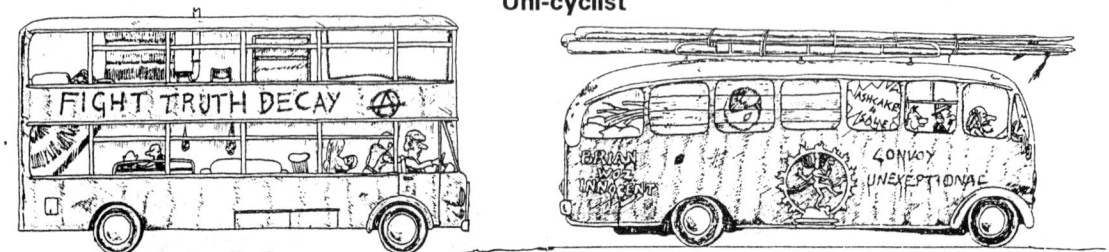

The old family circuses continue a circuit of seasonal performances, retiring to winter quarters annually. These are often on land which has been bought specifically to cater for the circus needs. Performers develop their skills, equipment is repaired and repainted, children have a chance to attend local state schools. In contrast, Travellers may use their skills for busking, site entertainment, or cabaret; as well as participating in organised circus - which often spend a great deal of time in Europe.

One such company, under Pierrot Pillot-Bidon originated in France, but picked up performers in Britain and elsewhere to join the motley collection of tents, caravans and trailers on the road. They referred to their Archaos as "The Life" and Pierrot said:
> *"If we lived safe bourgeois lives in a safe bourgeois town,*
> *how could we push our imagination to the limit?"*

Instead, until a fire destroyed their big tent, they took pyrotechnics, chainsaws, motorcycles, fumes and decibel limits to the absolute limit.

◆ ◆ ◆ ◆ ◆

At the winter quarters of three circuses we talked about the changes precipitated by Travellers. One circus had just 'opened' for the season, but nobody on the winter site anticipated any hassle from the new legislation. The circuit is always organised well in advance, and land is usually council-owned, near town centres, and protected from squatting. The winter site itself had been bought many years ago, and was a disused airfield and P.O.W. camp. The circus Travellers pointed out that they were subject to the wild animal laws, and all paid council tax, vehicle tax etc.

Having said that Travellers had not affected them, though, there was quite deep condemnation:
> *"They leave crap everywhere...."*
> *"They make Gypsies seem respectable-that's the one*
> *good thing they've done."*
> *"Ask Bob about them, he knows, he slept with one and regretted it later....!"*

On the prospect of new age performers without animals, there was similar lack of interest:
> *"People won't come if there's no animals, see."*

And it was pointed out that the nearest the circus came to hassle from Travellers was the arrival of 'hippy' protesters waving placards about animal rights at the turnstile. The circus Travellers have found a secure niche within the community, and have little time to consider or debate the problems of a group of nomads whose paths never cross theirs.

WATER TRAVELLERS

Hundreds of thousands holiday each year on Britain's rivers and canals. British Waterways Board has promoted what was a major 19th century. form of industrial communication as a major holiday resource. Narrow-boats and barges, the traditional form of transportation on the

canal network are frequently emblazoned with waterway's folk art, castles and roses painted in the same styles as the artwork on Gypsy vardos. However, beneath the romanticised image of the 'Water-Gypsy,' often used in advertising brochures, the reality facing people wanting to live full-time afloat, is far from unhassled.

There are no official figures for people living permanently on the canals and rivers. Some pay fees for a mooring, which can be an exorbitant £40 p.w., all year round, whether they are there or not. Others keep on the move, and moor up on legal and illegal quays and riverbanks. The theory is that if you move a full boat's length each day, you cannot be moved on. However, BWB officials often operate differently. Many of the canal and riverbanks are private property, and holidaymakers in tupperware boats and anglers enjoy much more tolerance than permanent Water-Travellers.

Unlike most of the land-based Travellers described elsewhere in this book, the vast majority of Water-Travellers do not identify with those on the road. The narrowboat and barge dwellers are probably the elite, because it is the traditional form of canal transport; but people are living full-time in everything from half-submerged 12 foot fibreglass cabin cruisers through to yachts (wind and steam powered) coal butties, house boats and even ex-life boats.

In some areas of the country, particularly around Worcester, Gloucester and Tewkesbury, there has been a fluid movement of Travellers between the land and the water, and much more 'new age' associated interest in travelling traditions, the environment, and all things mystical and spiritual. The Shropshire Union, Staffs & Worcester, and Worcester-Birmingham canals are probably 'home' to more Water Travellers than elsewhere.

The similarities and differences within the water-travelling fraternity is akin to the range encountered amongst house-dwellers. Some have every electronic gadget which can be powered by battery or generator; others have no loo, no electric power, and make do with candles or paraffin for light, and a range or wood burner for cooking and heating. We know of a number of Travellers who work from their boats in a range of occupations from coal person

Narrowboat Life on the cut

to writers, boat-builders and painters to actors - performing shows from their two narrowboats. As with Travellers on the land, the sense of community, self-help and shared support is much in evidence; as are the dogs, children, wooding tools and the tat of park ups and sites.

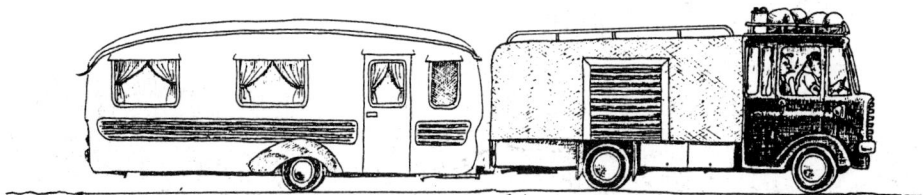

Kathy, whose boat has moved round various moorings between Worcester and Gloucester, works intermittently in shops, and has lived in a caravan with Travellers for other years of her life. This free movement between land and water travel happens naturally, but with little help from the various authorities who licence boats. They try to insist on ever more rigorous rules of compliance - like a road vehicle's M.O.T. - but covering health and safety factors, as well as maintenance of hull, steerage and engine.

◆ ◆ ◆ ◆ ◆

As has been shown, Travellers are, to a certain extent, adopting the traditional skills of other types of nomadic people. And just as legislation has persecuted them in the past, so new Travellers have taken on the role of scapegoat now.

Legislative action against Gypsies and Showmen is being repeated and increased against Travellers; rumours of the deviant behaviour of those past Travellers existed, but modern media makes the myths about new Travellers more exaggerated. Parents warned their children about not running away to join the Gypsies, fairgrounds and circuses - as they warn today about crusties, ravers and hippies.

Yet all these cultures have grown and developed in time; have become more acceptable to the settled communities who once felt threatened by them. With understanding and tolerance on all sides, this could happen again. Fighting is negative energy, whilst co-operating is positive. Travellers have a great deal to learn from the legal, social and moral battles fought by nomads in the past, but would benefit from a greater sharing of knowledge and ideas. Civil Rights groups fight for every oppressed minority, and we can only hope that they succeed in helping support all Travellers at this time of repressive legislation.

WOBBLE F.C.

Chapter Seven:
What Future?

There is an awful lot of travelling to be done, and someone has got to do it.

— Woodie Guthrie.

Do Travellers have a future in Britain? Several thousand obviously believe that they do, but lives are being adapted to suit the harsh conditions of continuing a way of life established by a bunch of dreamers twenty years ago. There are all sorts of problems to be overcome, yet there are endless possibilities for compromise. Those complacently watching the harassment of this minority, would do well to remember that everybody should have a right to live the way they choose - deviance does not necessarily mean dangerous! Changes in attitude, policy and practice are needed on all counts - from public to media, to the most extreme Travellers - if any kind of harmony is ever to be achieved.

Civil Liberties

The current Government campaigns against Travellers have been likened to the Nazi persecution of Gypsies during the second world war. Whilst the seventeenth century laws making it illegal to be a Gypsy were repealed during the following century, the proposed new legislation is a major infringement of basic human rights.

> _"What perturbs me is that if 'hippies' can be sent packing, who is next? The Gypsies? The Irish? The Asians? The West Indians?"_
> _Dennis Binns. 'How to de-commission a lifestyle.'_

The Declaration of Human Rights states in article 13 that everyone has the right to freedom of movement and residence within the borders of each State. Yet the new police surveillance on vehicles and their drivers is in conflict with this.

> _"It's a fundamental infringement of civil liberties to put someone under surveillance because there is a chance they might break the law."_ Andrew Puddephat. Liberty.

> _"Under these laws it's going to be illegal to be nomadic. We will all be criminals overnight."_ Charlie Smith. National Gypsy Council.

Article 20 of the Declaration states that: everyone has the rights to peaceful assembly and association. The proposed limit of six vehicles parking up together; the banning of processions (i.e. more than one person) walking towards Stonehenge; the turning- back of cars within a five-mile radius of a gathering; the confiscation of sound systems. All seem to be contraventions of this basic right. The Stonehenge Peoples' Free Festival was a 'peaceful assembly' until the police became involved from 1985 onwards.

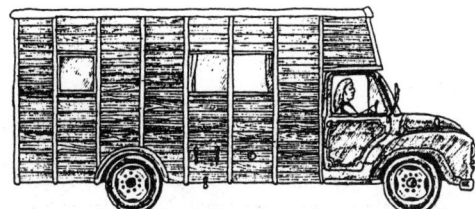

*"There should be a proper balance between the civil liberties and freedom of
people to travel without hindrance on their legitimate business, and the rights of
people to live their lives without having their peace and quiet infringed by a
sudden influx of people."*   Alan Michael. Labour M.P.

Six vehicles limits most Travellers to family units only:

*"We have a bus, a truck, two vans and a motorbike between us - so that's
the limit; we can't visit anyone, and they can't visit us either."*   Fiona.

The Government makes much of caring for the dispossessed in the former Yugoslavia, and of
establishing safe havens for the Kurds, yet are prepared to do nothing about the problem on
their own doorstep.

*"It's all very well having legislation, but Travellers are not going to
disappear in a cloud of smoke, so they and the way they wish to
live need to be accommodated in some way."*
                     Pat Merrick, Malvern D.C. Chairman.

In 1991, more than 1,000,000 private houses and flats were deemed unfit for human
habitation; an increasing number of homes are repossessed as the recession continues;
squatting has been made almost impossible; young people cannot claim housing benefit.
So where are these Travellers supposed to go? With laws impounding their homes; authorities
dividing their families, and imprisonment for resisting arrest; the future seems bleak, but
Travellers do have their own solutions, if only the Government would listen to them. Arrests,
bed and breakfast accommodation, and finding permanent homes for maybe 5,000 individuals
could cost the Government £250,000 p.w. It would be much cheaper and more practical to
come to some arrangement about site provision.

*"Travellers are not just festival goers, they wish to live a normal lifestyle 365 days a
year in peace like any other family."*   John Harrison.

As Travellers cannot be classified as an ethnic minority, having no common cultural or religious
bond, this cannot strictly speaking be called ethnic cleansing. But it is certainly a heavy-handed
approach to solving what the Government deems a problem.

*"They don't just inhibit us, they inhibit everybody. The general public has
lost the use of common land, not just the Travellers. And if they hadn't restricted
us from common land, there wouldn't be a problem."*   Gary.

Sites

Wary of being treated as the Gypsies were after the Caravan Sites Act of 1968, Travellers are
careful about their requests for land. Under present designation, a Gypsy accepting a place on
a council site generally has to reside there semi-permanently. The sites are often quite bleak,
with concrete standing, and basic blocks of toilets/standpipes etc. A fellow Gypsy is usually in
charge of the site, many of which are in places that other members of the population would
find undesirable - such as near motorways and on the outskirts of hard-to-let council estates.
Travellers are careful about how they define a site:

• It should be transit - for short or long stay, depending on the needs of
individuals;

• Hard standing and grass should be available;
• Basic amenities should be provided;
• Visitors should not be registered constantly.

Bar at Wrekin site

There are many areas of potentially suitable land in Britain, which include:

-Green lanes / commons where Travellers have traditionally stopped for centuries. Both can be used by small numbers without damage being done.

-Disused council land - areas either awaiting development, or just lying empty would be suitable.

-M.O.D land - acres of green land, well away from houses and settled communities are reserved for occasional M.O.D use. The areas with most potential are the hundreds of disused airfields abandoned after W.W.II, and much of Salisbury Plain.

-Sympathetic landowners - there have been several cases in which landowners have fought local authorities for the right of Travellers to live on their land. Proposed legislation states that: "It is a criminal offence to park any living vehicle on any land without the consent of the owner." Yet even with this consent, the owner may be subject to fines up to £20,000 if there is no planning permission. Councils usually oppose such permission.

Those Travellers who have managed to buy a small piece of land have generally been harassed off it, as they have no planning permission to be there. A national network of sites would be beneficial on all counts.

"I want to live, I don't want to be forever fighting. I can't get anything together if I'm being hassled from pillar to post."   Gary.

Travellers could build up their skills, and become involved with local communities. Police forces

could then direct their energies towards preventing crime, rather than moving on nomadic people. Children would have the option of settled schooling.

Of course Travellers will continue to migrate abroad, to sites in Europe, and festivals in India, where legislation is less restrictive .

> *"Yet for every Traveller that quits Britain for the continent,*
> *there's likely to be masses of replacements."*   Media commentary. 8/5/93.

In the long run, transit site provision would be much cheaper than relentless persecution and potential cost of re-housing those who own nothing and have nowhere to go.

Spain

In Denmark and Holland there are settled communities of buses where wood, water and hygiene are provided. These self-help initiatives have built into very successful groups which are self-sufficient and comfortable.

Talley, the alternative community of tipi dwellers near Cwmdu in Wales, has been fighting legal battles since the mid-seventies. Although the hundred or so acres are owned by the inhabitants of the nomadic homes, local authorities have persistently tried to clear the land over the last decade. One official admitted that:

> *"I can't honestly see the authority ever being in a position to get rid of them."*

But it takes dedication and persistence to maintain such a challenge. In future, those on their own land may find it even more awkward.

Groups such as the Rainbow Circle maintain their nomadic lifestyle through safe havens, where parking up is tolerated or even invited. They arrange their own series of special spiritual celebrations throughout the year. These take place on borrowed land, and are highly organised,

drawing punters who want a peaceful alternative experience. However, in order to continue these, the Rainbow Circle, which started

"with a jar full of 50p pieces" Sid.

has had to become a company, or forfeit insurance cover.

Some Travellers are committed to preventing unnecessary road construction:

"The land is my birthright and it is my duty to protect it." Mark.

They are dedicated to peaceful protest:

"We would just sit on their machinery for 30 minutes and the workers would just knock off for the day." Jo.

- The World can live without us.
- We cannot live without it.
- We are the problem.
- We must be the solution.
- We will destroy the world along with ourselves.

"It's time to save our lives"

Icewalk International Student Expedition, 1989

So the way forward in terms of site provision and needs are varied. Some want to be in urban areas; some in rural; some want to stay in one area; others to keep moving; some have a cause, others don't. But there is no way that legislation can make several thousand people disappear. Coercion and intimidation often have the effect of creating unity within Traveller groups and even more resolve against authorities and oppression. Sites of some kind must be provided, and the reform of the Caravan Sites Act is a step backwards, rather than forwards; a negative solution, rather than positive one.

"The proposed changes in the law are going to cost a lot of money. For the police and local authorities it's going to have implications for seizing vehicles, storing them, as well as taking children into care and providing homes for them. What should be happening is local authorities should be making sure that sites are provided, both temporary and permanent." Jenny Smith. Shelter.

Festivals

Paying music festivals are very anti-Traveller involvement now, even though a lot of the initial setting-up and the later clearing-up is completed by paid Travellers.

> *"Gone are the days of spontaneity where stars were born; bands are now booked months in advance." Big Issue. 14/5/93.*

Proposed legislation will make illegal raves almost impossible to organise, with police having powers of seizing property and arresting individuals.

> *"Free festivals were set up as an antidote to the increasing commerciality which has beset Glastonbury, Reading and the like. They've spawned bands who've now crossed over and enjoy sell-out tours in their own right." Big Issue.*

An increasing number of Travellers are attracted to Vintage and Steam fairs and Bike Rallies. There is generally great appreciation of old vehicles and their restoration. A classic vehicle on site stands out, especially if it has been rescued and rebuilt.

> *"At the Great Dorset Steam Fair, there were a few dozen Traveller vehicles in the camping car parks. The whole event was really peaceful and without prejudice, People who love their vehicles also love anyone who takes an interest in them."*
>
> *Fiona.*

Stonehenge

English Heritage has launched a campaign to improve facilities for tourists to the monument, through the creation of a massive car park and a visitor centre.

> *"....that's destruction on a scale the hippies could never hope to achieve." Richard W.*

Whilst no-one would deny that the greatest access possible to this amazing monument should be allowed, there has been no indication of restoring the rights of people wanting to celebrate the solstice ceremonies there. Many Travellers would still like the spiritual access which has a profound effect on their lives.

The Stonehenge campaign continues - how can anyone own an ancient monument?

Internal Survival

The increasing difficulty of receiving the social security benefits to which they are entitled, and a reluctance to be owned and controlled by the State, has encouraged the establishment of many successful businesses run by Travellers. These may be the traditional rides of showmen, or the alternative presentations of new circuses and cabarets. Some have built up sound systems, and others have established a mechanic's trade. They are as diverse as the people running them, but are an important aspect in a move towards independence from Government intervention. Some benefits include the chance to qualify as a showman's rig, and be subjected to less rigorous trespass laws if a show is provided.

Sharon's life:
"We travel 7 months out of the year, attending Fayres, Festivals and Rallies with our hand turned juvenile rides. It is hard work, but compatible and fun for us and our kids, who help and have fun. This is one of the trades we've built up over the years and we hope to hand over to our kids to carry on with when they are ready to.

We try our hands at most things to earn enough to be self- sufficient. I sometimes work for other people such as farmers, picking fruit or tractor driving."

Fire

Fire has had a fascination for humankind from the dawn of time to our modern age, and its manipulation is a thrilling experience for audiences of all ages.

Fiery Tales

Sacred Flame Fire Theatre uses circus fire skills and stunning pyrotechnics in a dramatic setting to spin tales of mystery and adventure. These dazzling one-woman shows appeal to a wide variety of audiences and are suitable for daytime events, but work best of all at night. The various fiery tales are all 20 minutes in length.

Ancient Fires

Some of Sacred Flame's fiery tales have become very popular at historical and re-enactment events. Taking inspiration from myth and legend, with an imaginative mix of atmospheric period music, these shows make a unique addition to any historical event. Entertainment can also be provided for banquets.

Ring of Fire

Sacred Flame can offer a dramatic and dazzling contribution to any small circus in the best of new circus style, using an unusual range of fire skills and breathtaking effects. This show is set to up-to-the-minute music and lasts a breathless five minutes!

By taking on business responsibilities, people have more to risk, and are not inclined to become involved in conflict. They need a semi-permanent base, and still have the means to travel as necessary. This way forward is positive, but is being threatened by the proposed complex and damaging new laws. Lizzy, for example, of Sacred Flame, is moving to Ireland this summer, rather than fight legal battles as well as performing her trade.

Education

The future funding of Traveller Education Service departments is under much debate, and it is generally agreed that a policy of integration will predominate. The T.S.C. must therefore accept a new responsibility to provide adequate information and resources for Traveller parents to provide a responsible alternative to State education.

If leading a nomadic life is criminalised, parents will face losing their children if they cannot prove efficient care and education at home. With much media exposure of abuse within the child care system, and the statistics showing how State care can encourage criminal behaviour; it is surprising that it could be deemed better than a secure communal base with at least one parent, siblings and friends.

Traveller Groups

There are a multitude of Traveller help groups. These include the Traveller-initiated organisations, such as T.A.T., FFT and the T.S.C., as well as those financed by charitable groups , such as S.C.F. and Shelter. The first group supply various needs, but funds depend on efficient grant applications and fund raising events. It is sometimes difficult to co-ordinate a group of Travellers, and ensure that meetings go ahead. The other groups have been increasingly affected by Government legislation and pressure to ensure that help is not made available for the Traveller minority. The S.C.F mailing provided for T.S.C., for example, is likely to be abandoned.

Also important are the efforts of dedicated volunteers or poorly paid workers who have offered advice and aid throughout the country. These include a number of the Gypsy organisations and small-scale publishers like Monolith, Unique, Bridestone and Fevered Imaginings.

Various areas have regional support groups which help with legal advice, health care, etc, and there is a support group for parents and families of Travellers which meets quite frequently. All these and other advice bases, will be crucial in the next few years if the Traveller community is to survive the legislative onslaught from the Conservative Government.

Politics

Future survival of this lifestyle is quite dependent on the policies of Governments to come. The various parties have made different statements regarding the needs of Travellers. the Labour party, in particular, has a positive campaign for providing adequate and efficient sites, and includes Travellers within its working parties. They believe in the fundamental right to travel.

Travellers believe they have a right to continue a nomadic life, and the community gains strength as it unites to fight for survival in the face of media and legislative opposition. The future is uncertain, but there will be one. Travellers will not just vanish, and whatever oppressive measures are taken, those who believe in the right to live as nomads and Travellers will continue to live their lifestyle.

The role of Travellers within communities and the country as a whole needs clarification and positive encouragement, rather than the negative persecution which only brings out the worst in everyone.

◆ ◆ ◆ ◆ ◆

To end the book in an appropriate way we asked some Travellers and workers with Travellers for their answer to the question: **"What future?"**.

What Future.....words from Travellers, our friends and others.

Sharon:
"The future would look bright with prospects of more work through the spring/summer/autumn, and maybe earn enough some day to buy a plot of land for our homes;

and have time to establish cultural, educational and resource facilities (or centres) to preserve our way of living. I believe have a tribal recognition with most other Travellers. But, future laws and legislation threaten our rights to travel and also to gather for Fayres; this will certainly make the future more difficult than it already is for all of us.

Travellers do not need criminalisation, just a right to stay. I'm a Traveller, not a criminal. A little respect from settled communities wouldn't cost a penny."

♦ ♦ ♦ ♦ ♦

Glen:
"I have been living on the ROAD as a Traveller for a number of years and in the last five years the whole scene has deteriorated immensely i.e. loads of dickhead from council estates inheritance and general Doughnuts, who think it is all owed them. That us **real** people owe them for some reason or another, and they don't have to do anything except sit around all day picking their noses. You've seen 'em, the types who think that para boots and baggy jumpers are some sort of designer wear.

They walk with their heads down; have they not got the strength to hold their heads up? I may be a self-opinionated bastard, but they are dragging the rest of us down, when we are living this way for a reason. They just think it's an easy way to live, 'cos they don't have to be responsible for even themselves. The only good thing about the new laws is that this'll weed out the wankers, and the rest of us can get on with our lives without the handbag brigade."

♦ ♦ ♦ ♦ ♦

Lou:
"I'm not sure what's to happen come April with these new laws; I hope nothing too sad goes down. I'm so glad I'm staying in a house just now, as living on the road is shit now with everyone on the verges and lay-bys. Things just aren't what they used to be. Loads of people are so lunched out now compared to a few years ago - Spain or houses seem to be the plan for everyone I know."

♦ ♦ ♦ ♦ ♦

John, aged 11:
"It's getting harder for us to stop anywhere and I think in the future it's just going to be illegal to have a vehicle that moves around on the road that you live in. I'm gonna fight against them. If they win I'll just go somewhere else; carry on travelling. I won't live in a house."

♦ ♦ ♦ ♦ ♦

Fiona:
"The future legislation is under debate, but I believe that there will always be a core of Travellers in Britain, and that one day, our vision of life will be acknowledged and appreciated."

♦ ♦ ♦ ♦ ♦

Friends, Families and Travellers' Support Group
Steve Staines:
"This was formed by Steve Staines who is an ex-soil scientist turned teacher with a son and grand-daughter on the road. the idea of getting people like himself involved in Traveller issues started when he visited his Traveller family on a number of sites and realised that their life had much to offer, and was under threat. The group has grown from small beginnings and may be able to become a significant national voice bringing together Travellers, their friends and supporters as well as professionals in the field. As well as significant publicity, particularly in the south and west, the group has produced a newsletter and also held the first of a planned

series of meetings in major centre of population. Plans for the future include:
- the creation of a networked crisis line for Travellers;
- provision of advice and information;
- promotion of a positive view of Travellers and their culture;
- development of model policies for local authorities to use;
- development of a resource base for Travellers.

What future?..... At the time of writing it seems likely that the Criminal Justice and Public Order Bill will go through parliament without major revision to the clauses which relate to Travellers. The increased powers will mean that the whole of England and Wales will become effectively designated, and the local authorities and police will have summary eviction powers for all illegal camping. The future very much depends on how these powers are used. The worst case scenario would be of groups of Travellers being harried from pillar to post until they are unable to move through exhaustion or lack of money for diesel. Travellers may be arrested, fined and/or imprisoned and their homes seized. Their homes may end up being destroyed if they are unable to find the money for vehicle pound charges.

The best case scenario, which FFT will try to help with, would be positive co-operation between councils, Travellers and police so that a policy of toleration was pursued. Tolerated sites could be serviced by councils via facilities agreements for which Travellers would make a contribution to costs. These would apply to short-term sites where Travellers would agree to move on after a stated time period. Councils could also provide limited period planning permissions for sites on farmland where permanent settlement would not be envisaged. Farmers could make a charge for such sites. Councils should, according to recently issued planning guidelines, offer advice and practical help with planning procedures to Gypsies who wish to acquire their own land for development. This assumes, of course, that all Travellers be given the status of Gypsies under these planning guidelines. I fear that this scenario will not happen without a great change of attitude on the part of councils and officials, and a willingness of Travellers to take part in the planning process."

♦ ♦ ♦ ♦ ♦

Ann Bagehot:
"I was born and raised in Kenya, which was a cosmopolitan place, buzzing with many races, languages and cultures. Perhaps it explains my view that people being different does not threaten my culture or way of life. It is not necessary to destroy them to ensure that my ideas survive.

I've worked with Gypsies and Travellers since 1974, being a part of the gradual increase in site provision and then the horrors of the Beanfield and the need to extend my work to newer Travellers and their children. I am sad and anxious about the future, because it is almost certain that the Criminal Justice and Public Order Bill will become an Act by July/August 1994 and then the evictions will start in earnest.

However, I do see several large chinks of light, in that large organisations from Child Care to Barristers and Public Relations, are concerned and want to help. Churches, journalists, TV programmes and interested individuals are succeeding in raising the issues, exposing the distortions and the unacceptable consequences of the new law, and more people **are** becoming aware of the truth. That is where we will succeed in getting other voters to back the sensible,

cost-effective and socially responsible alternatives: Transit sites; Facilities Agreements; Housing Association accommodation; more Council sites, and positive help for those who can afford a private site. Public opinion will win the day and we need to educate that opinion. Democratic accountability will win in the end."

◆ ◆ ◆ ◆ ◆

John Harrison:
"Although I've spent most of my life living in seven different houses, I have lived in a caravan for six months and attended many festivals all over the country since I attended the 1984 Stonehenge Free Festival. I'm a Traveller in the sense that I travel around a lot. I've travelled all over this country as well as Ireland, Europe, Greece, India and Egypt. I've been very much involved in the Stonehenge campaign since 1985 and promoting Travellers'/Human Rights via my magazine 'Monolith News.' I have also published other booklets on the subjects of Travellers and Stonehenge and recently written a children's story titled 'Gnorman and the Gnomon.'

*What Future?......*I first met the so-called New Age Travellers ten years ago at the Stonehenge free festival in June 1984. I remember at some festivals how friendly the police were and Welsh farmers joining us for the evening's entertainment. It makes me feel old talking about 'the good old days.' I remember waking up to beautiful sunrises, birds singing and the wind rustling in the trees. I remember waking up to see a different view form the van window of ancient sites; Stonehenge, Glastonbury Tor, Uffington White Horse and Rollright stones. I remember sitting around bonfires late at night until early morning with friends under the stars, discussing the meaning of life and being able to hear ourselves talk and the kids asleep in bed in their mobile homes.

Site meeting

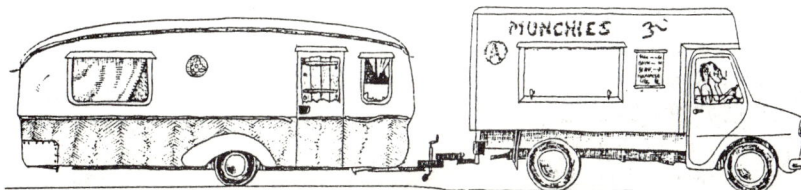

The numbers increased though, as well as the noise. Many of the ravers had good intentions, others not. The Travellers' children were forgotten, as well as the locals in their houses. Norman Tebbit said 'Get on your bike' to look for work. The Travellers were already on four wheels, but most still couldn't find work. Technology is taking the jobs away. The pied piper of the industrial revolution brought people off the land and into the cities. The Travellers returned to that land.

The Government said we should all help ourselves. The Travellers provided their own self-sufficient mobile homes, saving the tax-payer money by not claiming housing benefit, yet still got called scroungers. The Conservatives say they are for the family values, yet now they plan to disrupt and possibly split up travelling families. They say there is no suitable land for Travellers, yet want more set-aside land from farmers. Now, they are cutting the defence budget and making soldiers unemployed, so perhaps they will have some spare MOD land for the Travellers on Salisbury Plain or elsewhere.

And, of course, there seems to be plenty of available land to build new roads and motorways!

The Travellers have a lot to offer if only given a chance. They are skilled and willing to work, just like the unemployed in the cities. They can cook you a good vegetarian meal, mend your car, make all sorts of crafts, paint you a beautiful picture or dig your garden. I say; selfish ignorant politicians......Not in this age, not in any age. Let others speak for these selfish ignorant politicians."

◆　◆　◆　◆　◆

George Firsoff (FIN):

"I feel let down by the Traveller movement. The Free Festival movement and the issue of religious access to Stonehenge, for which I have campaigned for years, and continue to campaign, have been totally taken over in the media and the academic world by the issue of 'Travellers' and I am annoyed that no attention whatever is paid to the needs of CITY DWELLERS having open access to the countryside. To some extent, supporters of the Travellers' rights and enthusiasts for the Traveller way of life are responsible for this false attitude, although of course, I accept the police and media propaganda are also responsible for looking upon us as 'Travellers.' Perhaps Travellers should pay some attention to our existence?

Once upon a time, Free Festivals attracted thousands of young people from cities and I think that the main reason they stopped coming, and the festivals themselves died, is because the festivals and the Travellers' movement within it, were unable and often unwilling to cope with the violence and banditry of a minority of their number, and NOT because of police harassment. This happened in the late '80's. There is a big alternative movement within which Travellers are not particularly a source of inspiration at the moment, and my own needs are served nowadays by organising our own, legal, green spiritual camps. At the request of the owners we deal with, these do not usually accommodate living vehicles and usually do not permit dogs, certainly not unrestrained dogs.

having cleared up any misconception about my own role, I must of course say that our network publicises police abuses of the law, and the Government's current attacks on the Traveller life style through legislation, along with all the other abuses and attacks motivated by

the landowners' lobby and the *'back to the 1950's'* movement in the Tory party. Thus, we support the rights of Travellers and their right to be treated as citizens with regard to the law, being treated as being innocent until proved guilty, for instance. Instead, we have a Society without understanding or any education in the fundamental principles of human rights, believing in *'collective guilt''* and *'collective punishment''* of minorities, including Travellers. This is the same as fascism."

Gubby:

I came to travelling in 1979 from squatting houses to squatting land. Part of the late seventies unemployment boom, I was looking to make the best of it + Stonehenge '79 gave me a glimpse of something better than the traps + trappin' of conformity. I work as an artist tho' am mainly supported/paid off by the state.

As to what future ; I should imagine that, as in the past, the lot of travellers will be dependent on the conditions imposed from without, + will adapt accordingly. Whatever happens it is sure to be entirly different from either the intentions of government or the aspirations of travellers, it might help if the government accepted the existence of travellers + that they cannot legislate it out. ●

The present government agenda supposedly is to make it easier for travellers to buy land with one hand, while squeezing out the illegal/'official' sites with the other, this will go though the usual run of appeasing local opposition, official inertia etc. etc. also the obvious problem that most travellers can't afford to buy land anyway.

One positive outcome might be some relaxing of the planning laws that prevent residence on agricultural/common land, this being the main obstruction to freindly landowners allowing travellers to occupy otherwise useless bits of land. I hope that might result in more people living in fields + on droves + less on lay-bys.

Unfortunately there seems little opportunity for travellers to travel now, this seems to have taken a lot of the fun /exchange of ideas out of it, a few good festivals might help

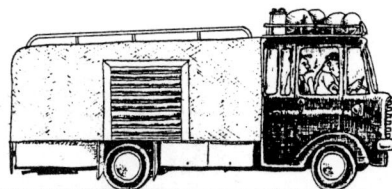

Tammy, aged 8:
"I want to keep travelling with my dad. I live in a trailer and I've got a van to tow the trailer. When I am older I am going to be horse-drawn. I was living in a house with my mummy, but I came to live with my dad in a caravan. I like living with my dad in a caravan more than a house, because I can be with the horses and I've got more friends with my dad and more room to play. I like living on a site more than a house."

◆ ◆ ◆ ◆ ◆

Luke:
It has got to the stage now where travelling is a way of life for a large number of people, many of whom are families. With a second generation who know no other existence, it is strange for the powers that be to think that by changing a few laws they will be rid of the problem. This is a fallacy. Many a time I've been questioned as to what I do in the winter, 'why don't I go home?' The future needs to hold a greater understanding of our ways of life and accepting the fact that a culture cannot be destroyed. Travellers also need greater integration with Society, of whom, the majority still think that we are all one band of special brew swigging layabouts. We don't need to be isolated even more.

We have a lot to offer Society, if all parties were just a little more tolerant. In truth, the future scares me, and I can't see any way forward unless my idealistic views were shared by many more people, but all I can do now is sit and wait until such a time as these new laws are implemented, and I dread to think what may happen."

◆ ◆ ◆ ◆ ◆

Steve:
"I am twenty nine years old and have been travelling for almost ten years. For nearly half of this time I have been travelling with horses, but now my horses are moved by means of a horse-box and I reside in a twenty one foot trailer.

I have spent these years in various forms of employment, from cartwrighting to stockman on various hill farms. I have even been kennelman for a pack of foxhounds.

The future in this country for me at the moment seems very bleak. Our freedom as Travellers over the years has been eroded in various ways and means. The Government has tried many draconian methods to remove us from the face of the earth i.e. the Beanfield, Stoney Cross etc. But these approaches caused such a public outrage, that they are now trying a more covert approach, almost using the 'give them enough rope' scenario, with a gentle (or not so gentle) shove in the wrong direction.

With the introduction of the CJB, we been pinpointed as convenient scapegoats for the whole of the traditional travelling fraternity. It is our fault, with our loud rave music and unruly convoys that it is becoming illegal to live in a caravan, or so the Government would have you believe.
Personally, though, I dislike rave music immensely and I am only forced through circumstance to live and travel in large groups, through the general intolerance of people which seems greatly media-induced. So, at the moment there seems very few reasonable avenues open to any of my travelling family in this country. It saddens me greatly to have to admit this, as in the whole of my life I have done nothing more illegal than live in a caravan and work and play hard.

But it seems that in the near future our lives stand to be made very miserable, with planned witch-hunts; also with emergence of some very frightening travelling elites, working along purity of race lines. So it seems the options available are either move into a house or leave this beautiful country of ours."

◆   ◆   ◆   ◆   ◆

Roddy Glasse, Traveller and photographer:
"To be honest, with all the appalling things that happen in the world each day, the wars, the starving, the endless list of socially and ecologically dreadful human conduct and suffering, I feel rather uncomfortable with all the attention focused on our lifestyle. Maybe if this attention was focused on more important issue, people might start to think rather than judge.

The only benefit I've been able to see in this level of attention paid to our lives is that it might serve to highlight a few issues completely central to the future of the planet and all its people. In recent years, the media hype, the social conditions in Britain and the resulting several-fold increase in the numbers of people travelling has left the important issues lost in a mass of Bullshit. However, one thing is almost certain; for whatever reason people may be travelling, we live, either deliberately or unintentionally, more sustainable lives than most of those who are presently considered 'normal.' It is not perfect, but, nonetheless, living how we do consumes a lot less of the world's resources and causes a lot less pollution than normal civilised Western lifestyles.

And just how civilised is it to be.......living the Modern Life in the 1990's? the writing has long been on the wall, and it says: 'Live More Simply.' The chronic damage done to the rivers, seas, forests, lakes, the atmosphere, our world - damage made worse every day in pursuit of western style progress and growth. But this 'growth 'really means 'consumption,' and soon there will be nothing left worth having.

Even in the meantime, whilst this reckless abuse of the earth continues, it has only been possible for things to last like this for as long as they have done because most people in the world live much more simple lives, including many starving in dust bowls. In contrast, a real, genuine sharing of the world's resources could provide a decent life for all the world's people. This planet definitely cannot provide and sustain western style civilisation for six and a half billion humans. This is an 'I'm all right, Jack - Fuck You' attitude on a global scale, and an intrinsic lack of respect for the peoples of the world, their cultures and lifestyles.

The only numerically significant group of people in the U.K, with something approaching a sustainable lifestyle are Travellers, yet we're set up as the bad guys and proposals to give us a hard time are given priority. Wake up....Let's get our priorities right...the adult population has the opportunity to change how we live. Children alive already may find that when they have grown up, it is already too late. Do we want to tell the kids in a few years time, how we lived through decades of destruction and poisoning of our environment?

Or, are we going to do something different, instead of just scapegoating others?

Take responsibility for our lives
Planet Death only occurs with our complicity.
75,000 acres of Rainforest logged every day.
The air and sea, a soup of chemicals.
More and more land disappears under concrete and tarmac.
50-100 species extinct each day and on and on,
    all in pursuit of western style prosperity;
Surely it's time to start learning.......
    ....from our mistakes?
I don't expect or desire everyone to become a Traveller, but rather than being up-tight about the people who may try something different, let's first consider just how good you can feel about the status quo."

◆ ◆ ◆ ◆ ◆

Landrover Tom:
What future indeed! With the present authoritarianism, it would appear that the lifestyle of many is seriously under threat. With the state of existing laws and laws to be, hundreds will be searching for a direction in which to turn.

Children, for whom the travelling life is the norm, will certainly be disillusioned with a changing and eventually alien existence. The changes will be sudden, and the impact and the implications immeasurable. Our choice, Our voices and Our way of life denied. What Future?

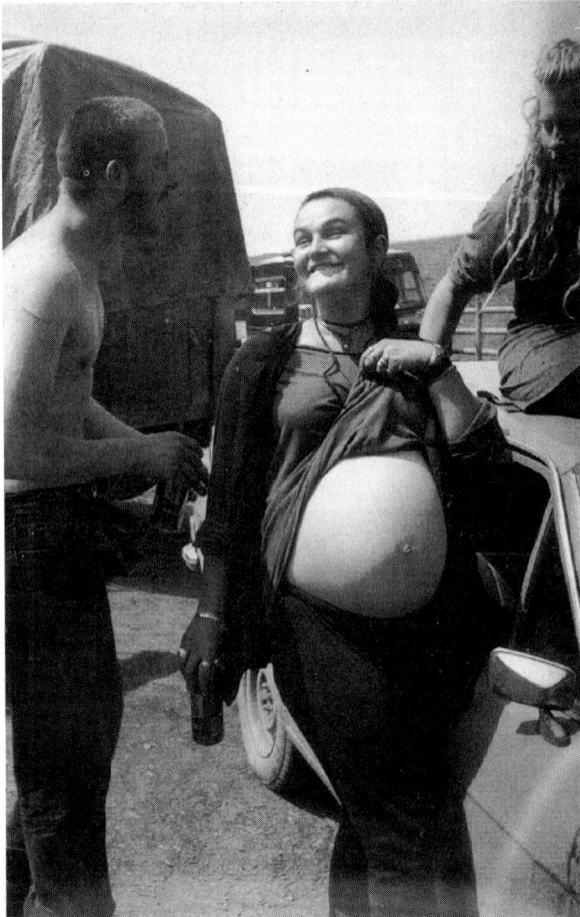

◆ ◆ ◆ ◆ ◆

Pregnant and proud

Jeremy Sandford:
Best known, so far, for his plays including 'Cathy Come Home' and 'Edna the Inebriate
Woman.' An ex-member of the national Gypsy Council, he currently runs a green and 'New
Age' conference facility at his home, and provides music and teaching of folk and sacred circle
dancing at Oak Dragon and Rainbow Circle Camps. He is currently working on collecting
traditional and modern Gypsy music, funded by the Arts Council.

*What future?......*In time of war they come to be conscripted to fight and die for their green
and pleasant land, and in peace time it seems only fair that we should find them the small
amount of land to live on that they ask of us; whether they be traditional or new Travellers.

There has not been an agrarian revolution in this country. The distribution of land is unfair.
Some people own hundreds of thousands of acres, some a small garden or backyard; huge
numbers of people are dispossessed. They own nothing at all.

Divided out equally, there would in this country be two acres for every child, woman, man;
enough for a small family group to live off, especially if they enjoy a vegetarian or vegan diet.

So, how to find them these small margins of land that they ask of us? Travellers live on my
land and on the land of friendly farmers. That's where they've always lived, as well as on
those bits of land that, in an increasingly enclosed country, still belong to all of us - the verges,
the lay-bys and commons. What makes it increasingly hard for them now is the network of
laws, operated by 'no-no people,' and which seem designed to stop anyone living differently to
anyone else.

Yet there is a surge of anxiety among many local taxpayers at the expense of the endless
evictions, blocking and ditching of lay-bys, and court actions and some stirrings of guilt that
their money is being used to finance the harassing of pregnant mothers, new born babies, and
sometimes invalids - as well as less vulnerable Travellers. My hope is that, with so many
farmers being paid not to farm their land, and so many Travellers prepared to pay for a little
space to place their tents of living vehicles, we can find a way to bring the two together."

◆ ◆ ◆ ◆ ◆

Huw Wynne-Jones:
(an extract from 'First Hand'. Independent. 20/3/94)
"The first Travellers arrived back in 1987. There were 12 of them, and they parked on an old
trackway about three miles out of the village. Theoretically it was common land - it's been
used for centuries by Gypsies and Travellers - but a farmer turned up and told them to get off
because he'd been storing hay bales on it.......He got quite friendly with them in the end.
Because they had horsedrawn carts they even joined in the local hunt; they just jumped on
their old nags and galloped off with the plummy types."

"....Of course there are odd farmers in Wales with a genuine cause to grumble, and some
Traveller settlements are disgusting - one in a lay-by by the A46 for example couldn't even be
lived in by pigs. But I don't think that most people are against them as much as has always
been made out. A lot of it is just media rubbish....."

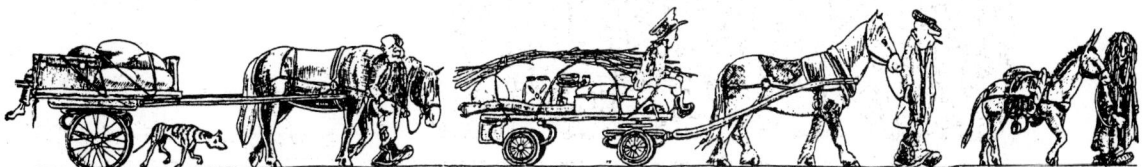

".....I employ Travellers to work for me, and some of them are allowed to park their buses on my land. My two young children like them - they provide entertainment, and because they value children they like playing with them. Some are saints, some are thugs......I had a cart stolen by one of them: the fact he was a Traveller was irrelevant - he's just a bastard...."

"....Thanks to the new Government legislation, by just being a Traveller you will be made a criminal.......I'm a taxpayer. Personally I would rather pay someone to drive around in a colourful bus, than pay some civil servant in Whitehall to make their life hell."

And so, in conclusion.........

Whatever the perception of Travellers - as refugees, romantic wanderers, outcasts, hippies etc. - we are humans with emotions and needs the same as anyone else.

True, there are petty criminals, drug addicts and idiots amongst us, but they are a minority. Most of them, given the chance to rehabilitate without persecution, can become as independent and efficient as the majority. Daily, the media reports horrendous crimes such as murder, rape and child abuse - yet the house-dwelling perpetrators do not precipitate draconian laws banning all people from inhabiting houses!

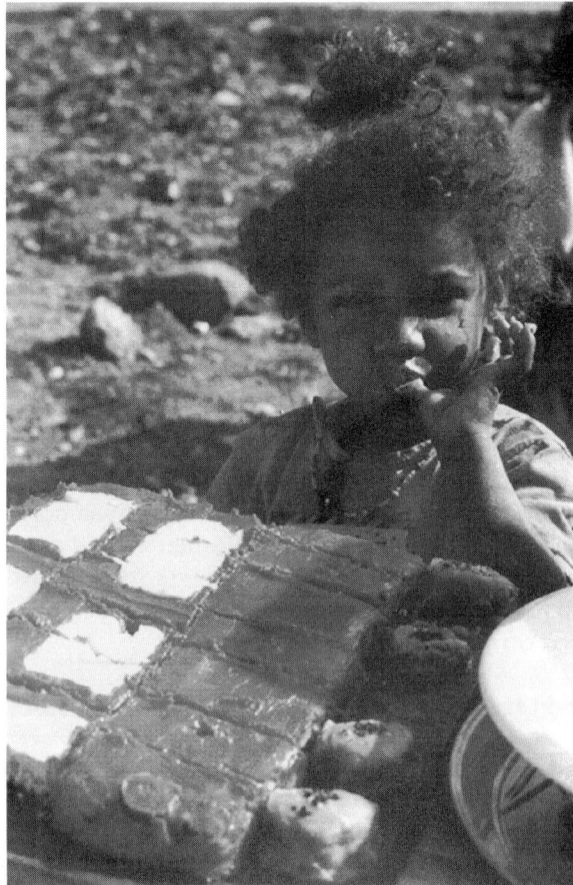

Our children - Our future

We do not seek confrontation; and are almost the only group in Britain against whom discrimination is legal. A nomadic lifestyle can be ideal for the educational and emotional development of children, learning through experience, rather than from books, unfettered by pre-conceived notions of success.

♦ ♦ ♦ ♦ ♦

We hope that this book has provided some insight into our history, our lives and the challenges we face. Do not judge us by the media reportage, or a panicking Government; but talk to us, and help us all build a unity amongst people of all cultures.

> **"Do not follow where the path may lead.**
> **Go, instead, where there is no path**
> **and leave a trail."**

BIBLIOGRAPHY

Books, Journals, etc.

The Action Man Explains, dedicated to Robert Calvert

Alphabet Activity Book, Fiona Earle, Wheel Life, 1991

Alternative News Digest, edited by Bruce Garrard, Unique Publications

Ancient Mysteries of Britain, Janet and Coin Bord, Harper Collins, 1986

Anywhere but here, Mary Daly, London Race and Housing Research Unit, 1990

Children's Rights: A Participative Exercise, Peter Jenkins, Longman, 1993

A Dartmoor Journey, Andrew P

Butterworths Police law, 3rd edition, Jack English and Michael Hurd, Butterworths, 1991

Days in the Life: Voices from the English Underground 1961 - 71, Jonathan Green, Minerva, 1989

Destiny of Europe's Gypsies, Donald Kennrick and Gratton Puxon, Basic Books, 1972

Dread Zone No. 3, Dave and the Posse, Dread Zone Arts, 1992 (?)

The Drugs Menace, Mary Manning, Columbus, 1985

The Education of Gypsy and Traveller Children, Edited by A.C.E.R.T., University of Herts Press, 1993

Earth Harmony, Nigel Pennick, Century ,1987

Earth Magic, Francis Hitching, Picador,1976

Fads, Fashions and Cults, Tony Thorne, Bloomsbury, 1993

Fevered Imaginings magazine, Kudu Komix, Norwich

Fourth People's Free Festival: Watchfield, compiled by Suburban Guerrillas, 1989

Gathered All Around: A Collection of Gypsy Poetry, edited by Dennis Binns, T.T.S., 1987

The Glastonbury Festivals, Lynne Elstrobe & Anne Howes, Gothic Image, 1987

Glastonbury '92 Caravan Classroom, Children's work compiled by Fiona Earle, TSC, 1992

Gnomon, Issue 6, John Harrison, Monolith Publications

The Green Collective, Mailing 1985, edited by Bruce Garrard, Unique Publications, 1985/86

Greenlands Farm, edited by Bruce Garrard, Unique Publications, 1986

The Gypsies, Angus Fraser, Blackwell, 1992

Gypsies, Jeremy Sandford, Abacus, 1975

The Gypsies, Jan Yoors, Waveland Press Inc

Gypsies of the World, A Journey into the Hidden World of Gypsy Life and Culture, Nebojsa Baro Tomasevic and Rajko Djuric, Flint River Press, 1988

The Gypsies: Wagon Time and After, Dennis Harvey, Batsford, 1979

Gypsy Camera, Tony Boxall, Creative Monochrome, 1992

Gypsy Folk Tales, Diane Tong, HJB

Guide to Prehistoric England, Nicholas Thomas, Batsford, 1976

A Guide to Prehistoric and Roman Monumnets in England and Wales, Jacquetta Hawkes, Cardinal 1973

The Hard Way Up, edited by Geoffrey Mitchell, Virago, 1984

How to de-commission a lifestyle, Dennis Binns, Traveller Education, Manchester, 1986

Interface: Gypsies and Travellers Education, Nos 1 - 12

The Last Night of Rainbow Fields Village at Molesworth, Bruce Garrard, Unique Publications, 1985

Lurchers and Longdogs, E. G. Walsh, Standfast Press

May the Devil Walk Behind You, Scottish Traveller Tales, Duncan Willimson, Canongate

Medieval Brigands: Pictures in a year of the 'hippie' convoy, Peter Gardner, Redcliffe, 1987

Monolith News: various issues, John Harrison, Monolith Publications

Mother Earth, Father Sky, Marcia Keegan, Clearlight Publishers, 1988

Musicians Network 22, MN, 1993

New Travellers, Kent Traveller Education Service, 1992

NGC Response to Grant Proposals to reform CSA '68, October 1992

Nott Fin, Free Info Network, July 1992

On the Verge: The Gypsies of England, Donald Kennrick, Romanestan Publications

People on the Move: 1992 and the New World, edited by Rhys Evans, Leicester-Malaysia
Link Group

Policy on Gypsies, CJB and PO Research Paper 94/3 7/1/94, Christopher Barclay

Portable North American Reader, edited by Frederick W. Turner III, Penguin 1974

Prehistoric England, Richard Cavendish, Artus Books, 1983

Rainbow Village on the Road: Poems and Writings from Rainbow Fields in Exile,
    Feb/Mar 1985, edited by Bruce Garrard, Rainbow Jo, Alistair McKay, Unique publications, 1986

Rave Off, Steve Redhead, Avebury

Reefer Madness 1, 2, 3, Hawk Frends, 1988, 1989, 1990

Rehearal for the Year 2000, Alan Beam, 1976

Resurgence magazine, Hartland , Devon

Right to travel and Right to stop, Jenny Smith, Shelter Publications

Romani Rokkeripen Todivus, Thomas Acton and Donald Kennrick, Romanestan Publications

Romano Lavo Lil and Lavengro, (and other books) George Borrow, Allan Sutton Publishing

School Provision for Gypsy and Traveller Children: orientation document for reflection
and for action, Jean-Pierre Liegeois, Commission of European Communities, Traveller Education Service

Select, August 1993

A Series of Shock Slogans and Mindless Token Tantrums, Crass, Existential Press, 1982

Solstice Ritual, Alan Lodge

The Spirit of the Flame: poems by Charlie Smith, Charlie Smith, S. March Resources Centre, 1990

The Stone Faerie and Other Friends, Andrew P

Stonehenge, NCCL, Yale Penn Ltd, 1986

Stonehenge Campaign, leaflets

The Stonehenge Conflict: Experiences and Opinions, John Harrison, Monolith Publications, 1989

Stonehenge Solstice '89, Suburban Guerrilla, 1989

Stonehenge: The Indo-European Heritage, Jean E. Stover and Bruce King, Nelson Hall, 1978

Stonehenge: Who Knows?, Suburban Guerrilla, 1989

Stonehenge '85, edited by Sheila Craig, Unique Publications, 1986

Stonehenge, edited by Bruce Gaward and Steve Hieronymous, Unique Publications, 1986

Stonehenge '90: assorted contributors, Suburban Guerrilla, 1990

Spring, Katie Daniels, TSC, 1991

The Sun in the East: Norfolk & Suffolk Fairs, compiled by Richard Barnes, F. Crowe & Sons, 1983

Tales of a Gypsy: Poems by Julia Gentle, Julia Gentle, T.E.S., 1989

Tipi Living, Patrick Whitefield, Unique Publications, 1987

Touch the Earth: a self portrait of Indian existence, compiled by T.C. McLuhan, Abacus, 1978

Travellers: An Introduction, Jon Cannon, Interchange Books, 1989

Traveller Education, Journals 25, 26

Travellers at Appleby Fair, Alisha Heron, Dennis Binns Publications, 1988

Travellers in Glastonbury, Ann Morgan and Bruce Garrard, Unique Publications, 1989

Travellers' Handbook, Bill Forrester, Interchange Press, 1985

Travellers: Voices of the New Age Nomads, Richard Lowe and William Shaw, 4th Estate, 1993

The Travelling People, Duncan Dallas, MacMillan, 1977

Tribal Messenger, edited by John Pendragon

Very Heaven: Looking Back at the 60s, edited Sara Maitland, Virago, 1988

What shall we do with the children?, Cathy Kiddle

The Willing Victim: A Parent's guide to Drug Abuse, George Birdwood, Secker and Warburg, 1969

Yorkshire Gypsy Fairs, customs and caravans, Alan Jones, Hulton Press, 1980

Research Writing

Education of the Road: Travellers Old and New, J.M. Forest. May 1990

From Myth to Reality, Gypsy Survey 1993, N.G.C.

Investigation into Policies, Priorities and resources Available to N.A.T.S. the Hippy Convoy, Vicki Strangroome
Neglected Minority? Investigative Study of Marchwood Site: Research Project, Jackie Grant, Nov 1991
New Age Travellers: North Cornwall District, Tessa Barratt
The Road to Nowhere: Report on the Government's Proposals to Reform CSA 1968, Liberty, 1993
Study Assignment of 'Travellers', David Lovegrove, 1988

USEFUL ADDRESSES

ACERT: Moot House, The Stow, Harlow, Essex CM20 3AG

British Romani Union, Hever Rd., Edenbridge, Kent TH8 5DJ

Cottage Books, Gelsmoor, Coloerton, Leicestershire LE67 8HQ

Fevered Imaginings: Kudu Komix, 38-40 Exchange St. Norwich, Norfolk NR2 1AX

FFT: Friends and Families of Travellers, 33 Bryanston Street, Blandford, Dorset DT11 7AZ

Freedom Network: (CJA related activities) the Old Dole House, 372 Coldharbour lane, London SW9 8PP

TSC: PO Box 36, Grantham NG31 6EW

LCTR: 84 Bankside St., Leeds LS8 5AD

Liberty: 21 Tabbard St.., London SE1 4LA

Monolith Publications: PO Box 4, Syston, Leicestershire LE74 4RD

National Gypsy Council: Greenhills Caravan Site, Greengate St., Oldham, Manchester OL4 1DG

NATT: Broad lane, Bilston, Wolverhampton WV14 0SB

Resurgence: Ford House, Hartland, Bideford, Devon EX39 6EE

Romanestan Publications: 22 North End, Warley, Brentwood, Essex CM14 5LA

Save the Children, Traveller Information, 17 Grove Lane, London SE5 8RD

Unicorn and Bridestone Publications: PO Box 18, Hessle, East Yorks HU13 0HW

Unique Publications: High St., Glastonbury, Somerset

Zine: PO Box 288, Shere, Guildford, Surry GU5 9JS

Postcript

Those people reading this who have other stories to tell, are welcome to send them for possible inclusion in later editions of 'A Time to Travel.' Similarly, photos drawings, poems, songs etc.

Fiona and the rest of the authors
c/o Enabler Publications
Russell House
Lym Close
Lyme Regis
Dorset DT7 3DE.

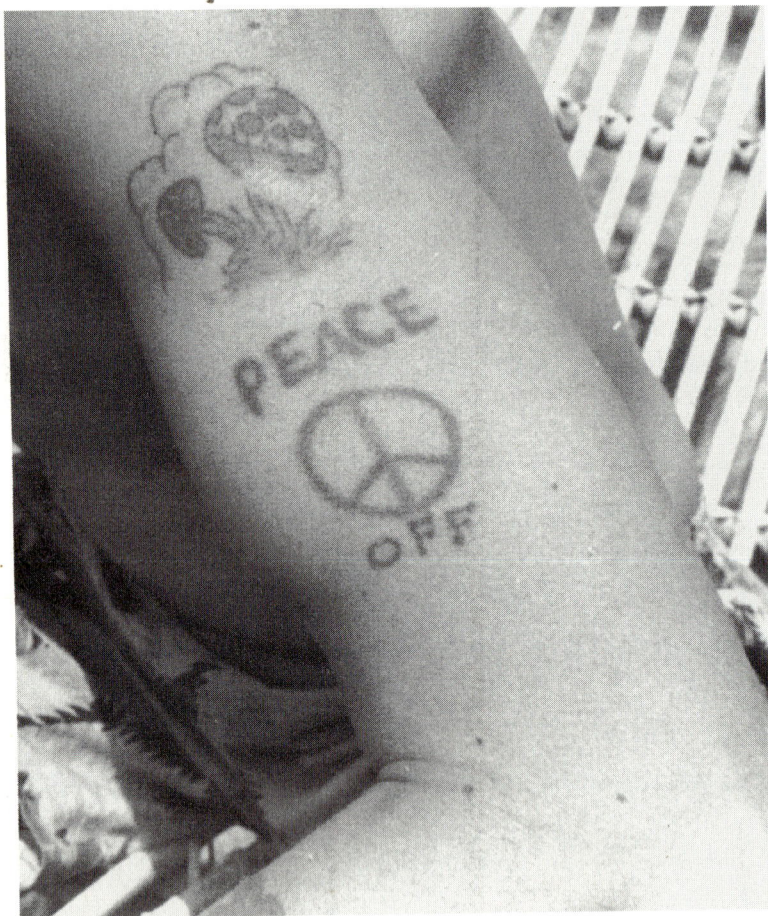